ABOUT THIS PUBLICATION

FOR SERVICE ASSISTANCE

Customer Service Department
1.704.898.0770

North Carolina General Statues is published by The Muliti-Media Group of Greater Charlotte in Charlotte, North Carolina. Copyright 2015 by the Multi-Media Group of Greater Charlotte. This book or parts thereof may not be reproduced in any form, stored in a retrieval system, or transmitted in any form by any means—electronic, mechanical, photocopy, recording or otherwise—without prior written permission of the publisher, except as provided by United States of America copyright law.

The records required by U.S. Code 2257(a) through (c) and the pertinent regulations 28 C.F.R. Cli. 1, Part 75 with respect to this publication and all materials associated with such records are maintained by The Multi-Media Group of Greater Charlotte, Publisher and available for review by Attorney General.

www.visionbooks.org

Copyright © 2015 by MMGGC
All rights reserved!

TID: 4993148
ISBN (10) digit: 1502331063
ISBN (13) digit: 978-1502331069

123-4-56789-01234-Paperback
123-4-56789-01234-Hardback

First Edition

090520140547

Printed in the United States of America

2015 EDITION

North Carolina Criminal Law And Procedure-Pamphlet # 9

Printed In conjunction with the Administration of the Courts

North Carolina Criminal Law and Procedure
Pamphlet Reference Guide

Chapters	Pamphlet
Chapter 1 Civil Procedure	1
Chapter 1 Civil Procedure (Continue)	2
Chapter 1A Rules of Civil Procedure	2
Chapter 1B Contribution.	2
Chapter 1C Enforcement of Judgments.	2
Chapter 1D Punitive Damages.	2
Chapter 1E Eastern Band of Cherokee Indians.	2
Chapter 1F North Carolina Uniform Interstate Depositions and Discovery Act.	2
Chapter 2 - Clerk of Superior Court [Repealed and Transferred.]	3
Chapter 3 - Commissioners of Affidavits and Deeds [Repealed.]	3
Chapter 4 - Common Law	3
Chapter 5 - Contempt [Repealed.]	3
Chapter 5A - Contempt	3
Chapter 6 - Liability for Court Costs	3
Chapter 7 - Courts [Repealed and Transferred.]	3
Chapter 7A – Judicial Department	3
Chapter 7A – Continuation (Judicial Department)	4
Chapter 7A – Continuation (Judicial Department)	5
Chapter 7B - Juvenile Code	5
Chapter 8 - Evidence	6
Chapter 8A - Interpreters for Deaf Persons [Recodified.]	6
Chapter 8B - Interpreters for Deaf Persons	6
Chapter 8C - Evidence Code	6
Chapter 9 - Jurors	6
Chapter 10 - Notaries [Repealed.]	6
Chapter 10A - Notaries [Recodified.]	6
Chapter 10B - Notaries	6
Chapter 11 - Oaths	6
Chapter 12 - Statutory Construction	6
Chapter 13 - Citizenship Restored	6
Chapter 14 - Criminal Law	7
Chapter 14 –Criminal Law (Continuation)	8
Chapter 15 - Criminal Procedure	9
Chapter 15A - Criminal Procedure Act (Continuation)	10
Chapter 15A - Criminal Procedure Act (Continuation)	11
Chapter 15B - Victims Compensation	11
Chapter 15C - Address Confidentiality Program	11
Chapter 16 - Gaming Contracts and Futures	11
Chapter 17 - Habeas Corpus	11

Chapter 17A - Law-Enforcement Officers [Recodified.]	11
Chapter 17B - North Carolina Criminal Justice Education and Training System [Recodified.] Chapter 17C - North Carolina Criminal Justice Education and Training Standards Commission	11
	11
Chapter 17D - North Carolina Justice Academy	11
Chapter 17E - North Carolina Sheriffs' Education and Training Standards Commission	11
Chapter 18 - Regulation of Intoxicating Liquors [Repealed.]	12
Chapter 18A - Regulation of Intoxicating Liquors [Repealed.]	12
Chapter 18B - Regulation of Alcoholic Beverages	12
Chapter 18C - North Carolina State Lottery	12
Chapter 19 - Offenses against Public Morals	12
Chapter 19A - Protection of Animals	12
Chapter 20 - Motor Vehicles	13
Chapter 20 - Motor Vehicles (Continuation)	14
Chapter 20 - Motor Vehicles (Continuation)	15
Chapter 20 - Motor Vehicles (Continuation)	16
Chapter 21 - Bills of Lading	17
Chapter 22 - Contracts Requiring Writing	17
Chapter 22A - Signatures	17
Chapter 22B - Contracts Against Public Policy	17
Chapter 22C - Payments to Subcontractors	17
Chapter 23 - Debtor and Creditor	17
Chapter 24 – Interest	17
Chapter 25 – Uniform Commercial Code	18
Chapter 25 – Uniform Commercial Code (Continuation)	19
Chapter 25A – Retail Installment Sales Act	20
Chapter 25B - Credit	20
Chapter 25C - Sales of Artwork	20
Chapter 26 - Suretyship	20
Chapter 27 - Warehouse Receipts [Repealed.]	20
Chapter 28 - Administration [Repealed.]	20
Chapter 28A - Administration of Decedents' Estates	20
Chapter 28B - Estates of Absentees in Military Service	20
Chapter 28C - Estates of Missing Persons	20
Chapter 29 - Intestate Succession	21
Chapter 30 - Surviving Spouses	21
Chapter 31 - Wills	21
Chapter 31A - Acts Barring Property Rights	21
Chapter 31B - Renunciation of Property and Renunciation of Fiduciary Powers Act	21
Chapter 31C - Uniform Disposition of Community Property Rights at Death Act	21
Chapter 32 - Fiduciaries	21
Chapter 32A - Powers of Attorney	21
Chapter 33 - Guardian and Ward [Repealed and Recodified.]	21

Chapter 33A - North Carolina Uniform Transfers to Minors Act	21
Chapter 33B - North Carolina Uniform Custodial Trust Act	21
Chapter 34 - Veterans' Guardianship Act	22
Chapter 35 - Sterilization Procedures	22
Chapter 35A - Incompetency and Guardianship	22
Chapter 36 - Trusts and Trustees [Repealed]	22
Chapter 36A - Trusts and Trustees	22
Chapter 36B - Uniform Management of Institutional Funds Act [Repealed.]	22
Chapter 36C - North Carolina Uniform Trust Code	22
Chapter 36D - North Carolina Community Third Party Trusts, Pooled Trusts	23
Chapter 36E - Uniform Prudent Management of Institutional Funds Act	23
Chapter 37 - Allocation of Principal and Income [Repealed.]	23
Chapter 37A - Uniform Principal and Income Act	23
Chapter 38 - Boundaries	23
Chapter 38A - Landowner Liability	23
Chapter 39 - Conveyances	23
Chapter 39A - Transfer Fee Covenants Prohibited	23
Chapter 40 - Eminent Domain [Repealed.]	23
Chapter 40A - Eminent Domain	23
Chapter 41 - Estates	23
Chapter 41A - State Fair Housing Act	23
Chapter 42 - Landlord and Tenant	23
Chapter 42A - Vacation Rental Act	23
Chapter 43 - Land Registration	23
Chapter 44 - Liens	24
Chapter 44A - Statutory Liens and Charges	24
Chapter 45 - Mortgages and Deeds of Trust	24
Chapter 45A - Good Funds Settlement Act	24
Chapter 46 - Partition	24
Chapter 47 - Probate and Registration	25
Chapter 47A - Unit Ownership	25
Chapter 47B - Real Property Marketable Title Act	25
Chapter 47C - North Carolina Condominium Act	25
Chapter 47D - Notice of Settlement Act [Expired.]	25
Chapter 47E - Residential Property Disclosure Act	25
Chapter 47F - North Carolina Planned Community Act	25
Chapter 47G - Option to Purchase Contracts	25
Chapter 47H - Contracts for Deed	25
Chapter 48 - Adoptions	26
Chapter 48A - Minors	26
Chapter 49 - Bastardy	26
Chapter 49A - Rights of Children	26
Chapter 50 - Divorce and Alimony	26
Chapter 50A - Uniform Child-Custody Jurisdiction and	

Enforcement Act	26
Chapter 50B - Domestic Violence	26
Chapter 50C - Civil No-Contact Orders	26
Chapter 51 - Marriage	26
Chapter 52 - Powers and Liabilities of Married Persons	27
Chapter 52A - Uniform Reciprocal Enforcement of Support Act [Repealed.]	27
Chapter 52B - Uniform Premarital Agreement Act	27
Chapter 52C - Uniform Interstate Family Support Act	27
Chapter 53 - Banks	27
Chapter 53A - Business Development Corporations and North Carolina Capital Resource Corporations	28
Chapter 53B - Financial Privacy Act	28
Chapter 54 - Cooperative Organizations	28
Chapter 54A - Capital Stock Savings and Loan Associations [Repealed.]	28
Chapter 54B - Savings and Loan Associations	29
Chapter 54C - Savings Banks	29
Chapter 55 - North Carolina Business Corporation Act	30
Chapter 55A - North Carolina Nonprofit Corporation Act	31
Chapter 55B - Professional Corporation Act	31
Chapter 55C - Foreign Trade Zones	31
Chapter 55D - Filings, Names, and Registered Agents for Corporations, Nonprofit Corporations, and Partnerships	31
Chapter 56 - Electric, Telegraph and Power Companies [Repealed.]	31
Chapter 57 - Hospital, Medical and Dental Service Corporations [Recodified.]	31
Chapter 57A - Health Maintenance Organization Act [Recodified.]	31
Chapter 57B - Health Maintenance Organization Act [Recodified.]	31
Chapter 57C - North Carolina Limited Liability Company Act.	31
Chapter 58 - Insurance.	32
Chapter 58 - Insurance (Continuation)	33
Chapter 58 - Insurance (Continuation)	34
Chapter 58 - Insurance (Continuation)	35
Chapter 58 - Insurance (Continuation)	36
Chapter 58 - Insurance (Continuation)	37
Chapter 58 - Insurance (Continuation)	38
Chapter 58A - North Carolina Health Insurance Trust Commission [Recodified.]	38
Chapter 59 - Partnership.	39
Chapter 59B - Uniform Unincorporated Nonprofit Association Act.	39
Chapter 60 - Railroads and Other Carriers [Repealed and Transferred.]	39
Chapter 61 - Religious Societies	39
Chapter 62 - Public Utilities	39

Chapter 62 - Public Utilities (Continuation)	40
Chapter 62A - Public Safety Telephone Service And Wireless Telephone Service	40
Chapter 63 - Aeronautics	40
Chapter 63A - North Carolina Global TransPark Authority	40
Chapter 64 - Aliens	40
Chapter 65 – Cemeteries	40
Chapter 66 - Commerce and Business	41
Chapter 67 - Dogs	41
Chapter 68 - Fences and Stock Law	41
Chapter 69 - Fire Protection	41
Chapter 70 - Indian Antiquities, Archaeological Resources and Unmarked Human Skeletal Remains Protection	42
Chapter 71 - Indians [Repealed.]	42
Chapter 71A - Indians	42
Chapter 72 - Inns, Hotels and Restaurants	42
Chapter 73 - Mills	42
Chapter 74 - Mines and Quarries	42
Chapter 74A - Company Police [Repealed.]	42
Chapter 74B - Private Protective Services Act [Repealed.]	42
Chapter 74C - Private Protective Services	42
Chapter 74D - Alarm Systems	42
Chapter 74E - Company Police Act	42
Chapter 74F - Locksmith Licensing Act	42
Chapter 74G - Campus Police Act	42
Chapter 75 - Monopolies, Trusts and Consumer Protection	42
Chapter 75A - Boating and Water Safety	43
Chapter 75B - Discrimination in Business	43
Chapter 75C - Motion Picture Fair Competition Act	43
Chapter 75D - Racketeer Influenced and Corrupt Organizations	43
Chapter 75E - Unlawful Activities in Connection With Certain Corporate Transactions	43
Chapter 76 - Navigation	43
Chapter 76A - Navigation and Pilotage Commissions	43
Chapter 77 - Rivers, Creeks, and Coastal Waters	43
Chapter 78 - Securities Law [Repealed.]	43
Chapter 78A - North Carolina Securities Act	43
Chapter 78B - Tender Offer Disclosure Act [Repealed.]	43
Chapter 78C - Investment Advisers	43
Chapter 78D - Commodities Act	43
Chapter 79 - Strays [Repealed.]	43
Chapter 80 - Trademarks, Brands, etc.	44
Chapter 81 - Weights and Measures [Recodified.]	44
Chapter 81A - Weights and Measures Act of 1975.	44
Chapter 82 - Wrecks [Repealed.]	44
Chapter 83 - Architects [Recodified.]	44

Chapter 83A - Architects	44
Chapter 84 - Attorneys-at-Law	44
Chapter 84A - Foreign Legal Consultants	44
Chapter 85 - Auctions and Auctioneers [Repealed.]	44
Chapter 85A - Bail Bondsmen and Runners [Recodified.]	44
Chapter 85B - Auctions and Auctioneers	44
Chapter 85C - Bail Bondsmen and Runners [Recodified.]	44
Chapter 86 - Barbers [Recodified.]	44
Chapter 86A - Barbers	44
Chapter 87 - Contractors	44
Chapter 88 - Cosmetic Art [Repealed.]	44
Chapter 88A - Electrolysis Practice Act	44
Chapter 88B - Cosmetic Art	45
Chapter 89 - Engineering and Land Surveying [Recodified.]	45
Chapter 89A - Landscape Architects	45
Chapter 89B - Foresters	45
Chapter 89C - Engineering and Land Surveying	45
Chapter 89D - Landscape Contractors	45
Chapter 89E - Geologists Licensing Act	45
Chapter 89F - North Carolina Soil Scientist Licensing Act	45
Chapter 89G - Irrigation Contractors	45
Chapter 90 - Medicine and Allied Occupations	45
Chapter 90 - Medicine and Allied Occupations (Continuation)	46
Chapter 90 - Medicine and Allied Occupations (Continuation)	47
Chapter 90 - Medicine and Allied Occupations (Continuation)	48
Chapter 90A - Sanitarians and Water and Wastewater Treatment Facility Operators	48
Chapter 90B - Social Worker Certification and Licensure Act	48
Chapter 90C - North Carolina Recreational Therapy Licensure Act	48
Chapter 90D - Interpreters and Transliterators	48
Chapter 91 - Pawnbrokers [Repealed.]	48
Chapter 91A - Pawnbrokers Modernization Act of 1989	48
Chapter 92 - Photographers [Deleted.]	48
Chapter 93 - Certified Public Accountants	48
Chapter 93A - Real Estate License Law	49
Chapter 93B - Occupational Licensing Boards	49
Chapter 93C - Watchmakers [Repealed.]	49
Chapter 93D - North Carolina State Hearing Aid Dealers and Fitters Board.	49
Chapter 93E - North Carolina Appraisers Act	49
Chapter 94 - Apprenticeship	49
Chapter 95 - Department of Labor and Labor Regulations	49
Chapter 95 - Department of Labor and Labor Regulations (Continuation)	50
Chapter 96 - Employment Security	50
Chapter 97 - Workers' Compensation Act	50
Chapter 97 - Workers' Compensation Act (Continuation)	51

Chapter 98 - Burnt and Lost Records	51
Chapter 99 - Libel and Slander	51
Chapter 99A - Civil Remedies for Criminal Actions	51
Chapter 99B - Products Liability	51
Chapter 99C - Actions Relating to Winter Sports Safety and Accidents	51
Chapter 99D - Civil Rights	51
Chapter 99E - Special Liability Provisions	51
Chapter 100 - Monuments, Memorials and Parks	51
Chapter 101 - Names of Persons	51
Chapter 102 - Official Survey Base	51
Chapter 103 - Sundays, Holidays and Special Days	51
Chapter 104 - United States Lands	51
Chapter 104A - Degrees of Kinship	51
Chapter 104B - Hurricanes or Other Acts of Nature	51
Chapter 104C - Atomic Energy, Radioactivity and Ionizing Radiation [Repealed and Recodified.]	51
Chapter 104D - Southern States Energy Compact	51
Chapter 104E - North Carolina Radiation Protection Act	51
Chapter 104F - Southeast Interstate Low-Level Radioactive Waste Management Compact [Repealed]	51
Chapter 104G - North Carolina Low-Level Radioactive Waste Management Authority Act of 1987 [Repealed]	51
Chapter 105 - Taxation	51
Chapter 105 - Taxation (Continuation)	52
Chapter 105 - Taxation (Continuation)	53
Chapter 105 - Taxation (Continuation)	54
Chapter 105A - Setoff Debt Collection Act	55
Chapter 105B - Defaulted Student Loan Recovery Act	55
Chapter 106 - Agriculture	55
Chapter 106 - Agriculture (Continue)	56
Chapter 106 - Agriculture (Continue)	57
Chapter 107 - Agricultural Development Districts [Repealed.]	57
Chapter 108 - Social Services [Repealed and Recodified.]	57
Chapter 108A - Social Services	57
Chapter 108B - Community Action Programs	58
Chapter 108C Medicaid and Health Choice Provider Requirements.	58
Chapter 108D Medicaid Managed Care for Behavioral Health Services.	58
Chapter 109 - Bonds [Recodified.]	58
Chapter 110 - Child Welfare	58
Chapter 111 - Aid to the Blind	58
Chapter 112 - Confederate Homes and Pensions [Repealed.]	58
Chapter 113 - Conservation and Development	58
Chapter 113 - Conservation and Development (Continuation)	59

Chapter 113A - Pollution Control and Environment	59
Chapter 113A - Pollution Control and Environment (Continuation)	60
Chapter 113B - North Carolina Energy Policy Act of 1975	60
Chapter 114 - Department of Justice	60
Chapter 115 - Elementary and Secondary Education [Repealed.]	60
Chapter 115A - Community Colleges, Technical Institutes, and Industrial Education Centers [Repealed.]	60
Chapter 115B - Tuition and Fee Waivers	60
Chapter 115C - Elementary and Secondary Education	60
Chapter 115C - Elementary and Secondary Education (Continuation)	61
Chapter 115C - Elementary and Secondary Education (Continuation)	62
Chapter 115C - Elementary and Secondary Education (Continuation)	63
Chapter 115D - Community Colleges	63
Chapter 115E - Private Educational Facilities Finance Act [Recodified]	63
Chapter 116 - Higher Education	63
Chapter 116 - Higher Education (Continuation)	63
Chapter 116A - Escheats and Abandoned Property [Repealed.]	64
Chapter 116B - Escheats and Abandoned Property	64
Chapter 116C - Continuum of Education Programs	64
Chapter 116D - Higher Education Bonds	64
Chapter 116E -Education Longitudinal Data System	64
Chapter 117 - Electrification	64
Chapter 118 - Firemen's and Rescue Squad Workers' Relief and Pension Funds [Recodified.]	64
Chapter 118A - Firemen's Death Benefit Act [Repealed.]	64
Chapter 118B - Members of a Rescue Squad Death Benefit Act [Repealed.]	64
Chapter 119 - Gasoline and Oil Inspection and Regulation	64
Chapter 120 - General Assembly	65
Chapter 120 - General Assembly (Continuation)	66
Chapter 120 - General Assembly (Continuation)	67
Chapter 120C - Lobbying	67
Chapter 121 - Archives and History	67
Chapter 122 - Hospitals for the Mentally Disordered [Repealed.]	67
Chapter 122A - North Carolina Housing Finance Agency	67
Chapter 122B - North Carolina Agricultural Facilities Finance Act [Repealed.]	67
Chapter 122C - Mental Health, Developmental Disabilities, and Substance Abuse Act of 1985	67
Chapter 122C - Mental Health, Developmental Disabilities, and Substance Abuse Act of 1985 (Continuation)	68

Chapter 122D - North Carolina Agricultural Finance Act	68
Chapter 122E - North Carolina Housing Trust and Oil Overcharge Act	68
Chapter 123 - Impeachment	69
Chapter 123A - Industrial Development [Repealed.]	69
Chapter 124 - Internal Improvements	69
Chapter 125 - Libraries	69
Chapter 126 - State Personnel System	69
Chapter 127 - Militia [Repealed.]	69
Chapter 127A - Militia	69
Chapter 127B - Military Affairs	69
Chapter 127C - Advisory Commission on Military Affairs	69
Chapter 128 - Offices and Public Officers	69
Chapter 128 - Offices and Public Officers (Continuation)	70
Chapter 129 - Public Buildings and Grounds	70
Chapter 130 - Public Health [Repealed.]	70
Chapter 130A - Public Health	70
Chapter 130A - Public Health (Continuation)	71
Chapter 130A - Public Health (Continuation)	72
Chapter 130B - Hazardous Waste Management Commission [Repealed.]	72
Chapter 131 - Public Hospitals [Repealed.]	72
Chapter 131A - Health Care Facilities Finance Act	72
Chapter 131B - Licensing of Ambulatory Surgical Facilities [Repealed.]	72
Chapter 131C - Charitable Solicitation Licensure Act [Repealed.]	72
Chapter 131D - Inspection and Licensing of Facilities	72
Chapter 131E - Health Care Facilities and Services	72
Chapter 131E - Health Care Facilities and Services (Continuation)	73
Chapter 131F - Solicitation of Contributions	73
Chapter 132 - Public Records	73
Chapter 133 - Public Works	74
Chapter 134 - Youth Development [Recodified.]	74
Chapter 134A - Youth Services [Repealed.]	74
Chapter 135 - Retirement System for Teachers and State Employees; Social Security; Health Insurance Program for Children	74
Chapter 135 - Retirement System for Teachers and State Employees; Social Security; Health Insurance Program for Children	75
Chapter 136 - Transportation	75
Chapter 136 - Transportation (Continuation)	76
Chapter 137 - Rural Rehabilitation [Repealed.]	76
Chapter 138 - Salaries, Fees and Allowances	76
Chapter 138A - State Government Ethics Act	76

Chapter 139 - Soil and Water Conservation Districts	76
Chapter 140 - State Art Museum; Symphony and Art Societies	76
Chapter 140A - State Awards System	76
Chapter 141 - State Boundaries	76
Chapter 142 - State Debt	76
Chapter 143 - State Departments, Institutions, and Commissions	77
Chapter 143 - State Departments, Institutions, and Commissions (Continuation)	78
Chapter 143 - State Departments, Institutions, and Commissions (Continuation)	79
Chapter 143 - State Departments, Institutions, and Commissions (Continuation)	80
Chapter 143A - State Government Reorganization	80
Chapter 143B - Executive Organization Act of 1973	80
Chapter 143B - Executive Organization Act of 1973 (Continuation)	81
Chapter 143B - Executive Organization Act of 1973 (Continuation)	82
Chapter 143C - State Budget Act	83
Chapter 143D - The State Governmental Accountability and Internal Control Act	83
Chapter 144 - State Flag, Official Governmental Flags, Motto, and Colors	83
Chapter 145 - State Symbols and Other Official Adoptions.	83
Chapter 146 - State Lands	83
Chapter 147 - State Officers	83
Chapter 148 - State Prison System	84
Chapter 149 - State Song and Toast	84
Chapter 150 - Uniform Revocation of Licenses [Repealed.]	84
Chapter 150A - Administrative Procedure Act [Recodified.]	84
Chapter 150B - Administrative Procedure Act	84
Chapter 151 - Constables [Repealed.]	84
Chapter 152 - Coroners	84
Chapter 152A - County Medical Examiner [Repealed.]	84
Chapter 152A - County Medical Examiner [Repealed.] (Continuation)	85
Chapter 153 - Counties and County Commissioners [Repealed.]	85
Chapter 153A - Counties	85
Chapter 153B - Mountain Resources Planning Act	85
Chapter 153C - Uwharrie Regional Resources Act	85
Chapter 154 - County Surveyor [Repealed.]	85
Chapter 155 - County Treasurer [Repealed.]	85
Chapter 156 - Drainage	85

Chapter 156 – Drainage (Continuation)	86
Chapter 157 - Housing Authorities and Projects	86
Chapter 157A - Historic Properties Commissions [Transferred.]	86
Chapter 158 - Local Development	86
Chapter 159 - Local Government Finance	86
Chapter 159 - Local Government Finance (Continuation)	87
Chapter 159A - Pollution Abatement and Industrial Facilities Financing Act [Unconstitutional.]	87
Chapter 159B - Joint Municipal Electric Power and Energy Act	87
Chapter 159C - Industrial and Pollution Control Facilities Financing Act	87
Chapter 159D - The North Carolina Capital Facilities Financing Act	87
Chapter 159E - Registered Public Obligations Act	87
Chapter 159F - North Carolina Energy Development Authority [Repealed.]	87
Chapter 159G - Water Infrastructure	87
Chapter 159H - [Reserved.]	87
Chapter 159I - Solid Waste Management Loan Program and Local Government Special Obligation Bonds	87
Chapter 160 - Municipal Corporations [Repealed And Transferred.]	87
Chapter 160A - Cities and Towns	88
Chapter 160A - Cities and Towns (Continuation)	89
Chapter 160B - Consolidated City-County Act	89
Chapter 160C - Baseball Park Districts [Repealed.]	90
Chapter 161 - Register of Deeds	90
Chapter 162 - Sheriff	90
Chapter 162A - Water and Sewer Systems	90
Chapter 162B Continuity of Local Government in Emergency.	90
Chapter 163 Elections and Election Laws.	90
Chapter 163 Elections and Election Laws. (Continuation)	91
Chapter 164 Concerning the General Statutes of North Carolina.	92
Chapter 165 Veterans.	92
Chapter 166 Civil Preparedness Agencies [Repealed.]	92
Chapter 166A North Carolina Emergency Management Act.	92
Chapter 167 State Civil Air Patrol [Repealed.]	92
Chapter 168 Persons with Disabilities.	92
Chapter 168A Persons With Disabilities Protection Act.	92

Chapter 15

Criminal Procedure.

Article 1.

General Provisions.

§ 15-1. Statute of limitations for misdemeanors.

The crimes of deceit and malicious mischief, and the crime of petit larceny where the value of the property does not exceed five dollars ($5.00), and all misdemeanors except malicious misdemeanors, shall be presented or found by the grand jury within two years after the commission of the same, and not afterwards: Provided, that if any indictment found within that time shall be defective, so that no judgment can be given thereon, another prosecution may be instituted for the same offense, within one year after the first shall have been abandoned by the State. (1826, c. 11; R.C., c. 35, s. 8; Code, s. 1177; Rev., s. 3147; 1907, c. 408; C.S., s. 4512; 1943, c. 543.)

§§ 15-2 through 15-3. Repealed by Session Laws 1973, c. 1286, s. 26.

§ 15-4. Accused entitled to counsel.

Every person, accused of any crime whatsoever, shall be entitled to counsel in all matters which may be necessary for his defense. (1777, c. 115, s. 85, P.R.; R.C., c. 35, s. 13; Code, s. 1182; Rev., s. 3150; C.S., s. 4515.)

§§ 15-4.1 through 15-5.1. Repealed by Session Laws 1969, c. 1013, s. 12.

§ 15-5.2. Repealed by Session Laws 1969, c. 1013, s. 6.

§§ 15-5.3 through 15-5.4. Repealed by Session Laws 1969, c. 1013, s. 12.

§ 15-6. Imprisonment to be in county jail.

No person shall be imprisoned except in the common jail of the county, unless otherwise provided by law: Provided, that whenever the sheriff of any county shall be imprisoned, he may be imprisoned in the jail of any adjoining county. (1797, c. 474, s. 3, P.R.; R.C., c. 35, s. 6; 1879, c. 12; Code, s. 1174; Rev., s. 3151; C.S., s. 4517; 1973, c. 1141, s. 1.)

§ 15-6.1. Changing place of confinement of prisoner committing offense.

In all cases where a defendant has been convicted in a court inferior to the superior court and sentenced to a term in the county jail or to serve in some county institution other than under the supervision of the State Division of Adult Correction of the Department of Public Safety, and such defendant is subsequently brought before such court for an offense committed prior to the expiration of the term to be served in such county institution, upon conviction, plea of guilty or nolo contendere, the judge shall have the power and authority to change the place of confinement of the prisoner and commit such defendant to work under the supervision of the Division of Adult Correction of the Department of Public Safety. This provision shall apply whether or not the terms of the new sentence are to run concurrently with or consecutive to the remaining portion of the old sentence. (1953, c. 778; 1957, c. 65, s. 11; 1967, c. 996, s. 16; 2011-145, s. 19.1(h); 2012-83, s. 20.)

§ 15-6.2. Concurrent sentences for offenses of different grades or to be served in different places.

When by a judgment of a court or by operation of law a prison sentence runs concurrently with any other sentence a prisoner shall not be required to serve any additional time in prison solely because the concurrent sentences are for different grades of offenses or that it is required that they be served in different places of confinement. (1955, c. 57.)

§ 15-6.3. Credit for service of sentence while in another jurisdiction.

When a person in actual confinement under sentence of another jurisdiction is brought for trial before a court of this State, the court may, upon sentencing, specifically impose a sentence to be concurrently served and direct that such person receive credit against the sentence imposed for all time subsequently served in the jurisdiction possessing physical custody of such person. (1971, c. 828.)

§ 15-7. Postmortem examinations directed.

In all cases of homicide, any officer prosecuting for the State may, at any time, direct a postmortem examination of the deceased to be made by one or more physicians to be summoned for the purpose; and the physicians shall be paid a reasonable compensation for such examination, the amount to be determined by the court and taxed in the costs, and if not collected out of the defendant the same shall be paid by the State. (R.C., c. 35, s. 49; Code, s. 1214; Rev., s. 3152; C.S., s. 4518; 1973, c. 1141, s. 2.)

§ 15-8. Stolen property returned to owner.

Upon the conviction of any person for robbing or stealing any money, goods, chattels, or other estate of any description whatever, the person from whom such goods, money, chattels or other estate were robbed or stolen shall be entitled to restitution thereof; and the court may award restitution of the articles so robbed or stolen, and make all such orders and issue such writs of restitution or otherwise as may be necessary for that purpose. (21 Hen. VIII, c. 11; R.C., c. 35, s. 34; Code, s. 1201; Rev., s. 3153; C.S., s. 4519; 1943, c. 543.)

§ 15-9. Repealed by Session Laws 1973, c. 1286, s. 26.

§ 15-10. Speedy trial or discharge on commitment for felony.

When any person who has been committed for treason or felony, plainly and specially expressed in the warrant of commitment, upon his prayer in open court to be brought to his trial, shall not be indicted some time in the next term of the superior or criminal court ensuing such commitment, the judge of the court, upon notice in open court on the last day of the term, shall set at liberty such prisoner upon bail, unless it appear upon oath that the witnesses for the State could not be produced at the same term; and if such prisoner, upon his prayer as aforesaid, shall not be indicted and tried at the second term of the court, he shall be discharged from his imprisonment: Provided, the judge presiding may, in his discretion, refuse to discharge such person if the time between the first and second terms of the court be less than four months. (1868-9, c. 116, s. 33; Code, s. 1658; Rev., s. 3155; 1913, c. 2; C.S., s. 4521.)

§ 15-10.1. Detainer; purpose; manner of use.

Any person confined in the State prison system of North Carolina, subject to the authority and control of the Division of Adult Correction of the Department of Public Safety, or any person confined in any other prison of North Carolina, may be held to account for any other charge pending against him only upon a written order from the clerk or judge of the court in which the charge originated upon a case regularly docketed, directing that such person be held to answer the charge pending in such court; and in no event shall the prison authorities hold any person to answer any charge upon a warrant or notice when the charge has not been regularly docketed in the court in which the warrant or charge has been issued: Provided, that this section shall not apply to any State agency exercising supervision over such person or prisoner by virtue of a judgment, order of court or statutory authority. (1949, c. 303; 1953, c. 603; 1957, c. 349, s. 10; 1967, c. 996, s. 13; 2011-145, s. 19.1(h); 2012-83, s. 21.)

§ 15-10.2. Mandatory disposition of detainers - request for final disposition of charges; continuance; information to be furnished prisoner.

(a)   Any prisoner serving a sentence or sentences within the State prison system who, during his term of imprisonment, shall have lodged against him a detainer to answer to any criminal charge pending against him in any court within the State, shall be brought to trial within eight months after he shall have caused to be sent to the district attorney of the court in which said criminal charge is pending, by registered mail, written notice of his place of confinement and request for a final disposition of the criminal charge against him; said request shall be accompanied by a certificate from the Secretary of Public Safety stating the term of the sentence or sentences under which the prisoner is being held, the date he was received, and the time remaining to be served; provided that, for good cause shown in open court, the prisoner or his counsel being present, the court may grant any necessary and reasonable continuance.

(b) The Secretary of Public Safety shall, upon request by the prisoner, inform the prisoner in writing of the source and contents of any charge for which a detainer shall have been lodged against such prisoner as shown by said detainer, and furnished the prisoner with the certificate referred to in subsection (a). (1957, c. 1067, s. 1; 1967, c. 996, s. 15; 1973, c. 47, s. 2; c. 1262, s. 10; 2011-145, s. 19.1(i).)

§ 15-10.3. Mandatory disposition of detainers - procedure; return of prisoner after trial.

The district attorney, upon receipt of the written notice and request for a final disposition as hereinbefore specified, shall make application to the court in which said charge is pending for a writ of habeas corpus ad prosequendum and the court upon such application shall issue such writ to the Secretary of Public Safety requiring the prisoner to be delivered to said court to answer the pending charge and to stand trial on said charge within the time hereinbefore provided; upon completion of said trial, the prisoner shall be returned to the State prison system to complete service of the sentence or sentences under which he was held at the time said writ was issued. (1957, c. 1067, s. 2; 1967, c. 996, s. 15; 1973, c. 47, s. 2; c. 1262, s. 10; 2011-145, s. 19.1(i).)

§ 15-10.4. Mandatory disposition of detainers - exception as to prisoners who are mentally ill.

The provisions of G.S. 15-10.2 and 15-10.3 shall not apply to any prisoner who has been transferred and assigned for observation or treatment to any unit of the prison system which is maintained for those prisoners who are mentally ill or are suffering from mental disorders. (1957, c. 1067, s. 3.)

Article 2.

Record and Disposition of Seized, etc., Articles.

§ 15-11. Sheriffs and police departments to maintain register of personal property confiscated, seized or found.

Each sheriff and police department in this State is hereby required to keep and maintain a book or register, and it shall be the duty of each sheriff and police department to keep a record therein of all articles of personal property which may be seized or confiscated by him or it, or of which he or it may have become possessed in any way in the discharge of his duty. Said sheriffs and police departments shall cause to be kept in said registers a description of such property, the name of the person from whom it was seized, if such name be known, the date and place of its seizure, and, where the article was not taken from the person of a suspect or prisoner, a brief recital of the place and circumstances concerning the possession thereof by such sheriff and police department. Such sheriff and police department shall also keep in said register appropriate entries showing the manner, date, and to whom said articles are disposed of or delivered, and, if sold as hereinafter provided, a record showing the disposition of the proceeds arising from such sale. (1939, c. 195, s. 1; 1973, c. 1141, s. 3.)

§ 15-11.1. Seizure, custody and disposition of articles; exceptions.

(a)   If a law-enforcement officer seizes property pursuant to lawful authority, he shall safely keep the property under the direction of the court or magistrate as long as necessary to assure that the property will be produced at and may be used as evidence in any trial. Upon application by the lawful owner or a person, firm or corporation entitled to possession or upon his own determination, the district attorney may release any property seized pursuant to his lawful authority if he determines that such property is no longer useful or necessary as evidence in a criminal trial and he is presented with satisfactory evidence of ownership. If the district attorney refuses to release such property, the lawful owner or a person, firm or corporation entitled to possession may make application to the court for return of the property. The court, after notice to all parties, including the defendant, and after hearing, may in its discretion order any or all of the property returned to the lawful owner or a person, firm or corporation entitled to possession. The court may enter such order as may be necessary to assure that the evidence will be available for use as evidence at the time of trial, and will otherwise protect the rights of all parties. Notwithstanding any other provision of law, photographs or other identification or analyses made of the property may be introduced at the time of the trial provided that the court determines that the introduction of such substitute evidence is not likely to substantially prejudice the rights of the defendant in the criminal trial.

(b)   In the case of unknown or unapprehended defendants or of defendants willfully absent from the jurisdiction, the court shall determine whether an attorney should be appointed as guardian ad litem to represent and protect the interest of such unknown or absent defendants. Appointment shall be in accordance with rules adopted by the Office of Indigent Defense Services. The judicial findings concerning identification or value that are made at such hearing whereby property is returned to the lawful owner or a person, firm, or corporation entitled to possession, may be admissible into evidence at the trial. After final judgment all property lawfully seized by or otherwise coming into the possession of law-enforcement authorities shall be disposed of as the court or magistrate in its discretion orders, and may be forfeited and either sold or destroyed in accordance with due process of law.

(b1) Notwithstanding subsections (a) and (b) of this section or any other provision of law, if the property seized is a firearm and the district attorney determines the firearm is no longer necessary or useful as evidence in a criminal trial, the district attorney, after notice to all parties known or believed by the district attorney to have an ownership or a possessory interest in the firearm, including the defendant, shall apply to the court for an order of disposition of the firearm. The judge, after hearing, may order the disposition of the firearm in one of the following ways:

(1)   By ordering the firearm returned to its rightful owner, when the rightful owner is someone other than the defendant and upon findings by the court (i) that the person, firm, or corporation determined by the court to be the rightful owner is entitled to possession of the firearm and (ii) that the person, firm, or corporation determined by the court to be the rightful owner of the firearm was unlawfully deprived of the same or had no knowledge or reasonable belief of the defendant's intention to use the firearm unlawfully.

(2)   By ordering the firearm returned to the defendant, but only if the defendant is not convicted of any criminal offense in connection with the possession or use of the firearm, the defendant is the rightful owner of the firearm, and the defendant is not otherwise ineligible to possess such firearm.

(3) By ordering the firearm turned over to be destroyed by the sheriff of the county in which the firearm was seized or by his duly authorized agent if the firearm does not have a legible, unique identification number or is unsafe for use because of wear, damage, age, or modification. The sheriff shall maintain a record of the destruction of the firearm.

(4) By ordering the firearm turned over to a law enforcement agency in the county of trial for (i) the official use of the agency or (ii) sale, trade, or exchange by the agency to a federally licensed firearm dealer in accordance with all applicable State and federal firearm laws. The court may order a disposition of the firearm pursuant to this subdivision only upon the written request of the head or chief of the law enforcement agency and only if the firearm has a legible, unique identification number. If the law enforcement agency sells the firearm, then the proceeds of the sale shall be remitted to the appropriate county finance officer as provided by G.S. 115C-452 to be used to maintain free public schools. The receiving law enforcement agency shall maintain a record and inventory of all firearms received pursuant to this subdivision.

This subsection (b1) is not applicable to seizures pursuant to G.S. 113-137 of firearms used only in connection with a violation of Article 22 of Chapter 113 of the General Statutes or any local wildlife hunting ordinance.

(c) Any property, the forfeiture and disposition of which is specified in any general or special law, shall be disposed of in accordance therewith. (1977, c. 613; 1979, c. 593; 1994, Ex. Sess., c. 16, s. 1; 2000-144, s. 27; 2005-287, s. 1; 2013-158, s. 1.)

§ 15-11.2. Disposition of unclaimed firearms not confiscated or seized as trial evidence.

(a) Definition. - For purposes of this section, the term "unclaimed firearm" means a firearm that is found or received by a law enforcement agency and that remains unclaimed by the person who may be entitled to it for a period of 30 days after the publication of the notice required by subsection (b) of this section. The term does not include a firearm that is seized and disposed of pursuant to G.S. 15-11.1 or a firearm that is confiscated and disposed of pursuant to G.S. 14-269.1.

(b) Published Notice of Unclaimed Firearm. - When a law enforcement agency finds or receives a firearm and the firearm remains unclaimed for a period of 180 days, the agency shall publish at least one notice in a newspaper published in the county in which the agency is located. The notice shall include all of the following:

(1) A statement that the firearm is unclaimed and is in the custody of the law enforcement agency.

(2) A statement that the firearm may be sold or otherwise disposed of unless the firearm is claimed within 30 days of the date of the publication of the notice.

(3) A brief description of the firearm and any other information that the chief or head of the law enforcement agency may consider necessary or advisable to reasonably inform the public about the firearm.

(c) Repealed by Session Laws 2013-158, s. 2, effective September 1, 2013, and applicable to any firearm found or received by a local law enforcement agency on or after that date and to any judicial order for the disposition of any firearm on or after that date.

(d) If the firearm remains unclaimed for a period of 30 days after the publication of the notice, then the head or chief of the law enforcement agency shall order the disposition of the firearm in one of the following ways:

(1) By having the firearm destroyed if the firearm does not have a legible, unique identification number or is unsafe for use because of wear, damage, age, or modification and will not be disposed of pursuant to subdivision (3) of this subsection. The head or chief of the law enforcement agency shall maintain a record of the destruction of the firearm.

(2) By sale, trade, or exchange by the agency to a federally licensed firearm dealer in accordance with all applicable State and federal firearm laws or by sale of the firearm at a public auction to persons licensed as firearms collectors, dealers, importers, or manufacturers. The head or chief of the law enforcement agency shall dispose of the firearm pursuant to this subdivision only if the firearm has a legible, unique identification number.

(3) By maintaining the firearm for training or experimental purposes or transferring the firearm to a museum or historical society.

(e) Repealed by Session Laws 2013-158, s. 2, effective September 1, 2013, and applicable to any firearm found or received by a local law enforcement agency on or after that date and to any judicial order for the disposition of any firearm on or after that date.

(f) Disbursement of Proceeds of Sale. - If the law enforcement agency sells the firearm pursuant to subdivision (2) of subsection (d) of this section, then the proceeds of the sale shall be retained by the law enforcement agency and used for law enforcement purposes. The receiving law enforcement agency shall maintain a record and inventory of all firearms received pursuant to this section, as well as the disposition of the firearm, including any funds received from a sale of a firearm or any firearms or other property received in exchange or trade of a firearm. (2005-287, s. 2; 2013-158, s. 2; 2013-410, s. 17(a).)

§ 15-12. Publication of notice of unclaimed property; advertisement and sale or donation of unclaimed bicycles.

(a) Unless otherwise provided herein, whenever such articles in the possession of any sheriff or police department have remained unclaimed by the person who may be entitled thereto for a period of 180 days after such seizure, confiscation, or receipt thereof in any other manner, by such sheriff or police department, the said sheriff or police department in whose possession said articles are may cause to be published one time in some newspaper published in said county a notice to the effect that such articles are in the custody of such officer or department, and requiring all persons who may have or claim any interest therein to make and establish such claim or interest not later than 30 days from the date of the publication of such notice or in default thereof, such articles will be sold and disposed of. Such notice shall contain a brief description of the said articles and such other information as the said officer or department may consider necessary or advisable to reasonably inform the public as to the kind and nature of the article about which the notice relates.

(b) Notwithstanding subsection (a) of this section or Article 12 of Chapter 160A of the General Statutes, when bicycles which are in the possession of any sheriff or police department, as provided for in this Article, have remained unclaimed by the person who may be entitled thereto for a period of 60 days after such seizure, confiscation or receipt thereof, the said sheriff or police department who has possession of any such bicycle may proceed to advertise and sell such bicycles as provided by this Article, or may donate such bicycles to a charitable organization exempt under section 501(c)(3) of the Internal Revenue Code. If the bicycles are to be donated, the notice shall state that as the intended disposition if they are not claimed. (1939, c. 195, s. 2; 1965, c. 807, s. 1; 1973, c. 1141, s. 4; 1997-180, s. 1.)

§ 15-13. Public sale 30 days after publication of notice.

If said articles shall remain unclaimed or satisfactory evidence of ownership thereof not be presented to the sheriff or police department, as the case may be, for a period of 30 days after the publication of the notice provided for in G.S. 15-12, then the said sheriff or police department in whose custody such articles may be is hereby authorized and empowered to sell the same at public auction for cash to the highest bidder, either at the courthouse door of the county, the county law enforcement headquarters if the sale is conducted by the sheriff, or at the police headquarters of the municipality in which the said articles of property are located, and at such sale to deliver the same to the purchaser or purchasers thereof. (1939, c. 195, s. 3; 1973, c. 1141, s. 5; 1991, c. 531, s. 2.)

§ 15-14. Notice of sale.

Before any sale of said property is made under the provisions of this Article, however, the said sheriff or police department making the same shall first advertise the sale by publishing a notice thereof in some newspaper published in the said county at least one time not less than 10 days prior to the date of sale, and by posting a notice of the sale at the courthouse door and at three other public places in the said county. Said notice shall specify the time and place of sale, and contain a sufficient description of the articles of property to be sold. It shall not be required that the sale lay open for increase bids or objections, but it may be deemed closed when the purchaser at the sale pays the amount of the accepted bid. (1939, c. 195, s. 4; 1973, c. 1141, s. 6.)

§ 15-14.1. Sale of property through electronic auction.

In addition to selling property as authorized in G.S. 15-13, a sheriff or police department may sell property in his or its possession through an electronic auction service. The sheriff or police department shall comply with the publication and notice requirements provided in G.S. 15-12 through G.S. 15-14 prior to any sale under this section. (2003-284, s. 18.6(c).)

§ 15-15. Disbursement of proceeds of sale.

From the proceeds realized from the sale of said property, the sheriff, police department or other officer making the same shall first pay the costs and expenses of the sale, and all other necessary expenses incident to a compliance with this Article, and any balance then remaining from the proceeds of said sale shall be paid within 30 days after the sale to the treasurer of the county board of education of the county in which such sale is made, for the benefit of the fund for maintaining the free public schools of such county. (1939, c. 195, s. 5; 1973, c. 1141, s. 7.)

§ 15-16. Nonliability of officers.

No sheriff, police department, or other officer shall be liable for any damages or claims on account of any such sale or disposition of such property, as provided in this Article. (1939, c. 195, s. 6; 1973, c. 1141, s. 8.)

§ 15-17. Construction of Article.

This Article shall not be construed to apply to the seizure and disposition of whiskey distilleries, game birds, and other property or articles which have been or may be seized, where the existing law now provides the method, manner, and extent of the disposition of such articles or of the proceeds derived from the sale thereof. (1939, c. 195, s. 7.)

Article 3.

Warrants.

§§ 15-18 through 15-24. Repealed by Session Laws 1973, c. 1286, s. 26.

§ 15-24.1. Amendment of warrant to show ownership of property.

Any criminal warrant may be amended in the superior court, before or during the trial, when there shall appear to be any variance between the allegations in the warrant and the evidence in setting forth the ownership of property if, in the opinion of the court, such amendment will not prejudice the defendant. This section shall be construed as enlarging and not limiting the conditions and situations under which a warrant may be amended. (1965, c. 285.)

Article 4.

Search Warrants.

§ 15-25. Repealed by Session Laws 1973, c. 1286, s. 26.

§§ 15-25.1 through 15-25.2. Repealed by Session Laws 1969, c. 869, s. 8.

§§ 15-26 through 15-27.1. Repealed by Session Laws 1973, c. 1286, s. 26.

Article 4A.

Administrative Search and Inspection Warrants.

§ 15-27.2. Warrants to conduct inspections authorized by law.

(a) Notwithstanding the provisions of Article 11 of Chapter 15A, any official or employee of the State or of a unit of county or local government of North

Carolina may, under the conditions specified in this section, obtain a warrant authorizing him to conduct a search or inspection of property if such a search or inspection is one that is elsewhere authorized by law, either with or without the consent of the person whose privacy would be thereby invaded, and is one for which such a warrant is constitutionally required.

(b) The warrant may be issued by any magistrate of the general court of justice, judge, clerk, or assistant or deputy clerk of any court of record whose territorial jurisdiction encompasses the property to be inspected.

(c) The issuing officer shall issue the warrant when he is satisfied the following conditions are met:

(1) The one seeking the warrant must establish under oath or affirmation that the property to be searched or inspected is to be searched or inspected as part of a legally authorized program of inspection which naturally includes that property, or that there is probable cause for believing that there is a condition, object, activity or circumstance which legally justifies such a search or inspection of that property;

(2) An affidavit indicating the basis for the establishment of one of the grounds described in (1) above must be signed under oath or affirmation by the affiant;

(3) The issuing official must examine the affiant under oath or affirmation to verify the accuracy of the matters indicated by the statement in the affidavit;

(d) The warrant shall be validly issued only if it meets the following requirements:

(1) Except as provided in subsection (e), it must be signed by the issuing official and must bear the date and hour of its issuance above his signature with a notation that the warrant is valid for only 24 hours following its issuance;

(2) It must describe, either directly or by reference to the affidavit, the property where the search or inspection is to occur and be accurate enough in description so that the executor of the warrant and the owner or the possessor of the property can reasonably determine from it what person or property the warrant authorizes an inspection of;

(3) It must indicate the conditions, objects, activities or circumstances which the inspection is intended to check or reveal;

(4) It must be attached to the affidavit required to be made in order to obtain the warrant.

(e) Any warrant issued under this section for a search or inspection shall be valid for only 24 hours after its issuance, must be personally served upon the owner or possessor of the property between the hours of 8:00 A.M. and 8:00 P.M. and must be returned within 48 hours. If the warrant, however, was procured pursuant to an investigation authorized by G.S. 58-79-1, the warrant may be executed at any hour, is valid for 48 hours after its issuance, and must be returned without unnecessary delay after its execution or after the expiration of the 48 hour period if it is not executed. If the owner or possessor of the property is not present on the property at the time of the search or inspection and reasonable efforts to locate the owner or possessor have been made and have failed, the warrant or a copy thereof may be affixed to the property and shall have the same effect as if served personally upon the owner or possessor.

(f) No facts discovered or evidence obtained in a search or inspection conducted under authority of a warrant issued under this section shall be competent as evidence in any civil, criminal or administrative action, nor considered in imposing any civil, criminal, or administrative sanction against any person, nor as a basis for further seeking to obtain any warrant, if the warrant is invalid or if what is discovered or obtained is not a condition, object, activity or circumstance which it was the legal purpose of the search or inspection to discover; but this shall not prevent any such facts or evidence to be so used when the warrant issued is not constitutionally required in those circumstances.

(g) The warrants authorized under this section shall not be regarded as search warrants for the purposes of application of Article 11 of Chapter 15A of the General Statutes of North Carolina. (1967, c. 1260; 1979, c. 729; 1983, c. 294, ss. 1, 2; c. 739, ss. 1, 2.)

Article 5.

Peace Warrants.

§§ 15-28 through 15-38. Repealed by Session Laws 1973, c. 1286, ss. 11, 26.

Article 6.

Arrest.

§§ 15-39 through 15-42. Repealed by Session Laws 1973, c. 1286, s. 26.

§ 15-43. House broken open to prevent felony.

All persons are authorized to break open and enter a house to prevent a felony about to be committed therein. (1868-9, c. 178, subch. 1, s. 4; Code, s. 1127; Rev., s. 3179; C.S., s. 4545.)

§§ 15-44 through 15-47. Repealed by Session Laws 1973, c. 1286, s. 26.

Article 7.

Fugitives from Justice.

§ 15-48. Repealed by Session Laws 1997-80, s. 10.

§ 15-49. Repealed by Session Laws 1975, c. 166, s. 26.

§§ 15-50 through 15-52. Repealed by Session Laws 1973, c. 1286, s. 26.

§ 15-53. Governor may employ agents, and offer rewards.

The Governor, on information made to the Governor of any person, whether the name of such person be known or unknown, having committed a felony or other infamous crime within the State, and of having fled out of the jurisdiction thereof, or who conceals himself or herself within the State to avoid arrest, or who, having been convicted, has escaped and cannot otherwise be apprehended, may either employ a special agent, with a sufficient escort, to pursue and apprehend such fugitive, or issue a proclamation, and therein offer a reward, not exceeding one hundred thousand dollars ($100,000), according to the nature of the case, as in the Governor's opinion may be sufficient for the purpose, to be paid to anyone who shall apprehend and deliver the fugitive to such person and at such place as in the proclamation shall be directed. (1800, c. 561, P.R.; R.C., c. 35, s. 4; 1866, c. 28; 1868-9, c. 52; 1870-1, c. 15; 1871-2, c. 29; Code, s. 1169; 1891, c. 421; Rev., s. 3188; C.S., s. 4554; 1925, c. 275, s. 6; 1967, c. 165, s. 1; 2013-276, s. 1.)

§ 15-53.1. Governor may offer rewards for information leading to arrest and conviction.

When it shall appear to the Governor, upon satisfactory information furnished to the Governor, that a felony or other infamous crime has been committed within the State, whether the name or names of the person or persons suspected of committing the said crime be known or unknown, the Governor may issue a proclamation and therein offer an award [reward] not exceeding one hundred thousand dollars ($100,000), according to the nature of the case as, in the Governor's opinion, may be sufficient for the purpose, to be paid to anyone who shall provide information leading to the arrest and conviction of such person or persons. The proclamation shall be upon such terms as the Governor may deem proper, but it shall identify the felony or felonies and the authority to whom the information is to be delivered and shall state such other terms as the Governor may require under which the reward is payable. (1967, c. 165, s. 2; 2013-276, s. 2.)

§ 15-54. Officer entitled to reward.

Any sheriff or other officer who shall make an arrest of any person charged with crime for whose apprehension a reward has been offered is entitled to such reward, and may sue for and recover the same in any court in this State having jurisdiction: Provided, that no reward shall be paid to any sheriff or other officer for any arrest made for a crime committed within the county of such sheriff or officer making such arrest. (1913, c. 132; 1917, c. 8; C.S., s. 4555.)

Article 8.

Extradition.

§§ 15-55 through 15-84. Transferred to G.S. 15A-721 to 15A-750 by Session Laws 1973, c. 1286, s. 16.

Article 9.

Preliminary Examination.

§§ 15-85 through 15-101. Repealed by Session Laws 1973, c. 1286, s. 26.

Article 10.

Bail.

§§ 15-102 through 15-103. Repealed by Session Laws 1973, c. 1286, s. 26.

§ 15-103.1. Repealed by Session Laws 1977, c. 711, s. 33.

§ 15-103.2. Repealed by Session Laws 1975, c. 166, s. 26.

§ 15-104. Repealed by Session Laws 1973, c. 1286, s. 26.

§ 15-104.1. Repealed by Session Laws 1975, c. 166, s. 26.

§§ 15-105 through 15-107. Repealed by Session Laws 1973, c. 1286, s. 26.

§ 15-107.1. Repealed by Session Laws 1975, c. 166, s. 26.

§§ 15-108 through 15-109. Repealed by Session Laws 1973, c. 1286, s. 26.

Article 11.

Forfeiture of Bail.

§§ 15-110 through 15-124. Repealed by Sessions Laws 1977, c. 711, s. 33.

Article 12.

Commitment to Prison.

§ 15-125. Repealed by Session Laws 1973, c. 1286, s. 26.

§ 15-126. Commitment to county jail.

All persons committed to prison before conviction shall be committed to the jail of the county in which the examination is had, or to that of the county in which the offense is charged to have been committed: Provided, if the jails of these counties are unsafe, or injurious to the health of prisoners, the committing magistrate may commit to the jail of any other convenient county. And every sheriff or jailer to whose jail any person shall be committed by any court or magistrate of competent jurisdiction shall receive such prisoner and give a receipt for him, and be bound for his safekeeping as prescribed by law. (1868-9, c. 178, subch. 2, s. 33; Code, s. 1164; Rev., s. 3231; C.S., s. 4598; 1973, c. 1286, s. 26; 1975, c. 166, s. 25.)

§ 15-127. Repealed by Session Laws 1973, c. 1286, s. 26.

Article 13.

Venue.

§ 15-128. Repealed by Session Laws 1973, c. 1286, s. 26.

§ 15-129. In offenses on waters dividing counties.

When any offense is committed on any water, or watercourse whether at high or low water, which water or watercourse, or the sides or shores thereof, divides counties, such offense may be dealt with, inquired of, tried and determined, and punished at the discretion of the court, in either of the two counties which may be nearest to the place where the offense was committed. (R.C., c. 35, s. 24; Code, s. 1193; Rev., s. 3234; C.S., s. 4601; 1973, c. 1286, s. 26; 1975, c. 166, s. 25.)

§ 15-130. Assault in one county, death in another.

In all cases of felonious homicide when the assault has been made in one county within the State, and the person assaulted dies in any other county thereof, the offender shall be indicted and punished for the crime in the county wherein the assault was made. (1831, c. 22, s. 1; R.C., c. 35, s. 27; Code, s. 1196; Rev., s. 3235; C.S., s. 4602.)

§ 15-131. Assault in this State, death in another.

In all cases of felonious homicide, when the assault has been made within this State, and the person assaulted dies without the limits thereof, the offender shall be indicted and punished for the crime in the county where the assault was made, in the same manner, to all intents and purposes, as if the person assaulted had died within the limits of this State. (1831, c. 22, s. 2; R.C., c. 35, s. 28; Code, s. 1197; Rev., s. 3236; C.S., s. 4603.)

§ 15-132. Person in this State injuring one in another.

If any person, being in this State, unlawfully and willfully puts in motion a force from the effect of which any person is injured while in another state, the person so setting such force in motion shall be guilty of the same offense in this State as he would be if the effect had taken place within this State. (1895, c. 169; Rev., s. 3237; C.S., s. 4604.)

§ 15-133. In county where death occurs.

If a mortal wound is given or other violence or injury inflicted or poison is administered on the high seas or land, either within or without the limits of this

State, by means whereof death ensues in any county thereof, the offense may be prosecuted and punished in the county where the death happens. (1891, c. 68; Rev., s. 3238; C.S., s. 4605.)

§§ 15-134 through 15-136. Repealed by Session Laws 1973, c. 1286, s. 26.

Article 14.

Presentment.

§§ 15-137 through 15-139. Repealed by Session Laws 1973, c. 1286, s. 26.

Article 15.

Indictment.

§§ 15-140 through 15-143. Repealed by Session Laws 1973, c. 1286, s. 26.

§ 15-144. Essentials of bill for homicide.

In indictments for murder and manslaughter, it is not necessary to allege matter not required to be proved on the trial; but in the body of the indictment, after naming the person accused, and the county of his residence, the date of the offense, the averment "with force and arms," and the county of the alleged commission of the offense, as is now usual, it is sufficient in describing murder to allege that the accused person feloniously, willfully, and of his malice aforethought, did kill and murder (naming the person killed), and concluding as is now required by law; and it is sufficient in describing manslaughter to allege that the accused feloniously and willfully did kill and slay (naming the person killed), and concluding as aforesaid; and any bill of indictment containing the averments and allegations herein named shall be good and sufficient in law as an indictment for murder or manslaughter, as the case may be. (1887, c. 58; Rev., s. 3245; C.S., s. 4614.)

§ 15-144.1. Essentials of bill for rape.

(a) In indictments for rape it is not necessary to allege every matter required to be proved on the trial; but in the body of the indictment, after naming the person accused, the date of the offense, the county in which the offense of rape was allegedly committed, and the averment "with force and arms," as is now usual, it is sufficient in describing rape to allege that the accused person unlawfully, willfully, and feloniously did ravish and carnally know the victim, naming her, by force and against her will and concluding as is now required by law. Any bill of indictment containing the averments and allegations herein named shall be good and sufficient in law as an indictment for rape in the first degree and will support a verdict of guilty of rape in the first degree, rape in the second degree, attempted rape or assault on a female.

(b) If the victim is a female child under the age of 13 years it is sufficient to allege that the accused unlawfully, willfully, and feloniously did carnally know and abuse a child under 13, naming her, and concluding as aforesaid. Any bill of indictment containing the averments and allegations herein named shall be good and sufficient in law as an indictment for the rape of a female child under the age of 13 years and all lesser included offenses.

(c) If the victim is a person who is mentally disabled, mentally incapacitated, or physically helpless it is sufficient to allege that the defendant unlawfully, willfully, and feloniously did carnally know and abuse a person who was mentally disabled, mentally incapacitated or physically helpless, naming such victim, and concluding as aforesaid. Any bill of indictment containing the averments and allegations herein named shall be good and sufficient in law for the rape of a mentally disabled, mentally incapacitated or physically helpless person and all lesser included offenses. (1977, c. 861, s. 1; 1979, c. 682, s. 10; 1983, c. 720, s. 1; 2002-159, s. 2(d).)

§ 15-144.2. Essentials of bill for sex offense.

(a) In indictments for sex offense it is not necessary to allege every matter required to be proved on the trial; but in the body of the indictment, after naming the person accused, the date of the offense, the county in which the sex offense was allegedly committed, and the averment "with force and arms," as is now usual, it is sufficient in describing a sex offense to allege that the accused person unlawfully, willfully, and feloniously did engage in a sex offense with the victim, naming the victim, by force and against the will of such victim and concluding as is now required by law. Any bill of indictment containing the averments and allegations herein named shall be good and sufficient in law as an indictment for a first degree sex offense and will support a verdict of guilty of a sex offense in the first degree, a sex offense in the second degree, an attempt to commit a sex offense or an assault.

(b)   If the victim is a person under the age of 13 years, it is sufficient to allege that the defendant unlawfully, willfully, and feloniously did engage in a sex offense with a child under the age of 13 years, naming the child, and concluding as aforesaid. Any bill of indictment containing the averments and allegations herein named shall be good and sufficient in law as an indictment for a sex offense against a child under the age of 13 years and all lesser included offenses.

(c)   If the victim is a person who is mentally disabled, mentally incapacitated, or physically helpless it is sufficient to allege that the defendant unlawfully, willfully, and feloniously did engage in a sex offense with a person who was mentally disabled, mentally incapacitated or physically helpless, naming such victim, and concluding as aforesaid. Any bill of indictment containing the averments and allegations herein named shall be good and sufficient in law for a sex offense against a mentally disabled, mentally incapacitated or physically helpless person and all lesser included offenses. (1979, c. 682, s. 11; 1983, c. 720, ss. 2, 3; 2002-159, s. 2(e).)

§ 15-145. Form of bill for perjury.

In every indictment for willful and corrupt perjury it is sufficient to set forth the substance of the offense charged upon the defendant, and by what court, or before whom, the oath was taken (averring such court or person to have competent authority to administer the same), together with the proper averments to falsify the matter wherein the perjury is assigned, without setting forth the bill, answer, information, indictment, declaration, or any part of any record or proceedings, either in law or equity, other than aforesaid, and without setting forth the commission or authority of the court or person before whom the perjury was committed. In indictments for perjury the following form shall be sufficient, to wit:

The jurors for the State, on their oath, present, that A.B., of_____ County, did unlawfully commit perjury upon the trial of an action in _____ court, in _____ County, wherein _____ was plaintiff and _____ was defendant, by falsely asserting, on oath (or solemn affirmation) (here set out the statement or statements alleged to be false), knowing the said statement, or statements, to be false, or being ignorant whether or not said statement was true. (1842, c. 49, s. 1; R.C., c. 35, s. 16; Code, s. 1185; 1889, c. 83; Rev., ss. 3246, 3247; C.S., s. 4615.)

§ 15-146. Bill for subornation of perjury.

In every indictment for subornation of perjury, or for corrupt bargaining or contracting with others to commit willful and corrupt perjury, it is sufficient to set forth the substance of the offense charged upon the defendant, without setting forth the bill, answer, information, indictment, declaration or any part of any record or proceedings, and without setting forth the commission or authority of the court or person before whom the perjury was committed or was agreed or promised to be committed. (1842, c. 49, s. 2; R.C., c. 35, s. 17; Code, s. 1186; Rev., s. 3248; C.S., s. 4616.)

§ 15-147. Repealed by Session Laws 1973, c. 1286, s. 26.

§ 15-148. Manner of alleging joint ownership of property.

In any indictment wherein it is necessary to state the ownership of any property whatsoever, whether real or personal, which belongs to, or is in the possession of, more than one person, whether such persons be partners in trade, joint tenants or tenants in common, it is sufficient to name one of such persons, and to state such property to belong to the person so named, and another or others as the case may be; and whenever, in any such indictment, it is necessary to mention, for any purpose whatsoever, any partners, joint tenants or tenants in common, it is sufficient to describe them in the manner aforesaid; and this provision shall extend to all joint-stock companies and trustees. (R.C., c. 35, s. 19; Code, s. 1188; Rev., s. 3250; C.S., s. 4618.)

§ 15-149. Description in bill for larceny of money.

In every indictment in which it is necessary to make any averment as to the larceny of any money, or United States treasury note, or any note of any bank whatsoever, it is sufficient to describe such money, or treasury note, or bank note, simply as money, without specifying any particular coin, or treasury note, or bank note; and such allegation, so far as regards the description of the property, shall be sustained by proof of any amount of coin, or treasury note, or bank note, although the particular species of coin, of which such amount was composed, or the particular nature of the treasury note, or bank note, shall not be proven. (1876-7, c. 68; Code, s. 1190; Rev., s. 3251; C.S., s. 4619.)

§ 15-150. Description in bill for embezzlement.

In indictments for embezzlement, except when the offense relates to a chattel, it is sufficient to allege the embezzlement to be of money, without specifying any particular coin or valuable security; and such allegation, so far as regards the description of the property, shall be sustained if the offender shall be proved to have embezzled any amount, although the particular species of coin or valuable security of which such amount was composed shall not be proved. (1871-2, c. 145, s. 2; Code, s. 1020; Rev., s. 3252; C.S., s. 4620.)

§ 15-151. Intent to defraud; larceny and receiving.

In any case where an intent to defraud is required to constitute the offense of forgery, or any other offense whatever, it is sufficient to allege in the indictment an intent to defraud, without naming therein the particular person or body corporate intended to be defrauded; and on the trial of such indictment, it shall be sufficient, and shall not be deemed a variance, if there appear to be an intent to defraud the United States, or any state, county, city, town, or parish, or body corporate, or any public officer in his official capacity, or any copartnership or member thereof, or any particular person. The defendant may be charged in the same indictment in several counts with the separate offenses of receiving stolen goods, knowing them to be stolen, and larceny. (1852, c. 87, s. 2; R.C., c. 35, ss. 21, 23; 1874-5, c. 62; Code, s. 1191; Rev., s. 3253; C.S., s. 4621.)

§ 15-152. Repealed by Session Laws 1973, c. 1286, s. 26.

§ 15-153. Bill or warrant not quashed for informality.

Every criminal proceeding by warrant, indictment, information, or impeachment is sufficient in form for all intents and purposes if it express the charge against the defendant in a plain, intelligible, and explicit manner; and the same shall not be quashed, nor the judgment thereon stayed, by reason of any informality or refinement, if in the bill or proceeding, sufficient matter appears to enable the court to proceed to judgment. (37 Hen. VIII, c. 8; 1784, c. 210, s. 2, P.R.; 1811, c. 809, P.R.; R.C., c. 35, s. 14; Code, s. 1183; Rev., s. 3254; C.S., s. 4623.)

§ 15-154. Repealed by Session Laws 1973, c. 1286, s. 26.

§ 15-155. Defects which do not vitiate.

No judgment upon any indictment for felony or misdemeanor, whether after verdict, or by confession, or otherwise, shall be stayed or reversed for the want of the averment of any matter unnecessary to be proved, nor for omission of the words "as appears by the record," or of the words "with force and arms," nor for the insertion of the words "against the form of the statutes" instead of the words "against the form of the statute," or vice versa; nor for omission of the words "against the form of the statute" or "against the form of the statutes," nor for omitting to state the time at which the offense was committed in any case where time is not of the essence of the offense, nor for stating the time imperfectly, nor for stating the offense to have been committed on a day subsequent to the finding of the indictment, or on an impossible day, or on a day that never happened; nor for want of a proper and perfect venue, when the court shall appear by the indictment to have had jurisdiction of the offense. (7 Hen. VIII, c. 8; R.C., c. 35, s. 20; Code, s. 1189; Rev., s. 3255; C.S., s. 4625.)

Article 15A.

Investigation of Offenses Involving Abandonment and Nonsupport of Children.

§ 15-155.1. Reports to district attorneys of Work First Family Assistance and out-of-wedlock births.

The Department of Health and Human Services by and through the Secretary of Health and Human Services shall promptly after June 19, 1959, make a report to each district attorney, setting out the names and addresses of all mothers who reside in his prosecutorial district as defined in G.S. 7A-60 and are recipients of assistance under the provisions of Part 2, Article 2, Chapter 108A of the General Statutes. Such report shall in some manner show the identity of the unwed mothers and shall set forth the number of children born to each said mother. Such a report shall also be made monthly thereafter setting out the names and addresses of all such mothers who reside in the district and who may have become recipients of assistance under the provisions of Part 2, Article 2, Chapter 108A of the General Statutes since the date of the last report. (1959, c. 1210, s. 1; 1973, c. 47, s. 2; c. 476, s. 138; 1987 (Reg. Sess., 1988), c. 1037, s. 50; 1997-443, ss. 11A.118(a), 12.23.)

§ 15-155.2. District attorney to take action on report of Work First Family Assistance and children born out of wedlock.

(a)   Upon receipt of such reports as are provided for in G.S. 15-155.1, the district attorney of superior court may make an investigation to determine whether the mother of an out-of-wedlock child or who is a recipient of Work First Family Assistance, has abandoned, is willfully neglecting or is refusing to support and maintain the child within the meaning of G.S. 14-326 or 49-2 or is diverting any part of the funds received as Work First Family Assistance to any purpose other than for the support and maintenance of a child in violation of G.S. 108-76.1. In making this investigation the district attorney is authorized to call upon:

(1)   Any county board of social services or the Department of Health and Human Services for personal, clerical or investigative assistance and for access to any records kept by either such board and relating to the matter under investigation and such boards are hereby directed to assist in all investigations hereunder and to furnish all records relating thereto when so requested by the district attorney;

(2)   The board of county commissioners of any county within his district for legal or clerical assistance in making any investigation or investigations in such county and such boards are hereby authorized to furnish such assistance in their discretion; and

(3) The district attorney of any inferior court in his district for personal assistance in making any investigation or investigations in the county in which the court is located and any district attorney so called upon is hereby authorized to furnish such assistance by and with the consent of the board of county commissioners of the county in which the court is located, which board shall provide and fix his compensation for assistance furnished.

(b) If following the investigation the district attorney has reasonable grounds to believe that a violation of G.S. 49-2, 14-326, 108-76.1 or any other criminal offense is being or has been committed, he shall send to the grand jury of the county in which he believes the offense is being or has been committed a bill of indictment charging the commission of the offense. Sole and exclusive jurisdiction of offenses discovered as a result of investigations under this section shall be vested in the superior court notwithstanding any other provisions of law, whether general, special or local. Provided nothing in this Article shall be construed to take from the inferior courts any authority or responsibility now vested in them by existing law or to compel the district attorney to again prosecute a crime that has been disposed of in the inferior courts.

(c) Repealed by Session Laws 1985, c. 589, s. 8. (1959, c. 1210, s. 1; 1969, c. 982; 1973, c. 47, s. 2; c. 476, s. 138; 1985, c. 589, s. 8; 1997-443, ss. 11A.118(a), 12.24; 2013-198, s. 4.)

§ 15-155.3. Disclosure of information by district attorney or agent.

No such district attorney, assistant district attorney, or any attorney-at-law especially appointed to assist the district attorney, or any agent or employee of the district attorney's office shall disclose any information, record, report, case history or any memorandum or document or any information contained therein, which may relate to or be connected with the mother or father of any child born out of wedlock, or any child born out of wedlock, unless in the opinion of the district attorney it is necessary or is required in the prosecution and performance of the district attorney's duties as set forth in the provisions of this Article. (1959, c. 1210, s. 4; 1973, c. 47, s. 2; 2013-198, s. 5.)

Article 15B.

Pretrial Examination of Witnesses and Exhibits of the State.

§§ 15-155.4 through 15-155.5. Repealed by Session Laws 1973, c. 1286, s. 26.

Article 16.

Trial before Justice.

§§ 15-156 through 15-158. Repealed by Session Laws 1973, c. 1286, s. 26.

§ 15-159. Repealed by Session Laws 1977, c. 711, s. 33.

§§ 15-160 through 15-161. Repealed by Session Laws 1973, c. 1286, s. 26.

Article 17.

Trial in Superior Court.

§ 15-162. Repealed by Session Laws 1973, c. 1286, s. 26.

§ 15-162.1. Repealed by Session Laws 1971, c. 1225.

§§ 15-163 through 15-165. Repealed by Session Laws 1967, c. 218, s. 4.

§ 15-166. Exclusion of bystanders in trial for rape and sex offenses.

In the trial of cases for rape or sex offense or attempt to commit rape or attempt to commit a sex offense, the trial judge may, during the taking of the testimony of the prosecutrix, exclude from the courtroom all persons except the officers of the court, the defendant and those engaged in the trial of the case. (1907, c. 21; C. S., s. 4636; 1973, c. 1141, s. 14; 1979, c. 682, s. 3; 1981, c. 682, s. 5.)

§ 15-167. Extension of session of court by trial judge.

Whenever a trial for a felony is in progress on the last Friday of any session of court and it appears to the trial judge that it is unlikely that such trial can be completed before 5:00 P.M. on such Friday, the trial judge may extend the session as long as in his opinion it shall be necessary for the purposes of the case, but he may recess court on Friday or Saturday of such week to such time on the succeeding Sunday or Monday as, in his discretion, he deems wise. The trial judge, in his discretion, may exercise the same power in the trial of any other cause under the same circumstances, except civil actions begun after Thursday of the last week. The length of time such court shall remain in session each day shall be in the discretion of the trial judge. Whenever a trial judge continues a session pursuant to this section, he shall cause an order to such effect to be entered in the minutes, which order may be entered at such time as the judge directs, either before or after he has extended the session. (1830, c. 22; R.C., c. 31, s. 16; C.C.P., s. 397; Code, s. 1229; 1893, c. 226; Rev., s. 3266; C.S., s. 4637; 1961, c. 181; 1973, c. 1141, s. 15.)

§ 15-168. Justification as defense to libel.

Every defendant who is charged by indictment with the publication of a libel may prove on the trial for the same the truth of the facts alleged in the indictment; and if it shall appear to the satisfaction of the jury that the facts are true, the defendant shall be acquitted of the charge. (R.C., c. 35, s. 26; Code, s. 1195; Rev., s. 3267; C.S., s. 4638.)

§ 15-169. Conviction of assault, when included in charge.

On the trial of any person for any felony whatsoever, when the crime charged includes an assault against the person, it is lawful for the jury to acquit of the felony and to find a verdict of guilty of assault against the person indicted, if the evidence warrants such finding; and when such verdict is found the court shall have power to imprison the person so found guilty of an assault, for any term now allowed by law in cases of conviction when the indictment was originally for the assault of a like character. (1885, c. 68; Rev., s. 3268; C.S., s. 4639; 1979, c. 682, s. 4.)

§ 15-170. Conviction for a less degree or an attempt.

Upon the trial of any indictment the prisoner may be convicted of the crime charged therein or of a less degree of the same crime, or of an attempt to commit the crime so charged, or of an attempt to commit a less degree of the same crime. (1891, c. 205, s. 2; Rev., s. 3269; C.S., s. 4640.)

§ 15-171. Repealed by Session Laws 1953, c. 100.

§ 15-172. Verdict for murder in first or second degree.

Nothing contained in the statute law dividing murder into degrees shall be construed to require any alteration or modification of the existing form of indictment for murder, but the jury before whom the offender is tried shall determine in their verdict whether the crime is murder in the first or second degree. (1893, c. 85, s. 3; Rev., s. 3271; C.S., s. 4642.)

§ 15-173. Demurrer to the evidence.

When on the trial of any criminal action in the superior or district court, the State has introduced its evidence and rested its case, the defendant may move to dismiss the action, or for judgment as in case of nonsuit. If the motion is allowed, judgment shall be entered accordingly; and such judgment shall have the force and effect of a verdict of "not guilty" as to such defendant. If the motion is refused and the defendant does not choose to introduce evidence, the case shall be submitted to the jury as in other cases, and the defendant may on appeal urge as ground for reversal, the trial court's denial of his motion without the necessity of the defendant's having taken exception to such denial.

If the defendant introduces evidence, he thereby waives any motion for dismissal or judgment as in case of nonsuit which he may have made prior to the introduction of his evidence and cannot urge such prior motion as ground for appeal. The defendant, however, may make such motion at the conclusion of all the evidence in the case, irrespective of whether or not he made a motion for dismissal or judgment as in case of nonsuit theretofore. If the motion is allowed, or shall be sustained on appeal, it shall in all cases have the force and effect of a verdict of "not guilty." If the motion is refused, the defendant may on appeal, after the jury has rendered its verdict, urge as ground for reversal the trial court's denial of his motion made at the close of all the evidence without the necessity of the defendant's having taken exception to such denial. (1913, c. 73; Ex. Sess. 1913, c. 32; C.S., s. 4643; 1951, c. 1086, s. 1; 1973, c. 1141, s. 16.)

§§ 15-173.1 through 15-174. Repealed by Session Laws 1977, c. 711, s. 33.

§ 15-175. Repealed by Session Laws 1973, c. 1286, s. 26.

§ 15-176. Prisoner not to be tried in prison uniform.

It shall be unlawful for any sheriff, jailer or other officer to require any person imprisoned in jail to appear in any court for trial dressed in the uniform or dress of a prisoner or convict, or in any uniform or apparel other than ordinary civilian's dress, or with shaven or clipped head. And no person charged with a criminal offense shall be tried in any court while dressed in the uniform or dress of a prisoner or convict, or in any uniform or apparel other than ordinary civilian's dress, or with head shaven or clipped by or under the direction and requirement of any sheriff, jailer or other officer, unless the head was shaven or clipped while such person was serving a term of imprisonment for the commission of a crime.

Any sheriff, jailer or other officer who violates the provisions of this section shall be guilty of a Class 1 misdemeanor. (1915, c. 124; C.S., s. 4646; 1993, c. 539, s. 296; 1994, Ex. Sess., c. 24, s. 14(c).)

§ 15-176.1. District attorney may argue for death penalty.

In the trial of capital cases, the district attorney or other counsel appearing for the State may argue to the jury that a sentence of death should be imposed and that the jury should not recommend life imprisonment. (1961, c. 890; 1973, c. 47, s. 2.)

§ 15-176.2. Repealed by Session Laws 1973, c. 44, s. 1.

Article 17A.

Informing Jury in Case Involving Death Penalty.

§ 15-176.3. Informing and questioning potential jurors on consequences of guilty verdict.

When a jury is being selected for a case in which the defendant is indicted for a crime for which the penalty is a sentence of death, the court, the defense, or the State may inform any person called to serve as a potential juror that the death penalty will be imposed upon the return of a verdict of guilty of that crime and may inquire of any person called to serve as a potential juror whether that person understands the consequences of a verdict of guilty of that crime. (1973, c. 1286, s. 12.)

§ 15-176.4. Instruction to jury on consequences of guilty verdict.

When a defendant is indicted for a crime for which the penalty is a sentence of death, the court, upon request by either party, shall instruct the jury that the death penalty will be imposed upon the return of a verdict of guilty of that crime. (1973, c. 1286, s. 12.)

§ 15-176.5. Argument to jury on consequences of guilty verdict.

When a case will be submitted to a jury on a charge for which the penalty is a sentence of death, either party in its argument to the jury may indicate the consequences of a verdict of guilty of that charge. (1973, c. 1286, s. 12.)

§§ 15-176.6 through 15-176.8. Reserved for future codification purposes.

Article 17B.

Informing Jury of Possible Punishment upon Conviction.

§ 15-176.9. Loss of motor vehicle driver's license.

When a case will be submitted to a jury on a charge for which the penalty involves the possibility of the loss of a motor vehicle driver's license, either party in its argument to the jury may indicate the consequences of a verdict of guilty of that charge. (1973, c. 1286, s. 25.)

Article 18.

Appeal.

§§ 15-177 through 15-178. Repealed by Session Laws 1973, c. 1141, s. 17.

§§ 15-179 through 15-186. Repealed by Session Laws 1977, c. 711, s. 33.

§ 15-186.1: Repealed by Session Laws 1973, c. 44, s. 1.

Article 19.

Execution.

§ 15-187. Death by administration of lethal drugs.

Death by electrocution under sentence of law and death by the administration of lethal gas under sentence of law are abolished. Any person convicted of a criminal offense and sentenced to death shall be executed only by the administration of a lethal quantity of an ultrashort-acting barbiturate in combination with a chemical paralytic agent. The warden of Central Prison may obtain and employ the drugs necessary to carry out the provisions of this Article, regardless of contrary provisions in Chapter 90 of the General Statutes. (1909, ch. 443, s. 1; C.S., s. 4657; 1935, c. 294, s. 1; 1983, c. 678, ss. 1, 4; 1998-212, s. 17.22(a).)

§ 15-188. Manner and place of execution.

In accordance with G.S. 15-187, the mode of executing a death sentence must in every case be by administering to the convict or felon an intravenous injection of a substance or substances in a lethal quantity sufficient to cause death and until the person is dead, and that procedure shall be determined by the Secretary of the Department of Public Safety, who shall ensure compliance with the federal and State constitutions; and when any person, convict or felon shall be sentenced by any court of the State having competent jurisdiction to be so executed, the punishment shall only be inflicted within a permanent death chamber which the superintendent of the State penitentiary is hereby authorized and directed to provide within the walls of the North Carolina penitentiary at Raleigh, North Carolina. The superintendent of the State penitentiary shall also cause to be provided, in conformity with this Article, the necessary appliances for the infliction of the punishment of death and qualified personnel to set up and prepare the injection, administer the preinjections, insert the IV catheter, and to perform other tasks required for this procedure in accordance with the requirements of this Article. (1909, c. 443, s. 2; C.S., s. 4658; 1935, c. 294, s. 2; 1983, c. 678, s. 2; 1998-212, s. 17.22(b); 2012-136, s. 1; 2013-154, s. 3(a).)

§ 15-188.1. Health care professional assistance.

(a) Any assistance rendered with an execution under this Article by any licensed health care professional, including, but not limited to, physicians, nurses, and pharmacists, shall not be cause for any disciplinary or corrective measures by any board, commission, or other authority created by the State or governed by State law which oversees or regulates the practice of health care professionals, including, but not limited to, the North Carolina Medical Board, the North Carolina Board of Nursing, and the North Carolina Board of Pharmacy.

(b) The infliction of the punishment of death by administration of the required lethal substances under this Article shall not be construed to be the practice of medicine. (2013-154, s. 1(a).)

§ 15-189. Sentence of death; prisoner taken to penitentiary.

Upon the sentence of death being pronounced against any person in the State of North Carolina convicted of a crime punishable by death, it shall be the duty of the judge pronouncing such death sentence to make the same in writing, which shall be filed in the papers in the case against such convicted person. The clerk of the superior court in which such death sentence is pronounced shall prepare a certified copy of said judgment or sentence of death, including therewith a copy of any notice or entries of appeal made in such case; if no entries or notice of appeal have been made or given in such case, a statement to the effect shall be included in the certificate of the clerk; it shall also be the duty of the district attorney, assistant district attorney, or attorney prosecuting in behalf of the State in the absence of the district attorney, to prepare and sign a certificate stating in substance that he prosecuted said case in behalf of the State and that notice or entries of appeal have or have not been made or given in said case, and further that he has examined a copy of said judgment or sentence of death certified by the clerk, including the copy of the notice or entries of appeal or statement to the effect that no appeal has been given, and to the best of his knowledge the same is correct; the certificate of said district attorney, or other prosecuting officer above named, shall be attached to the certified copy of said sentence of death, as prepared and certified by the clerk, and both certificates shall be transmitted by the clerk of the superior court in which said sentence of death is pronounced to the warden of the State penitentiary at Raleigh, North Carolina; at the same time and in the same manner, a duplicate original of said certificates shall be prepared by the clerk of the superior court and the district attorney, or other prosecuting officer above named, and the said duplicate original or said certificates shall be transmitted to the Attorney General of North Carolina. If notice of appeal is given or entries of appeal are made after the expiration of the term of superior court in which said sentence of death is pronounced, said certificates shall be prepared by the clerk of the superior court in which said sentence is pronounced and by the district attorney, or other prosecuting officer above named, prosecuting in behalf of the State, in the same manner and shall be transmitted as soon as possible to the warden of the State penitentiary at Raleigh, North Carolina, and to the Attorney General of North Carolina. The above certificates so prepared by the clerk of the superior court in which such sentence of death is pronounced and by the district attorney, or other prosecuting officer above named, shall be transmitted by the clerk of the superior court in which such sentence is pronounced to the warden of the State penitentiary at Raleigh, North Carolina, and to the Attorney General of North Carolina, not more than 20 or less than 10 days before the time fixed in the judgment of the court for the execution of the sentence; and in all cases where there is no appeal, said sentence of death shall not be carried out by the warden of the State penitentiary or by any of his deputies or agents until said certificates so prepared and transmitted by the clerk of the superior court in which said sentence of death is pronounced, and by the district attorney, or the prosecuting officer above named, have been received in the office of the warden of the State penitentiary at Raleigh, North Carolina. In all cases where there is no appeal from the sentence of death and in all cases where the sentence is pronounced against a prisoner convicted of the crime of rape it shall be the duty of the sheriff, together with at least one deputy, to convey to the penitentiary, at Raleigh, North Carolina, such condemned felon or convict forthwith upon the adjournment of the court in which the felon was tried, and deliver the convict or felon to the warden of the penitentiary. (1909, c. 443, s. 3; C.S., s. 4659; 1951, c. 899, s. 1; 1973, c. 47, s. 2.)

§ 15-190. Person or persons to be designated by warden to execute sentence; supervision of execution; who shall be present.

(a) Some guard or guards or other reliable person or persons to be named and designated by the warden from time to time shall cause the person, convict or felon against whom the death sentence has been so pronounced to be executed as provided by this Article and all amendments thereto. The execution shall be under the general supervision and control of the warden of the penitentiary, who shall from time to time, in writing, name and designate the guard or guards or other reliable person or persons who shall cause the person, convict or felon against whom the death sentence has been pronounced to be executed as provided by this Article and all amendments thereto. At such execution there shall be present the warden or deputy warden or some person designated by the warden in the warden's place, and a licensed physician. Four respectable citizens, two members of the victim's family, the counsel and any relatives of such person, convict or felon and a minister or member of the clergy or religious leader of the person's choosing may be present if they so desire. The identities, including the names, residential addresses, residential telephone numbers, and social security numbers, of witnesses or persons designated to carry out the execution shall be confidential and exempted from Chapter 132 of the General Statutes and are not subject to discovery or introduction as evidence in any proceeding. The Senior Resident Superior Court Judge for Wake County may order disclosure of names made confidential by this section after making findings that support a conclusion that disclosure is necessary to a proper administration of justice.

(b) The warden shall report to the Joint Legislative Oversight Committee on Justice and Public Safety by April 1, 2014, and thereafter on October 1 of each year, on the status of the persons required by subsection (a) of this section to be named and designated by the warden to execute death sentences under this Article. The report shall confirm that the required persons are properly trained and ready to serve as an execution team. Alternatively, the Chairs of the Joint Legislative Oversight Committee on Justice and Public Safety may direct that the reports required under this subsection be made on other dates consistent with the Committee's schedule. (1909, c. 443, s. 4; C.S., s. 4660; 1925, c. 123; 1935, c. 294, s. 3; 1983, c. 678, s. 3; 1997-70, s. 1; 2004-124, s. 17.6A; 2004-199, s. 52; 2004-203, s. 22; 2013-154, s. 4.)

§ 15-191. Pending sentences unaffected.

Nothing in G.S. 15-187, 15-188, and 15-190 shall be construed to alter in any manner the execution of the sentence of death imposed on account of any crime or crimes committed before July 1, 1935. (1935, c. 294, s. 4.)

§ 15-192. Certificate filed with clerk.

The warden, together with the surgeon or physician of the penitentiary, shall certify the fact of the execution of the condemned person, convict or felon to the clerk of the superior court in which such sentence was pronounced, and the clerk shall file such certificate with the papers of the case and enter the same upon the records thereof. (1909, c. 443, s. 5; C.S., s. 4661.)

§ 15-193. Notice of reprieve or new trial.

Should the condemned person, convict or felon be granted a reprieve by the Governor or obtain a writ of error, or a new trial be granted by the Supreme Court of the State of North Carolina, or should the execution of the sentence be stayed by any competent judicial tribunal or proceeding, notice of such reprieve, new trial, appeal, writ of error or stay of execution shall be served upon the warden or deputy warden of the penitentiary by the sheriff of Wake County, in case such condemned person is confined in the penitentiary, or upon any sheriff having the custody of any such condemned person, also upon the condemned person himself. (1909, c. 443, s. 6; C.S., s. 4662.)

§ 15-194. Time for execution.

(a) In sentencing a capital defendant to a death sentence pursuant to G.S. 15A-2000(b), the sentencing judge need not specify the date and time the execution is to be carried out by the Division of Adult Correction of the Department of Public Safety. The Attorney General of North Carolina shall provide written notification to the Secretary of the Department of Public Safety of the occurrence of any of the following not more than 90 days from that occurrence:

(1) The United States Supreme Court has filed an opinion upholding the sentence of death following completion of the initial State and federal postconviction proceedings, if any;

(2) The mandate issued by the Supreme Court of North Carolina on direct appeal pursuant to N.C.R. App. P. 32(b) affirming the capital defendant's death sentence and the time for filing a petition for writ of certiorari to the United States Supreme Court has expired without a petition being filed;

(3) The capital defendant, if indigent, failed to timely seek the appointment of counsel pursuant to G.S. 7A-451(c), or failed to file a timely motion for appropriate relief as required by G.S. 15A-1415(a);

(4) The superior court denied the capital defendant's motion for appropriate relief, but the capital defendant failed to file a timely petition for writ of certiorari to the Supreme Court of North Carolina pursuant to N.C.R. App. P. 21(f);

(5) The Supreme Court of North Carolina denied the capital defendant's petition for writ of certiorari pursuant to N.C.R. App. P. 21(f), or, if certiorari was granted, upheld the capital defendant's death sentence, but the capital defendant failed to file a timely petition for writ of certiorari to the United States Supreme Court; or

(6) Following State postconviction proceedings, if any, the capital defendant failed to file a timely petition for writ of habeas corpus in the appropriate federal district court, or failed to timely appeal or petition an adverse habeas corpus

decision to the United States Court of Appeals for the Fourth Circuit or the United States Supreme Court.

The Secretary of the Department of Public Safety shall immediately schedule a date for the execution of the original death sentence not less than 15 days or more than 120 days from the date of receiving written notification from the Attorney General under this section.

The Secretary shall send a certified copy of the document fixing the date to the clerk of superior court of the county in which the case was tried or, if venue was changed, in which the defendant was indicted. The certified copy shall be recorded in the minutes of the court. The Secretary shall also send certified copies to the capital defendant, the capital defendant's attorney, the district attorney who prosecuted the case, and the Attorney General of North Carolina.

(b) The Attorney General shall submit a written report to the Joint Legislative Oversight Committee on Justice and Public Safety by April 1, 2014, and thereafter on October 1 of each year, on the status of all pending postconviction capital cases. Alternatively, the Chairs of the Joint Legislative Oversight Committee on Justice and Public Safety may direct that the reports required under this subsection be made on other dates consistent with the Committee's schedule. (1909, c. 443, s. 6; C.S., s. 4663; 1925, c. 55; 1951, c. 244, ss. 1, 2; 1973, c. 47, s. 2; 1981, c. 900; 1995 (Reg. Sess., 1996), c. 719, s. 5; 1997-289, s. 1; 1999-358, s. 2; 2011-145, s. 19.1(h), (i); 2013-154, s. 2.)

§ 15-195. Prisoner taken to place of trial when new trial granted.

Should a new trial be granted the condemned person, convict or felon against whom sentence of death has been pronounced, after he has been conveyed to the penitentiary, he shall be conveyed back to the place of trial by such guard or guards as the warden of the penitentiary shall direct, their expenses to be paid as is now provided by law for the conveyance of convicts to the penitentiary. (1909, c. 443, s. 7; C.S., s. 4664.)

§ 15-196: Repealed by Session Laws 1989, c. 353, s. 3.

Article 19A.

Credits against the Service of Sentences and for Attainment of Prison Privileges.

§ 15-196.1. Credits allowed.

The minimum and maximum term of a sentence shall be credited with and diminished by the total amount of time a defendant has spent, committed to or in confinement in any State or local correctional, mental or other institution as a result of the charge that culminated in the sentence. The credit provided shall be calculated from the date custody under the charge commenced and shall include credit for all time spent in custody pending trial, trial de novo, appeal, retrial, or pending parole, probation, or post-release supervision revocation hearing: Provided, however, the credit available herein shall not include any time that is credited on the term of a previously imposed sentence to which a defendant is subject. (1973, c. 44, s. 1; 1977, c. 711, s. 16A; 1977, 2nd Sess., c. 1147, s. 30; 1997-237, s. 3.)

§ 15-196.2. Allowance in cases of multiple sentences.

In the event time creditable under this section shall have been spent in custody as the result of more than one pending charge, resulting in imprisonment for more than one offense, credit shall be allowed as herein provided. Consecutive sentences shall be considered as one sentence for the purpose of providing credit, and the creditable time shall not be multiplied by the number of consecutive offenses for which a defendant is imprisoned. Each concurrent sentence shall be credited with so much of the time as was spent in custody due to the offense resulting in the sentence. When both concurrent and consecutive sentences are imposed, both of the above rules shall obtain to the applicable extent. (1973, c. 44, s. 1.)

§ 15-196.3. Effect of credit.

Time creditable under this section shall reduce the minimum and maximum term of a sentence; and, irrespective of sentence, shall reduce the time required to attain privileges made available to inmates in the custody of the Division of Adult

Correction of the Department of Public Safety which are dependent, in whole or in part, upon the passage of a specific length of time in custody, including parole or post-release supervision consideration by the Post-Release Supervision and Parole Commission. However, nothing in this section shall be construed as requiring an automatic award of privileges by virtue of the passage of time. (1973, c. 44, s. 1; 1977, c. 711, s. 17; 1997-237, s. 4; 2011-145, s. 19.1(h); 2012-83, s. 22.)

§ 15-196.4. Procedures for judicial award.

Upon sentencing or activating a sentence, the judge presiding shall determine the credits to which the defendant is entitled and shall cause the clerk to transmit to the custodian of the defendant a statement of allowable credits. Upon committing a defendant upon the conclusion of an appeal, or a parole, probation, or post-release supervision revocation, the committing authority shall determine any credits allowable on account of these proceedings and shall cause to be transmitted, as in all other cases, a statement of the allowable credit to the custodian of the defendant. Upon reviewing a petition seeking credit not previously allowed, the court shall determine the credits due and forward an order setting forth the allowable credit to the custodian of the petitioner. (1973, c. 44, s. 1; 1997-237, s. 5.)

Article 20.

Suspension of Sentence and Probation.

§§ 15-197 through 15-200.1. Repealed by Session Laws 1977, c. 711, s. 33.

§ 15-200.2. Repealed by Session Laws 1975, c. 309, s. 2.

§§ 15-201 through 15-202. Repealed by Session Laws 1973, c. 1262, s. 10.

§ 15-203. Duties of the Secretary of Public Safety; appointment of probation officers; reports; requests for extradition.

The Secretary of Public Safety, or the Secretary's designee, shall direct the work of the probation officers appointed under this Article. Notwithstanding any other provision of law, the Secretary of Public Safety shall have sole discretion to establish the minimum experience requirements to receive an appointment as a probation officer. The Office of State Human Resources shall work with the Secretary to establish position classifications for probation officers based on the experience requirements established by the Secretary. The Secretary, or the Secretary's designee, shall consult and cooperate with the courts and institutions in the development of methods and procedure in the administration of probation, and shall arrange conferences of probation officers and judges. The Secretary shall make an annual written report with statistical and other information to the Governor. The Secretary is authorized to present to the Governor written applications for requisitions for the return of probationers who have broken the terms of their probation, and are believed to be in another state, and the Secretary shall follow the procedure outlined for requests for extradition as set forth in G.S. 15A-743. (1937, c. 132, s. 7; 1959, c. 127; 1963, c. 914, s. 2; 1973, c. 1262, s. 10; 2010-96, s. 2; 2011-145, s. 19.1(h), (i); 2012-83, s. 2; 2013-382, s. 9.1(c).)

§ 15-203.1. Repealed by Session Laws 1963, c. 914, s. 6.

§ 15-204. Assignment, compensation and oath of probation officers.

Probation officers appointed under this Article shall be assigned to serve in such courts or districts or otherwise as the Secretary of Public Safety may determine. They shall be paid annual salaries to be fixed by the Department of Public Safety, and shall also be paid traveling and other necessary expenses incurred in the performance of their official duties as probation officers when such expense accounts have been authorized and approved by the Secretary of Public Safety.

Each person appointed as a probation officer shall take an oath of office before the judge of the court or courts in which he is to serve, which oath shall be as follows:

"I, _____, do solemnly and sincerely swear that I will be faithful and bear true allegiance to the State of North Carolina, and to the constitutional powers and authorities which are or may be established for the government thereof; and that I will endeavor to support, maintain, and defend the Constitution of said State, not inconsistent with the Constitution of the United States, to the best of my knowledge and ability; so help me God," and shall be noted of record by the clerk of the court. (1937, c. 132, s. 8; 1973, c. 1262, s. 10; 2011-145, s. 19.1(h), (i); 2012-83, s. 23.)

§ 15-205. Duties and powers of the probation officers.

A probation officer shall investigate all cases referred to him for investigation by the judges of the courts or by the Secretary of Public Safety. Such officer shall keep informed concerning the conduct and condition of each person on probation under his supervision by visiting, requiring reports, and in other ways, and shall report thereon in writing as often as the court or the Secretary of Public Safety may require. Such officer shall use all practicable and suitable methods, not inconsistent with the conditions imposed by the court or the Secretary of Public Safety, to aid and encourage persons on probation to bring about improvement in their conduct and condition. Such officer shall keep detailed records of his work; shall make such reports in writing to the Secretary of Public Safety as he may require; and shall perform such other duties as the Secretary of Public Safety may require. A probation officer shall have, in the execution of his duties, the powers of arrest and, to the extent necessary for the performance of his duties, the same right to execute process as is now given, or that may hereafter be given by law, to the sheriffs of this State. (1937, c. 132, s. 9; 1973, c. 1262, s. 10; 1975, c. 229, s. 1; 1977, c. 711, s. 18; 2011-145, s. 19.1(h), (i); 2013-101, s. 3.)

§ 15-205.1. Repealed by Session Laws 1977, c. 711, s. 33.

§ 15-206. Cooperation with Division of Adult Correction of the Department of Public Safety and officials of local units.

It is hereby made the duty of every city, county, or State official or department to render all assistance and cooperation within the official's or the Department's fundamental power which may further the objects of this Article. The Division of Adult Correction of the Department of Public Safety, the Secretary of Public Safety, and the probation officers are authorized to seek the cooperation of such officials and departments, and especially of the county superintendents of social services and of the Department of Health and Human Services. (1937, c. 132, s. 10; 1961, c. 139, s. 2; 1969, c. 982; 1973, c. 476, s. 138; c. 1262, s. 10; 1997-443, s. 11A.118(a); 2011-145, ss. 19.1(h), (i); 2012-83, s. 24.)

§ 15-207. Records treated as privileged information.

All information and data obtained in the discharge of official duty by any probation officer shall be privileged information, shall not be receivable as evidence in any court, and shall not be disclosed directly or indirectly to any other than the judge or to others entitled under this Article to receive reports, unless and until otherwise ordered by a judge of the court or the Secretary of Public Safety. (1937, c. 132, s. 11; 1973, c. 1262, s. 10; 2011-145, s. 19.1(i).)

§ 15-208. Repealed by Session Laws 1975, c. 138.

§ 15-209. Accommodations for probation offices.

(a) The county commissioners in each county in which a probation office exists shall provide, in or near the courthouse, suitable office space for those probation officers assigned to the county who have probationary caseloads and their administrative support. This requirement does not include management staff of the Division of Adult Correction of the Department of Public Safety, nonprobation staff, or other Division of Adult Correction of the Department of Public Safety employees.

(b) If a county is unable to provide the space required under subsection (a) of this section for any reason, it may elect to request that the Division of Adult Correction of the Department of Public Safety lease space for the probation office and receive reimbursement from the county for the leased space. If a county fails to reimburse the Division for such leased space, the Secretary of Public Safety may request that the Administrative Office of the Courts transfer the unpaid amount to the Division from the county's court and jail facility fee remittances. (1937, c. 132, s. 13; 2009-451, s. 19.19; 2011-145, s. 19.1(h), (i).)

Article 21.

Segregation of Youthful Offenders.

§§ 15-210 through 15-216. Repealed by Session Laws 1967, c. 996, s. 17.

Article 22.

Review of Criminal Trials.

§ 15-217. Repealed by Session Laws 1977, c. 711, s. 33.

§ 15-217.1: Recodified as § 15A-1420(b1) by Session Laws 1995 (Regular Session, 1996), c. 719, s. 3.

§§ 15-218 through 15-222. Repealed by Session Laws 1977, c. 711, s. 33.

Article 23.

Expunction of Records.

§§ 15-223 through 15-224. Recodified as §§ 15A-145 and 15A-146 by Session Laws 1985, c. 636, s. 1, effective July 5, 1985.

Chapter 15A.

Criminal Procedure Act.

SUBCHAPTER I. GENERAL.

Article 1.

Definitions and General Provisions.

§§ 15A-1 through 15A-100. Reserved for future codification purposes.

§ 15A-101. Definitions.

Unless the context clearly requires otherwise, the following words have the listed meanings:

(1) Appeal. - When used in a general context, the term "appeal" also includes appellate review upon writ of certiorari.

(1a) Attorney of Record. - An attorney who, under Article 4 of this Chapter, Entry and Withdrawal of Attorney in Criminal Case, has entered a criminal proceeding and has not withdrawn.

(2) Clerk. - Any clerk of superior court, acting clerk, or assistant or deputy clerk.

(3) District Court. - The District Court Division of the General Court of Justice.

(4) District Attorney. - The person elected and currently serving as district attorney in his prosecutorial district.

(4a) Entry of Judgment. - Judgment is entered when sentence is pronounced. Prayer for judgment continued upon payment of costs, without more, does not constitute the entry of judgment.

(5) Judicial Official. - A magistrate, clerk, judge, or justice of the General Court of Justice.

(6) Officer. - Law-enforcement officer.

(7) Prosecutor. - The district attorney, any assistant district attorney or any other attorney designated by the district attorney to act for the State or on behalf of the district attorney.

(8) State. - The State of North Carolina, all land or water in respect to which the State of North Carolina has either exclusive or concurrent jurisdiction, and the airspace above that land or water. "Other state" means any state or territory of the United States, the District of Columbia or the Commonwealth of Puerto Rico.

(9) Superior Court. - The Superior Court Division of the General Court of Justice.

(10)   Superior Court Judge. - A superior court judge who has jurisdiction pursuant to G.S. 7A-47.1 or G.S. 7A-48 in the district or set of districts as defined in G.S. 7A-41.1.

(11)   Vehicle. - Aircraft, watercraft, or landcraft or other conveyance. (1973, c. 1286, s. 1; 1975, c. 166, s. 2; 1977, c. 711, s. 19; 1987 (Reg. Sess., 1988), c. 1037, s. 52; 1997-456, s. 27.)

§ 15A-101.1. Electronic technology in criminal process and procedure.

As used in this Chapter, in Chapter 7A of the General Statutes, in Chapter 15 of the General Statutes, and in all other provisions of the General Statutes that deal with criminal process or procedure:

(1)   "Copy" means all identical versions of a document created or existing in paper form, including the original and all other identical versions of the document in paper form.

(2)   "Document" means any pleading, criminal process, subpoena, complaint, motion, application, notice, affidavit, commission, waiver, consent, dismissal, order, judgment, or other writing intended in a criminal or contempt proceeding to authorize or require an action, to record a decision or to communicate or record information. The term does not include search warrants. A document may be created and exist in paper form or in electronic form or in both forms. Each document shall contain the legible, printed name of the person who signed the document.

(3)   "Electronic" means relating to technology having electrical, digital, magnetic, wireless, optical, electromagnetic, Internet, or similar capabilities.

(3a)   "Electronic monitoring" or "electronically monitor" or "satellite-based monitoring" means monitoring with an electronic monitoring device that is not removed from a person's body, that is utilized by the supervising agency in conjunction with a Web-based computer system that actively monitors, identifies, tracks, and records a person's location at least once every minute 24 hours a day, that has a battery life of at least 48 hours without being recharged, that timely records and reports or records the person's presence near or within a crime scene or prohibited area or the person's departure from a specified geographic location, and that has incorporated into the software the ability to automatically compare crime scene data with locations of all persons being electronically monitored so as to provide any correlation daily or in real time. In areas of the State where lack of cellular coverage requires the use of an alternative device, the supervising agency shall use an alternative device that works in concert with the software and records location and tracking data for later download and crime scene comparison.

(4) "Electronic Repository" means an automated electronic repository for criminal process created and maintained pursuant to G.S. 15A-301.1.

(5) "Electronic signature" means any electronic method of signing a document that meets each of the following requirements:

a. Identifies and authenticates a particular person as the signer of the document, is unique to the person using it, is capable of certification, and is under the sole control of the person using it.

b. Is attached to or logically associated with the document in such a manner that if the document is altered in any way without authorization of the signer, the signature is invalidated.

c. Indicates that person's intent to issue, enter or otherwise authenticate the document.

(6) "Entered" means signed and filed in the office of the clerk of superior court of the county in which the document is to be entered. A document may be entered in either paper form or electronic form.

(7) "Filing" or "filed" means:

a. When the document is in paper form, delivering the original document to the office where the document is to be filed. Filing is complete when the original document is received in the office where the document is to be filed.

b. When the document is in electronic form, creating and saving the document, or transmitting it, in such a way that it is unalterably retained in the electronic records of the office where the document is to be filed. A document is "unalterably retained" in an electronic record when it may not be edited or otherwise altered except by a person with authorization to do so. Filing is complete when the document has first been unalterably retained in the electronic records of the office where the document is to be filed.

(8) "Issued" applies to documents in either paper form or electronic form. A document that is first created in paper form is issued when it is signed. A document that is first created in electronic form is issued when it is signed, filed in the office of the clerk of superior court of the county for which it is to be issued, and retained in the Electronic Repository.

(9) "Original" means:

a. A document first created and existing only in paper form, bearing the original signature of the person who signed it. The term also includes each copy in paper form that is printed through the facsimile transmission of the copy bearing the original signature of the person who signed it.

b. A document existing in electronic form, including the electronic form of the document and any copy that is printed from the electronic form.

(10) "Signature" means any symbol, including, but not limited to, the name of an individual, which is executed by that individual, personally or through an authorized agent, with the intent to authenticate or to effect the issuance or entry of a document. The term includes an electronic signature. A document may be signed by the use of any manual, mechanical or electronic means that causes the individual's signature to appear in or on the document. Any party challenging the validity of a signature shall have the burden of pleading, producing evidence, and proving the following:

a. The signature was not the act of the person whose signature it appears to be.

b. If the signature is an electronic signature, the requirements of subdivision (5) of this section have not been met. (2002-64, s. 1; 2011-245, s. 2(a); 2012-194, s. 6.)

Article 2.

Jurisdiction.

§§ 15A-102 through 15A-130. Reserved for future codification purposes.

Article 3.

Venue.

§ 15A-131. Venue generally.

(a) Venue for pretrial and trial proceedings in district court of cases within the original jurisdiction of the district court lies in the county where the charged offense occurred.

(b) Except for the probable cause hearing, venue for pretrial proceedings in cases within the original jurisdiction of the superior court lies in the superior court district or set of districts as defined in G.S. 7A-41.1 embracing the county where the venue for trial proceedings lies.

(c) Except as otherwise provided in this subsection, venue for probable cause hearings and trial proceedings in cases within the original jurisdiction of the superior court lies in the county where the charged offense occurred. Except as otherwise provided in this subsection, if the alleged offense is committed within the corporate limits of a municipality which is the seat of superior court and is located in more than one county, venue lies in the superior court which sits within that municipality, but upon timely objection of the defendant or the district attorney in the county in which the alleged offense occurred the case must be transferred to the county in which the alleged offense occurred. However, for charges brought by municipal law enforcement officers only, if the alleged offense is committed within the corporate limits of a municipality that extends into four or more counties, each of which is in a separate superior court district, offenses committed within the corporate limits of the municipality but in a superior court district other than the one for which the municipality is the seat of superior court shall be disposed of in the municipality with no allowance for objections by the defendant or the district attorney.

(d) Venue for misdemeanors appealed for trial de novo in superior court lies in the county where the misdemeanor was first tried.

(e) An offense occurs in a county if any act or omission constituting part of the offense occurs within the territorial limits of the county.

(f) For the purposes of this Article, pretrial proceedings are proceedings occurring after the initial appearance before the magistrate and prior to arraignment. (1973, c. 1286, s. 1; 1975, 2nd Sess., c. 983, s. 134; 1983, c. 727; 1987 (Reg. Sess., 1988), c. 1037, s. 53; 2009-398, s. 3.)

§ 15A-132. Concurrent venue.

(a) If acts or omissions constituting part of the commission of the charged offense occurred in more than one county, each county has concurrent venue.

(b) If charged offenses which may be joined in a single criminal pleading under G.S. 15A-926 occurred in more than one county, each county has concurrent venue as to all charged offenses.

(c) When counties have concurrent venue, the first county in which a criminal process is issued in the case becomes the county with exclusive venue. (1973, c. 1286, s. 1.)

§ 15A-133. Waiver of venue; motion for change of venue; indictment may be returned in other county.

(a) A waiver of venue must be in writing and signed by the defendant and the prosecutor indicating the consent of all parties to the waiver. The waiver must specify what stages of the proceedings are affected by the waiver, and the county to which venue is changed. If the venue is to be laid in a county in another prosecutorial district, the consent in writing of the prosecutor in that district must be filed with the clerks of both counties.

(b) Repealed by Session Laws 1989, c. 688, s. 2.

(c) Motions for change of venue by the defendant are made under G.S. 15A-957. If venue is laid in a county in another prosecutorial district by order of the judge ruling on the motion, no consent of any prosecutor is required.

(d) If venue is changed to a county in another prosecutorial district, whether upon waiver of venue or by order of a judge, the prosecutor of the prosecutorial district where the case originated must prosecute the case unless the prosecutor of the district to which venue has been changed consents to conduct the prosecution.

(e) If venue is changed, whether upon waiver of venue or by order of a judge, the grand jury in the county to which venue has been transferred has the power to return an indictment in the case. If an indictment has already been returned before the change of venue, no new indictment is necessary and prosecution may be had in the new county under the original indictment. (1921, c. 12, ss. 1, 2; C.S., ss. 4606(a), 4606(b); 1973, c. 1286, s. 1; 1975, c. 166, s. 27; 1987 (Reg. Sess., 1988), c. 1037, s. 54; 1989, c. 688, s. 2.)

§ 15A-134. Offense occurring in part outside North Carolina.

If a charged offense occurred in part in North Carolina and in part outside North Carolina, a person charged with that offense may be tried in this State if he has not been placed in jeopardy for the identical offense in another state. (1973, c. 1286, s. 1.)

§ 15A-135. Allegation of venue conclusive in absence of timely motion.

Allegations of venue in any criminal pleading become conclusive in the absence of a timely motion to dismiss for improper venue under G.S. 15A-952. A defendant may move to dismiss for improper venue upon trial de novo in superior court, provided he did not in the district court with benefit of counsel stipulate venue or expressly waive his right to contest venue. (1973, c. 1286, s. 1.)

§ 15A-136. Venue for sexual offenses.

If a person is transported by any means, with the intent to violate any of the provisions of Article 7A of Chapter 14 (§ 14-27.1 et seq.) of the General Statutes and the intent is followed by actual violation thereof, the defendant may be tried in the county where transportation was offered, solicited, begun, continued or ended. (1979, c. 682, s. 2.)

§§ 15A-137 through 15A-140. Reserved for future codification purposes.

Article 4.

Entry and Withdrawal of Attorney in Criminal Case.

§ 15A-141. When entry of attorney in criminal proceeding occurs.

An attorney enters a criminal proceeding when he:

(1)   Files a written notice of entry with the clerk indicating an intent to represent a defendant in a specified criminal proceeding; or

(2)   Appears in a criminal proceeding without limiting the extent of his representation; or

(3)   Appears in a criminal proceeding for a limited purpose and indicates the extent of his representation by filing written notice thereof with the clerk; or

(4)   Accepts assignment to represent an indigent defendant under the terms of Article 36 of Chapter 7A of the General Statutes; or

(5)   Files a written waiver of arraignment, except that representation in this instance may not be limited pursuant to subdivision (3). (1973, c. 1286, s. 1; 1975, 2nd Sess., c. 983, s. 135.)

§ 15A-142. Requirement that clerk record entry.

The clerk must note each entry by an attorney in the records of the proceeding. (1973, c. 1286, s. 1.)

§ 15A-143. Attorney making general entry obligated to represent defendant at all subsequent stages.

An attorney who enters a criminal proceeding without limiting the extent of his representation pursuant to G.S. 15A-141(3) undertakes to represent the defendant for whom the entry is made at all subsequent stages of the case until entry of final judgment, at the trial stage. An attorney who appears for a limited purpose under the provisions of G.S. 15A-141(3) undertakes to represent the defendant only for that purpose and is deemed to have withdrawn from the proceedings, without the need for permission of the court, when that purpose is fulfilled. (1973, c. 1286, s. 1; 1977, c. 1117.)

§ 15A-144. Withdrawal of attorney with permission of court.

The court may allow an attorney to withdraw from a criminal proceeding upon a showing of good cause. (1973, c. 1286, s. 1.)

Article 5.

Expunction of Records.

§ 15A-145. Expunction of records for first offenders under the age of 18 at the time of conviction of misdemeanor; expunction of certain other misdemeanors.

(a) Whenever any person who has not previously been convicted of any felony, or misdemeanor other than a traffic violation, under the laws of the United States, the laws of this State or any other state, (i) pleads guilty to or is guilty of a misdemeanor other than a traffic violation, and the offense was committed before the person attained the age of 18 years, or (ii) pleads guilty to or is guilty of a misdemeanor possession of alcohol pursuant to G.S. 18B-302(b)(1), and the offense was committed before the person attained the age of 21 years, he may file a petition in the court where he was convicted for expunction of the misdemeanor from his criminal record. The petition cannot be filed earlier than: (i) two years after the date of the conviction, or (ii) the completion of any period of probation, whichever occurs later, and the petition shall contain, but not be limited to, the following:

(1) An affidavit by the petitioner that he has been of good behavior for the two-year period since the date of conviction of the misdemeanor in question and has not been convicted of any felony, or misdemeanor other than a traffic violation, under the laws of the United States or the laws of this State or any other state.

(2) Verified affidavits of two persons who are not related to the petitioner or to each other by blood or marriage, that they know the character and reputation

of the petitioner in the community in which he lives and that his character and reputation are good.

(3) A statement that the petition is a motion in the cause in the case wherein the petitioner was convicted.

(4) Repealed by Session Laws 2010-174, s. 2, effective October 1, 2010, and applicable to petitions for expunctions filed on or after that date.

(4a) An application on a form approved by the Administrative Office of the Courts requesting and authorizing a name-based State and national criminal record check by the Department of Justice using any information required by the Administrative Office of the Courts to identify the individual and a search of the confidential record of expunctions maintained by the Administrative Office of the Courts. The application shall be forwarded to the Department of Justice and to the Administrative Office of the Courts, which shall conduct the searches and report their findings to the court.

(5) An affidavit by the petitioner that no restitution orders or civil judgments representing amounts ordered for restitution entered against him are outstanding.

The petition shall be served upon the district attorney of the court wherein the case was tried resulting in conviction. The district attorney shall have 10 days thereafter in which to file any objection thereto and shall be duly notified as to the date of the hearing of the petition.

The judge to whom the petition is presented is authorized to call upon a probation officer for any additional investigation or verification of the petitioner's conduct during the two-year period that he deems desirable.

(b) If the court, after hearing, finds that the petitioner had remained of good behavior and been free of conviction of any felony or misdemeanor, other than a traffic violation, for two years from the date of conviction of the misdemeanor in question, the petitioner has no outstanding restitution orders or civil judgments representing amounts ordered for restitution entered against him, and (i) petitioner was not 18 years old at the time of the offense in question, or (ii) petitioner was not 21 years old at the time of the offense of possession of alcohol pursuant to G.S. 18B-302(b)(1), it shall order that such person be restored, in the contemplation of the law, to the status he occupied before such arrest or indictment or information. No person as to whom such order has been entered shall be held thereafter under any provision of any laws to be guilty of perjury or otherwise giving a false statement by reason of his failure to recite or acknowledge such arrest, or indictment, information, or trial, or response to any inquiry made of him for any purpose.

(c)   The court shall also order that the misdemeanor conviction, or a civil revocation of a drivers license as the result of a criminal charge, be expunged from the records of the court. The court shall direct all law-enforcement agencies, the Division of Adult Correction of the Department of Public Safety, the Division of Motor Vehicles, and any other State or local government agencies identified by the petitioner as bearing record of the same to expunge their records of the petitioner's conviction or a civil revocation of a drivers license as the result of a criminal charge. This subsection does not apply to civil or criminal charges based upon the civil revocation, or to civil revocations under G.S. 20-16.2. The clerk shall notify State and local agencies of the court's order as provided in G.S. 15A-150. The clerk shall forward a certified copy of the order to the Division of Motor Vehicles for the expunction of a civil revocation provided the underlying criminal charge is also expunged. The civil revocation of a drivers license shall not be expunged prior to a final disposition of any pending civil or criminal charge based upon the civil revocation.

(d)   The clerk shall notify State and local agencies of the court's order as provided in G.S. 15A-150.

(d1)   Repealed by Session Laws 2012-191, s. 3, effective December 1, 2012.

(e)   A person who files a petition for expunction of a criminal record under this section must pay the clerk of superior court a fee of one hundred seventy-five dollars ($175.00) at the time the petition is filed. Fees collected under this subsection are payable to the Administrative Office of the Courts. The clerk of superior court shall remit one hundred twenty-two dollars and fifty cents ($122.50) of each fee to the North Carolina Department of Justice for the costs of criminal record checks performed in connection with processing petitions for expunctions under this section. The remaining fifty-two dollars and fifty cents ($52.50) of each fee shall be retained by the Administrative Office of the Courts and used to pay the costs of processing petitions for expunctions under this section. This subsection does not apply to petitions filed by an indigent. (1973, c. 47, s. 2; c. 748; 1975, c. 650, s. 5; 1977, c. 642, s. 1; c. 699, ss. 1, 2; 1979, c. 431, ss. 1, 2; 1985, c. 636, s. 1; 1999-406, s. 8; 2002-126, ss. 29A.5(a), (b); 2004-133, s. 1; 2005-276, s. 43.1(e); 2007-509, s. 1; 2008-187, s. 35; 2009-510,

s. 4(a), (b); 2009-577, s. 10; 2010-174, ss. 2, 3; 2011-145, s. 19.1(h); 2012-191, s. 3; 2013-360, s. 18B.16(a).)

§ 15A-145.1. Expunction of records for first offenders under the age of 18 at the time of conviction of certain gang offenses.

(a) Whenever any person who has not previously been convicted of any felony or misdemeanor other than a traffic violation under the laws of the United States or the laws of this State or any other state pleads guilty to or is guilty of (i) a Class H felony under Article 13A of Chapter 14 of the General Statutes or (ii) an enhanced offense under G.S. 14-50.22, or has been discharged and had the proceedings against the person dismissed pursuant to G.S. 14-50.29, and the offense was committed before the person attained the age of 18 years, the person may file a petition in the court where the person was convicted for expunction of the offense from the person's criminal record. Except as provided in G.S. 14-50.29 upon discharge and dismissal, the petition cannot be filed earlier than (i) two years after the date of the conviction or (ii) the completion of any period of probation, whichever occurs later. The petition shall contain, but not be limited to, the following:

(1) An affidavit by the petitioner that the petitioner has been of good behavior (i) during the period of probation since the decision to defer further proceedings on the offense in question pursuant to G.S. 14-50.29 or (ii) during the two-year period since the date of conviction of the offense in question, whichever applies, and has not been convicted of any felony or misdemeanor other than a traffic violation under the laws of the United States or the laws of this State or any other state.

(2) Verified affidavits of two persons who are not related to the petitioner or to each other by blood or marriage, that they know the character and reputation of the petitioner in the community in which the petitioner lives, and that the petitioner's character and reputation are good.

(3) If the petition is filed subsequent to conviction of the offense in question, a statement that the petition is a motion in the cause in the case wherein the petitioner was convicted.

(4) Repealed by Session Laws 2010-174, s. 4, effective October 1, 2010, and applicable to petitions for expunctions filed on or after that date.

(4a)   An application on a form approved by the Administrative Office of the Courts requesting and authorizing a name-based State and national criminal record check by the Department of Justice using any information required by the Administrative Office of the Courts to identify the individual and a search of the confidential record of expunctions maintained by the Administrative Office of the Courts. The application shall be forwarded to the Department of Justice and to the Administrative Office of the Courts, which shall conduct the searches and report their findings to the court.

(5)   An affidavit by the petitioner that no restitution orders or civil judgments representing amounts ordered for restitution entered against the petitioner are outstanding.

The petition shall be served upon the district attorney of the court wherein the case was tried resulting in conviction. The district attorney shall have 10 days thereafter in which to file any objection thereto and shall be duly notified as to the date of the hearing of the petition.

The judge to whom the petition is presented is authorized to call upon a probation officer for any additional investigation or verification of the petitioner's conduct during the probationary period or during the two-year period after conviction.

(b)   If the court, after hearing, finds that (i) the petitioner was dismissed and the proceedings against the petitioner discharged pursuant to G.S. 14-50.29 and that the person had not yet attained 18 years of age at the time of the offense or (ii) the petitioner has remained of good behavior and been free of conviction of any felony or misdemeanor other than a traffic violation for two years from the date of conviction of the offense in question, the petitioner has no outstanding restitution orders or civil judgments representing amounts ordered for restitution entered against the petitioner, and the petitioner had not attained the age of 18 years at the time of the offense in question, it shall order that such person be restored, in the contemplation of the law, to the status occupied by the petitioner before such arrest or indictment or information, and that the record be expunged from the records of the court. No person as to whom such order has been entered shall be held thereafter under any provision of any laws to be guilty of perjury or otherwise giving a false statement by reason of the person's failure to recite or acknowledge such arrest, or indictment or information, or trial, or response to any inquiry made of the person for any purpose. The court shall also direct all law enforcement agencies, the Division of Adult Correction of the Department of Public Safety, the Division of Motor Vehicles, and any other State or local government agencies identified by the petitioner as bearing record of the same to expunge their records of the petitioner's criminal charge and any conviction resulting from the charge. The clerk shall notify State and local agencies of the court's order as provided in G.S. 15A-150.

(c)   This section is supplemental and in addition to existing law and shall not be construed so as to repeal any existing provision contained in the General Statutes of North Carolina.

(d)   A person who files a petition for expunction of a criminal record under this section must pay the clerk of superior court a fee of one hundred seventy-five dollars ($175.00) at the time the petition is filed. Fees collected under this subsection are payable to the Administrative Office of the Courts. The clerk of superior court shall remit one hundred twenty-two dollars and fifty cents ($122.50) of each fee to the North Carolina Department of Justice for the costs of criminal record checks performed in connection with processing petitions for expunctions under this section. The remaining fifty-two dollars and fifty cents ($52.50) of each fee shall be retained by the Administrative Office of the Courts and used to pay the costs of processing petitions for expunctions under this section. This subsection does not apply to petitions filed by an indigent. (2009-577, s. 1; 2010-174, s. 4; 2011-145, s. 19.1(h); 2013-360, s. 18B.16(b).)

§ 15A-145.2. Expunction of records for first offenders not over 21 years of age at the time of the offense of certain drug offenses.

(a)   Whenever a person is discharged, and the proceedings against the person dismissed, pursuant to G.S. 90-96(a) or (a1), and the person was not over 21 years of age at the time of the offense, the person may apply to the court for an order to expunge from all official records, other than the confidential files retained under G.S. 15A-151, all recordation relating to the person's arrest, indictment or information, trial, finding of guilty, and dismissal and discharge pursuant to this section. The applicant shall attach to the application the following:

(1)   An affidavit by the petitioner that he or she has been of good behavior during the period of probation since the decision to defer further proceedings on the offense in question and has not been convicted of any felony or misdemeanor other than a traffic violation under the laws of the United States or the laws of this State or any other state;

(2) Verified affidavits by two persons who are not related to the petitioner or to each other by blood or marriage, that they know the character and reputation of the petitioner in the community in which he or she lives, and that the petitioner's character and reputation are good;

(3) Repealed by Session Laws 2010-174, s. 5, effective October 1, 2010, and applicable to petitions for expunctions filed on or after that date.

(3a) An application on a form approved by the Administrative Office of the Courts requesting and authorizing a name-based State and national criminal record check by the Department of Justice using any information required by the Administrative Office of the Courts to identify the individual and a search of the confidential record of expunctions maintained by the Administrative Office of the Courts. The application shall be forwarded to the Department of Justice and to the Administrative Office of the Courts, which shall conduct the searches and report their findings to the court.

The judge to whom the petition is presented is authorized to call upon a probation officer for any additional investigation or verification of the petitioner's conduct during the probationary period deemed desirable.

If the court determines, after hearing, that such person was discharged and the proceedings against him or her dismissed and that the person was not over 21 years of age at the time of the offense, it shall enter such order. The effect of such order shall be to restore such person in the contemplation of the law to the status the person occupied before such arrest or indictment or information. No person as to whom such order was entered shall be held thereafter under any provision of any law to be guilty of perjury or otherwise giving a false statement by reason of the person's failures to recite or acknowledge such arrest, or indictment or information, or trial in response to any inquiry made of him or her for any purpose.

The court shall also order that all records of the proceeding be expunged from the records of the court and direct all law enforcement agencies, the Division of Adult Correction, the Division of Motor Vehicles, and any other State and local government agencies identified by the petitioner as bearing records of the same to expunge their records of the proceeding. The clerk shall notify State and local agencies of the court's order as provided in G.S. 15A-150.

(b) Whenever any person is charged with a misdemeanor under Article 5 of Chapter 90 of the General Statutes by possessing a controlled substance included within Schedules I through VI of Article 5 of Chapter 90 of the General Statutes or a felony under G.S. 90-95(a)(3), upon dismissal by the State of the charges against the person, upon entry of a nolle prosequi, or upon a finding of not guilty or other adjudication of innocence, such person may apply to the court for an order to expunge from all official records all recordation relating to his or her arrest, indictment or information, or trial. If the court determines, after hearing, that such person was not over 21 years of age at the time the offense for which the person was charged occurred, it shall enter such order. The clerk shall notify State and local agencies of the court's order as provided in G.S. 15A-150. No person as to whom such order has been entered shall be held thereafter under any provision of any law to be guilty of perjury or otherwise giving a false statement by reason of the person's failures to recite or acknowledge such arrest, or indictment or information, or trial in response to any inquiry made of him or her for any purpose.

(c) Whenever any person who has not previously been convicted of (i) any felony offense under any state or federal laws; (ii) any offense under Chapter 90 of the General Statutes; or (iii) an offense under any statute of the United States or any state relating to controlled substances included in any schedule of Chapter 90 of the General Statutes or to that paraphernalia included in Article 5B of Chapter 90 of the General Statutes, pleads guilty to or has been found guilty of a misdemeanor under Article 5 of Chapter 90 of the General Statutes by possessing a controlled substance included within Schedules I through VI of Chapter 90, or by possessing drug paraphernalia as prohibited by G.S. 90-113.22 or pleads guilty to or has been found guilty of a felony under G.S. 90-95(a)(3), the court may, upon application of the person not sooner than 12 months after conviction, order cancellation of the judgment of conviction and expunction of the records of the person's arrest, indictment or information, trial, and conviction. A conviction in which the judgment of conviction has been canceled and the records expunged pursuant to this subsection shall not be thereafter deemed a conviction for purposes of this subsection or for purposes of disqualifications or liabilities imposed by law upon conviction of a crime, including the additional penalties imposed for second or subsequent convictions of Article 5 of Chapter 90 of the General Statutes. Cancellation and expunction under this subsection may occur only once with respect to any person. Disposition of a case under this subsection at the district court division of the General Court of Justice shall be final for the purpose of appeal.

The granting of an application filed under this subsection shall cause the issue of an order to expunge from all official records, other than the confidential files retained under G.S. 15A-151, all recordation relating to the petitioner's arrest, indictment or information, trial, finding of guilty, judgment of conviction, cancellation of the judgment, and expunction of records pursuant to this subsection.

The judge to whom the petition is presented is authorized to call upon a probation officer for additional investigation or verification of the petitioner's conduct since conviction. If the court determines that the petitioner was convicted of (i) a misdemeanor under Article 5 of Chapter 90 of the General Statutes for possessing a controlled substance included within Schedules I through VI of Article 5 of Chapter 90 of the General Statutes or for possessing drug paraphernalia as prohibited in G.S. 90-113.22 or (ii) a felony under G.S. 90-95(a)(3), that the petitioner has no disqualifying previous convictions as set forth in this subsection, that the petitioner was not over 21 years of age at the time of the offense, that the petitioner has been of good behavior since his or her conviction, that the petitioner has successfully completed a drug education program approved for this purpose by the Department of Health and Human Services, and that the petitioner has not been convicted of a felony or misdemeanor other than a traffic violation under the laws of this State at any time prior to or since the conviction for the offense in question, it shall enter an order of expunction of the petitioner's court record. The effect of such order shall be to restore the petitioner in the contemplation of the law to the status the petitioner occupied before arrest or indictment or information or conviction. No person as to whom such order was entered shall be held thereafter under any provision of any law to be guilty of perjury or otherwise giving a false statement by reason of the person's failures to recite or acknowledge such arrest, or indictment or information, or conviction, or trial in response to any inquiry made of him or her for any purpose. The judge may waive the condition that the petitioner attend the drug education school if the judge makes a specific finding that there was no drug education school within a reasonable distance of the defendant's residence or that there were specific extenuating circumstances which made it likely that the petitioner would not benefit from the program of instruction.

The court shall also order all law enforcement agencies, the Department of Correction, the Division of Motor Vehicles, and any other State or local agencies identified by the petitioner as bearing records of the conviction and records relating thereto to expunge their records of the conviction. The clerk shall notify State and local agencies of the court's order as provided in G.S. 15A-150.

(d) A person who files a petition for expunction of a criminal record under this section must pay the clerk of superior court a fee of one hundred seventy-five dollars ($175.00) at the time the petition is filed. Fees collected under this subsection are payable to the Administrative Office of the Courts. The clerk of superior court shall remit one hundred twenty-two dollars and fifty cents ($122.50) of each fee to the North Carolina Department of Justice for the costs of criminal record checks performed in connection with processing petitions for expunctions under this section. The remaining fifty-two dollars and fifty cents ($52.50) of each fee shall be retained by the Administrative Office of the Courts and used to pay the costs of processing petitions for expunctions under this section. This subsection does not apply to petitions filed by an indigent. (2009-577, s. 2; 2010-174, s. 5; 2011-145, s. 19.1(h); 2011-192, s. 5(b); 2011-412, s. 2.6(a); 2013-360, s. 18B.16(c).)

§ 15A-145.3. Expunction of records for first offenders not over 21 years of age at the time of the offense of certain toxic vapors offenses.

(a) Whenever a person is discharged and the proceedings against the person dismissed under G.S. 90-113.14(a) or (a1), such person, if he or she was not over 21 years of age at the time of the offense, may apply to the court for an order to expunge from all official records, other than the confidential files retained under G.S. 15A-151, all recordation relating to the person's arrest, indictment or information, trial, finding of guilty, and dismissal and discharge pursuant to this section. The applicant shall attach to the application the following:

(1) An affidavit by the petitioner that the petitioner has been of good behavior during the period of probation since the decision to defer further proceedings on the misdemeanor in question and has not been convicted of any felony or misdemeanor other than a traffic violation under the laws of the United States or the laws of this State or any other state;

(2) Verified affidavits by two persons who are not related to the petitioner or to each other by blood or marriage, that they know the character and reputation of the petitioner in the community in which the petitioner lives, and that his or her character and reputation are good;

(3) Repealed by Session Laws 2010-174, s. 6, effective October 1, 2010, and applicable to petitions for expunctions filed on or after that date.

(3a) An application on a form approved by the Administrative Office of the Courts requesting and authorizing a name-based State and national criminal record check by the Department of Justice using any information required by the Administrative Office of the Courts to identify the individual and a search of the confidential record of expunctions maintained by the Administrative Office of the Courts. The application shall be forwarded to the Department of Justice and to the Administrative Office of the Courts, which shall conduct the searches and report their findings to the court.

The judge to whom the petition is presented is authorized to call upon a probation officer for any additional investigation or verification of the petitioner's conduct during the probationary period deemed desirable.

If the court determines, after hearing, that such person was discharged and the proceedings against the person dismissed and that he or she was not over 21 years of age at the time of the offense, it shall enter such order. The effect of such order shall be to restore such person in the contemplation of the law to the status the person occupied before such arrest or indictment or information. No person as to whom such order was entered shall be held thereafter under any provision of any law to be guilty of perjury or otherwise giving a false statement by reason of the person's failures to recite or acknowledge such arrest, or indictment or information, or trial in response to any inquiry made of him or her for any purpose.

The court shall also order that all records of the proceeding be expunged from the records of the court and direct all law enforcement agencies bearing records of the same to expunge their records of the proceeding. The clerk shall notify State and local agencies of the court's order as provided in G.S. 15A-150.

(b) Whenever any person is charged with a misdemeanor under Article 5A of Chapter 90 of the General Statutes or possessing drug paraphernalia as prohibited by G.S. 90-113.22, upon dismissal by the State of the charges against the person or upon entry of a nolle prosequi or upon a finding of not guilty or other adjudication of innocence, such person may apply to the court for an order to expunge from all official records all recordation relating to the person's arrest, indictment or information, and trial. If the court determines, after hearing that such person was not over 21 years of age at the time the offense for which the person was charged occurred, it shall enter such order. The clerk shall notify State and local agencies of the court's order as provided in G.S. 15A-150. No person as to whom such order has been entered shall be held thereafter under any provision of any law to be guilty of perjury or otherwise giving a false statement by reason of the person's failures to recite or acknowledge such arrest, or indictment or information, or trial in response to any inquiry made of him or her for any purpose.

(c) Whenever any person who has not previously been convicted of an offense under Article 5 or 5A of Chapter 90 of the General Statutes or under any statute of the United States or any state relating to controlled substances included in any schedule of Article 5 of Chapter 90 of the General Statutes or to that paraphernalia included in Article 5B of Chapter 90 of the General Statutes pleads guilty to or has been found guilty of a misdemeanor under Article 5A of Chapter 90 of the General Statutes, the court may, upon application of the person not sooner than 12 months after conviction, order cancellation of the judgment of conviction and expunction of the records of the person's arrest, indictment or information, trial, and conviction. A conviction in which the judgment of conviction has been cancelled and the records expunged pursuant to this subsection shall not be thereafter deemed a conviction for purposes of this subsection or for purposes of disqualifications or liabilities imposed by law upon conviction of a crime, including the additional penalties imposed for second or subsequent convictions of violation of Article 5A of Chapter 90 of the General Statutes. Cancellation and expunction under this subsection may occur only once with respect to any person. Disposition of a case under this subsection at the district court division of the General Court of Justice shall be final for the purpose of appeal.

The granting of an application filed under this subsection shall cause the issue of an order to expunge from all official records, other than the confidential files retained under G.S. 15A-151, all recordation relating to the person's arrest, indictment or information, trial, finding of guilty, judgment of conviction, cancellation of the judgment, and expunction of records pursuant to this subsection.

The judge to whom the petition is presented is authorized to call upon a probation officer for additional investigation or verification of the petitioner's conduct since conviction. If the court determines that the petitioner was convicted of a misdemeanor under Article 5A of Chapter 90 of the General Statutes, or for possessing drug paraphernalia as prohibited by G.S. 90-113.22, that the petitioner was not over 21 years of age at the time of the offense, that the petitioner has been of good behavior since his or her conviction, that the petitioner has successfully completed a drug education program approved for this purpose by the Department of Health and Human Services, and that the petitioner has not been convicted of a felony or misdemeanor other than a traffic violation under the laws of this State at any time prior to or since the conviction for the misdemeanor in question, it shall enter an order of expunction of the petitioner's court record. The effect of such order shall be to restore the petitioner in the contemplation of the law to the status he occupied before such arrest or indictment or information or conviction. No person as to whom such order was entered shall be held thereafter under any provision of any law to be guilty of perjury or otherwise giving a false statement by reason of the person's failures to recite or acknowledge such arrest, or indictment or information, or conviction, or trial in response to any inquiry made of him or her for any purpose. The judge may waive the condition that the petitioner attend the drug education school if the judge makes a specific finding that there was no drug education school within a reasonable distance of the defendant's residence or that there were specific extenuating circumstances which made it likely that the petitioner would not benefit from the program of instruction.

The clerk shall notify State and local agencies of the court's order as provided in G.S. 15A-150.

(d) A person who files a petition for expunction of a criminal record under this section must pay the clerk of superior court a fee of one hundred seventy-five dollars ($175.00) at the time the petition is filed. Fees collected under this subsection are payable to the Administrative Office of the Courts. The clerk of superior court shall remit one hundred twenty-two dollars and fifty cents ($122.50) of each fee to the North Carolina Department of Justice for the costs of criminal record checks performed in connection with processing petitions for expunctions under this section. The remaining fifty-two dollars and fifty cents ($52.50) of each fee shall be retained by the Administrative Office of the Courts and used to pay the costs of processing petitions for expunctions under this section. This subsection does not apply to petitions filed by an indigent. (2009-577, s. 3; 2010-174, s. 6; 2013-360, s. 18B.16(d).)

§ 15A-145.4. Expunction of records for first offenders who are under 18 years of age at the time of the commission of a nonviolent felony.

(a) For purposes of this section, the term "nonviolent felony" means any felony except the following:

(1) A Class A through G felony.

(2) A felony that includes assault as an essential element of the offense.

(3) A felony that is an offense requiring registration pursuant to Article 27A of Chapter 14 of the General Statutes, whether or not the person is currently required to register.

(4) Repealed by Session Laws 2012-191, s. 2, effective December 1, 2012.

(5) Any felony offense under the following sex-related or stalking offenses: G.S. 14-27.7A(b), 14-190.7, 14-190.8, 14-202, 14-208.11A, 14-208.18, 14-277.3, 14-277.3A, 14-321.1.

(6) Any felony offense in Chapter 90 of the General Statutes where the offense involves methamphetamines, heroin, or possession with intent to sell or deliver or sell and deliver cocaine; except that if a prayer for judgment continued has been entered for an offense classified as either a Class G, H, or I felony, the prayer for judgment continued shall be subject to expunction under the procedures in this section.

(7) A felony offense under G.S. 14-12.12(b), 14-12.13, or 14-12.14, or any felony offense for which punishment was determined pursuant to G.S. 14-3(c).

(8) A felony offense under G.S. 14-401.16.

(9) Any felony offense in which a commercial motor vehicle was used in the commission of the offense.

(b) Notwithstanding any other provision of law, if the person is convicted of more than one nonviolent felony in the same session of court and none of the nonviolent felonies are alleged to have occurred after the person had already been served with criminal process for the commission of a nonviolent felony, then the multiple nonviolent felony convictions shall be treated as one nonviolent felony conviction under this section, and the expunction order issued under this section shall provide that the multiple nonviolent felony convictions shall be expunged from the person's record in accordance with this section.

(c) Whenever any person who had not yet attained the age of 18 years at the time of the commission of the offense and has not previously been convicted of any felony or misdemeanor other than a traffic violation under the laws of the United States or the laws of this State or any other state pleads guilty to or is guilty of a nonviolent felony, the person may file a petition in the court where the person was convicted for expunction of the nonviolent felony from the person's criminal record. The petition shall not be filed earlier than four years after the date of the conviction or when any active sentence, period of probation, and post-release supervision has been served, whichever occurs later. The person shall also perform at least 100 hours of community service, preferably related to the conviction, before filing a petition for expunction under this section. The petition shall contain the following:

(1) An affidavit by the petitioner that the petitioner has been of good moral character since the date of conviction of the nonviolent felony in question and has not been convicted of any other felony or any misdemeanor other than a traffic violation under the laws of the United States or the laws of this State or any other state.

(2) Verified affidavits of two persons who are not related to the petitioner or to each other by blood or marriage, that they know the character and reputation of the petitioner in the community in which the petitioner lives and that the petitioner's character and reputation are good.

(3) A statement that the petition is a motion in the cause in the case wherein the petitioner was convicted.

(4) An application on a form approved by the Administrative Office of the Courts requesting and authorizing (i) a State and national criminal history record check by the Department of Justice using any information required by the Administrative Office of the Courts to identify the individual; (ii) a search by the Department of Justice for any outstanding warrants or pending criminal cases; and (iii) a search of the confidential record of expunctions maintained by the Administrative Office of the Courts. The application shall be forwarded to the Department of Justice and to the Administrative Office of the Courts, which shall conduct the searches and report their findings to the court.

(5) An affidavit by the petitioner that no restitution orders or civil judgments representing amounts ordered for restitution entered against the petitioner are outstanding.

(6) An affidavit by the petitioner that the petitioner has performed at least 100 hours of community service since the conviction for the nonviolent felony. The affidavit shall include a list of the community services performed, a list of the recipients of the services, and a detailed description of those services.

(7) An affidavit by the petitioner that the petitioner possesses a high school diploma, a high school graduation equivalency certificate, or a General Education Development degree.

The petition shall be served upon the district attorney of the court wherein the case was tried resulting in conviction. The district attorney shall have 30 days thereafter in which to file any objection thereto and shall be duly notified as to the date of the hearing of the petition. The district attorney shall make his or her best efforts to contact the victim, if any, to notify the victim of the request for expunction prior to the date of the hearing.

(d) The court in which the petition was filed shall take the following steps and shall consider the following issues in rendering a decision upon a petition for expunction of records of a nonviolent felony under this section:

(1) Call upon a probation officer for additional investigation or verification of the petitioner's conduct during the four-year period since the date of conviction of the nonviolent felony in question.

(2) Review the petitioner's juvenile record, ensuring that the petitioner's juvenile records remain separate from adult records and files and are withheld from public inspection as provided under Article 30 of Chapter 7B of the General Statutes.

(3) Review the amount of restitution made by the petitioner to the victim of the nonviolent felony to be expunged and give consideration to whether or not restitution was paid in full.

(4) Review any other information the court deems relevant, including, but not limited to, affidavits or other testimony provided by law enforcement officers, district attorneys, and victims of nonviolent felonies committed by the petitioner.

(e) The court may order that the person be restored, in the contemplation of the law, to the status the person occupied before the arrest or indictment or information if the court finds all of the following after a hearing:

(1) The petitioner has remained of good moral character and has been free of conviction of any felony or misdemeanor, other than a traffic violation, for four years from the date of conviction of the nonviolent felony in question or any active sentence, period of probation, or post-release supervision has been served, whichever is later.

(2) The petitioner has not previously been convicted of any felony or misdemeanor other than a traffic violation under the laws of the United States or the laws of this State or any other state.

(3) The petitioner has no outstanding warrants or pending criminal cases.

(4) The petitioner has no outstanding restitution orders or civil judgments representing amounts ordered for restitution entered against the petitioner.

(5) The petitioner was less than 18 years old at the time of the commission of the offense in question.

(6) The petitioner has performed at least 100 hours of community service since the time of the conviction and possesses a high school diploma, a high school graduation equivalency certificate, or a General Education Development degree.

(7) The search of the confidential records of expunctions conducted by the Administrative Office of the Courts shows that the petitioner has not been previously granted an expunction.

(f) No person as to whom an order has been entered pursuant to subsection (e) of this section shall be held thereafter under any provision of any laws to be guilty of perjury or otherwise giving a false statement by reason of that person's failure to recite or acknowledge the arrest, indictment, information, trial, or conviction. Persons pursuing certification under the provisions of Chapter 17C or 17E of the General Statutes, however, shall disclose any and all felony convictions to the certifying Commission regardless of whether or not the felony convictions were expunged pursuant to the provisions of this section.

Persons required by State law to obtain a criminal history record check on a prospective employee shall not be deemed to have knowledge of any convictions expunged under this section.

(g) The court shall also order that the nonviolent felony conviction be expunged from the records of the court and direct all law enforcement agencies bearing record of the same to expunge their records of the conviction. The clerk shall notify State and local agencies of the court's order as provided in G.S. 15A-150.

(h) Any other applicable State or local government agency shall expunge from its records entries made as a result of the conviction ordered expunged under this section. The agency shall also vacate any administrative actions taken against a person whose record is expunged under this section as a result of the charges or convictions expunged. A person whose administrative action has been vacated by an occupational licensing board pursuant to an expunction under this section may then reapply for licensure and must satisfy the board's then current education and preliminary licensing requirements in order to obtain licensure. This subsection shall not apply to the Department of Justice for DNA records and samples stored in the State DNA Database and the State DNA Databank.

(i) Any person eligible for expunction of a criminal record under this section shall be notified about the provisions of this section by the probation officer assigned to that person. If no probation officer is assigned, notification of the provisions of this section shall be provided by the court at the time of the conviction of the felony which is to be expunged under this section.

(j) A person who files a petition for expunction of a criminal record under this section must pay the clerk of superior court a fee of one hundred seventy-five dollars ($175.00) at the time the petition is filed. Fees collected under this subsection are payable to the Administrative Office of the Courts. The clerk of superior court shall remit one hundred twenty-two dollars and fifty cents ($122.50) of each fee to the North Carolina Department of Justice for the costs of criminal record checks performed in connection with processing petitions for expunctions under this section. The remaining fifty-two dollars and fifty cents ($52.50) of each fee shall be retained by the Administrative Office of the Courts and used to pay the costs of processing petitions for expunctions under this section. This subsection does not apply to petitions filed by an indigent. (2011-278, s. 1; 2012-191, s. 2; 2013-53, s. 1; 2013-360, s. 18B.16(e).)

§ 15A-145.5. Expunction of certain misdemeanors and felonies; no age limitation.

(a) For purposes of this section, the term "nonviolent misdemeanor" or "nonviolent felony" means any misdemeanor or felony except the following:

(1) A Class A through G felony or a Class A1 misdemeanor.

(2)   An offense that includes assault as an essential element of the offense.

(3)   An offense requiring registration pursuant to Article 27A of Chapter 14 of the General Statutes, whether or not the person is currently required to register.

(4)   Any of the following sex-related or stalking offenses: G.S. 14-27.7A(b), 14-190.7, 14-190.8, 14-190.9, 14-202, 14-208.11A, 14-208.18, 14-277.3, 14-277.3A, 14-321.1.

(5)   Any felony offense in Chapter 90 of the General Statutes where the offense involves methamphetamines, heroin, or possession with intent to sell or deliver or sell and deliver cocaine.

(6)   An offense under G.S. 14-12.12(b), 14-12.13, or 14-12.14, or any offense for which punishment was determined pursuant to G.S. 14-3(c).

(7)   An offense under G.S. 14-401.16.

(8)   Any felony offense in which a commercial motor vehicle was used in the commission of the offense.

(b)   Notwithstanding any other provision of law, if the person is convicted of more than one nonviolent felony or nonviolent misdemeanor in the same session of court and none of the nonviolent felonies or nonviolent misdemeanors are alleged to have occurred after the person had already been served with criminal process for the commission of a nonviolent felony or nonviolent misdemeanor, then the multiple nonviolent felony or nonviolent misdemeanor convictions shall be treated as one nonviolent felony or nonviolent misdemeanor conviction under this section, and the expunction order issued under this section shall provide that the multiple nonviolent felony convictions or nonviolent misdemeanor convictions shall be expunged from the person's record in accordance with this section.

(c)   A person may file a petition, in the court where the person was convicted, for expunction of a nonviolent misdemeanor or nonviolent felony conviction from the person's criminal record if the person has no other misdemeanor or felony convictions, other than a traffic violation. The petition shall not be filed earlier than 15 years after the date of the conviction or when any active sentence, period of probation, and post-release supervision has been served, whichever occurs later. The petition shall contain, but not be limited to, the following:

(1) An affidavit by the petitioner that the petitioner has been of good moral character since the date of conviction for the nonviolent misdemeanor or nonviolent felony and has not been convicted of any other felony or misdemeanor, other than a traffic violation, under the laws of the United States or the laws of this State or any other state.

(2) Verified affidavits of two persons who are not related to the petitioner or to each other by blood or marriage, that they know the character and reputation of the petitioner in the community in which the petitioner lives and that the petitioner's character and reputation are good.

(3) A statement that the petition is a motion in the cause in the case wherein the petitioner was convicted.

(4) An application on a form approved by the Administrative Office of the Courts requesting and authorizing a name-based State and national criminal history record check by the Department of Justice using any information required by the Administrative Office of the Courts to identify the individual, a search by the Department of Justice for any outstanding warrants on pending criminal cases, and a search of the confidential record of expunctions maintained by the Administrative Office of the Courts. The application shall be forwarded to the Department of Justice and to the Administrative Office of the Courts, which shall conduct the searches and report their findings to the court.

(5) An affidavit by the petitioner that no restitution orders or civil judgments representing amounts ordered for restitution entered against the petitioner are outstanding.

Upon filing of the petition, the petition shall be served upon the district attorney of the court wherein the case was tried resulting in conviction. The district attorney shall have 30 days thereafter in which to file any objection thereto and shall be duly notified as to the date of the hearing of the petition. Upon good cause shown, the court may grant the district attorney an additional 30 days to file objection to the petition. The district attorney shall make his or her best efforts to contact the victim, if any, to notify the victim of the request for expunction prior to the date of the hearing.

The presiding judge is authorized to call upon a probation officer for any additional investigation or verification of the petitioner's conduct since the conviction. The court shall review any other information the court deems relevant, including, but not limited to, affidavits or other testimony provided by law enforcement officers, district attorneys, and victims of crimes committed by the petitioner.

If the court, after hearing, finds that the petitioner has not previously been granted an expunction under this section, G.S. 15A-145, 15A-145.1, 15A-145.2, 15A-145.3, or 15A-145.4; the petitioner has remained of good moral character; the petitioner has no outstanding warrants or pending criminal cases; the petitioner has no other felony or misdemeanor convictions other than a traffic violation; the petitioner has no outstanding restitution orders or civil judgments representing amounts ordered for restitution entered against the petitioner; and the petitioner was convicted of an offense eligible for expunction under this section and was convicted of, and completed any sentence received for, the nonviolent misdemeanor or nonviolent felony at least 15 years prior to the filing of the petition, it may order that such person be restored, in the contemplation of the law, to the status the person occupied before such arrest or indictment or information. If the court denies the petition, the order shall include a finding as to the reason for the denial.

(d)   No person as to whom an order has been entered pursuant to subsection (c) of this section shall be held thereafter under any provision of any law to be guilty of perjury or otherwise giving a false statement by reason of that person's failure to recite or acknowledge the arrest, indictment, information, trial, or conviction. Persons pursuing certification under the provisions of Chapter 17C or 17E of the General Statutes, however, shall disclose any and all convictions to the certifying Commission, regardless of whether or not the convictions were expunged pursuant to the provisions of this section.

Persons required by State law to obtain a criminal history record check on a prospective employee shall not be deemed to have knowledge of any convictions expunged under this section.

(e)   The court shall also order that the conviction be expunged from the records of the court and direct all law enforcement agencies bearing record of the same to expunge their records of the conviction. The clerk shall notify State and local agencies of the court's order, as provided in G.S. 15A-150.

(f)   Any other applicable State or local government agency shall expunge from its records entries made as a result of the conviction ordered expunged under this section upon receipt from the petitioner of an order entered pursuant to this section. The agency shall also vacate any administrative actions taken against a person whose record is expunged under this section as a result of the charges or convictions expunged. A person whose administrative action has been vacated by an occupational licensing board pursuant to an expunction under this section may then reapply for licensure and must satisfy the board's then current education and preliminary licensing requirements in order to obtain licensure. This subsection shall not apply to the Department of Justice for DNA records and samples stored in the State DNA Database and the State DNA Databank or to fingerprint records.

(g)   A person who files a petition for expunction of a criminal record under this section must pay the clerk of superior court a fee of one hundred seventy-five dollars ($175.00) at the time the petition is filed. Fees collected under this subsection shall be deposited in the General Fund. This subsection does not apply to petitions filed by an indigent. (2012-191, s. 1; 2013-53, s. 2; 2013-410, s. 4.)

§ 15A-145.6. Expunctions for certain defendants convicted of prostitution.

(a)   The following definitions apply in this section:

(1)   Prostitution offense. - A conviction for (i) violation of G.S. 14-204 or (ii) engaging in prostitution in violation of G.S. 14-204(7) for an offense that occurred prior to October 1, 2013.

(2)   Violent felony or violent misdemeanor. - A Class A through G felony or a Class A1 misdemeanor that includes assault as an essential element of the offense.

(b)   A person who has been convicted of a prostitution offense may file a petition in the court where the person was convicted for expunction of the prostitution offense from the person's criminal record provided that all the following criteria are met:

(1)   The person has not previously been convicted of any violent felony or violent misdemeanor under the laws of the United States or the laws of this State or any other state.

(2)   The person satisfies any one of the following criteria:

a. The person's participation in the prostitution offense was a result of having been a trafficking victim under G.S. 14-43.11 (human trafficking) or G.S. 14-43.13 (sexual servitude) or a victim of a severe form of trafficking under the federal Trafficking Victims Protection Act (22 U.S.C. § 7102(13)).

b. The person has no prior convictions for a prostitution offense and at least three years have passed since the date of conviction or the completion of any active sentence, period of probation, and post-release supervision, whichever occurs later.

c. The person received a conditional discharge pursuant to G.S. 14-204(b).

(c) The petition shall contain all of the following:

(1) An affidavit by the petitioner that the petitioner (i) has no prior conviction of a violent felony or violent misdemeanor, (ii) has been of good moral character since the date of conviction of the prostitution offense in question, and (iii) has not been convicted of any felony or misdemeanor under the laws of the United States or the laws of this State or any other state since the date of the conviction of the prostitution offense in question.

(2) Verified affidavits of two persons, who are not related to the petitioner or to each other by blood or marriage, that they know the character and reputation of the petitioner in the community in which the petitioner lives and that the petitioner's character and reputation are good.

(3) A statement that the petition is a motion in the cause in the case wherein the petitioner was convicted.

(4) An application on a form approved by the Administrative Office of the Courts requesting and authorizing (i) a State and national criminal history record check by the Department of Justice using any information required by the Administrative Office of the Courts to identify the individual; (ii) a search by the Department of Justice for any outstanding warrants or pending criminal cases; and (iii) a search of the confidential record of expunctions maintained by the Administrative Office of the Courts. The application shall be forwarded to the Department of Justice and to the Administrative Office of the Courts, which shall conduct the searches and report their findings to the court.

(5) An affidavit by the petitioner that no restitution orders or civil judgments representing amounts ordered for restitution entered against the petitioner are outstanding.

(d) The petition shall be served upon the district attorney of the court wherein the case was tried resulting in conviction. The district attorney shall have 30 days thereafter in which to file any objection thereto and shall be duly notified as to the date of the hearing of the petition.

(e) The court in which the petition was filed shall take the following steps and shall consider the following issues in rendering a decision upon a petition for expunction of records of a prostitution offense under this section:

(1) Call upon a probation officer for additional investigation or verification of the petitioner's conduct during the period since the date of conviction of the prostitution offense in question.

(2) Review any other information the court deems relevant, including, but not limited to, affidavits or other testimony provided by law enforcement officers and district attorneys.

(f) The court shall order that the person be restored, in the contemplation of the law, to the status the person occupied before the arrest or indictment or information if the court finds all of the following after a hearing:

(1) The criteria set out in subsection (b) of this section are satisfied.

(2) The petitioner has remained of good moral character and has been free of conviction of any felony or misdemeanor, other than a traffic violation, since the date of conviction of the prostitution offense in question.

(3) The petitioner has no outstanding warrants or pending criminal cases.

(4) The petitioner has no outstanding restitution orders or civil judgments representing amounts ordered for restitution entered against the petitioner.

(5) The search of the confidential records of expunctions conducted by the Administrative Office of the Courts shows that the petitioner has not been previously granted an expunction, other than an expunction for a prostitution offense.

(g) No person as to whom an order has been entered pursuant to subsection (f) of this section shall be held thereafter under any provision of any laws to be guilty of perjury or otherwise giving a false statement by reason of that person's failure to recite or acknowledge the arrest, indictment, information, trial, or conviction. Persons pursuing certification under the provisions of Chapter 17C or 17E of the General Statutes, however, shall disclose any and all prostitution convictions to the certifying Commission regardless of whether or not the prostitution convictions were expunged pursuant to the provisions of this section.

Persons required by State law to obtain a criminal history record check on a prospective employee shall not be deemed to have knowledge of any convictions expunged under this section.

(h) The court shall also order that the conviction of the prostitution offense be expunged from the records of the court and direct all law enforcement agencies bearing record of the same to expunge their records of the conviction. The clerk shall notify State and local agencies of the court's order as provided in G.S. 15A-150.

(i) Any other applicable State or local government agency shall expunge from its records entries made as a result of the conviction ordered expunged under this section. The agency shall also reverse any administrative actions taken against a person whose record is expunged under this section as a result of the charges or convictions expunged. This subsection shall not apply to the Department of Justice for DNA records and samples stored in the State DNA Database and the State DNA Databank.

(j) Any person eligible for expunction of a criminal record under this section shall be notified about the provisions of this section by the probation officer assigned to that person. If no probation officer is assigned, notification of the provisions of this section shall be provided by the court at the time of the conviction of the prostitution offense which is to be expunged under this section. (2013-368, s. 11.)

§ 15A-146. Expunction of records when charges are dismissed or there are findings of not guilty.

(a)   If any person is charged with a crime, either a misdemeanor or a felony, or was charged with an infraction under G.S. 18B-302(i) prior to December 1, 1999, and the charge is dismissed, or a finding of not guilty or not responsible is entered, that person may apply to the court of the county where the charge was brought for an order to expunge from all official records any entries relating to his apprehension or trial. The court shall hold a hearing on the application and, upon finding that the person had not previously received an expungement under this section, G.S. 15A-145, 15A-145.1, 15A-145.2, 15A-145.3, 15A-145.4, or 15A-145.5, and that the person had not previously been convicted of any felony under the laws of the United States, this State, or any other state, the court shall order the expunction. No person as to whom such an order has been entered shall be held thereafter under any provision of any law to be guilty of perjury, or to be guilty of otherwise giving a false statement or response to any inquiry made for any purpose, by reason of his failure to recite or acknowledge any expunged entries concerning apprehension or trial.

(a1)   Notwithstanding subsection (a) of this section, if a person is charged with multiple offenses and all the charges are dismissed, or findings of not guilty or not responsible are made, then a person may apply to have each of those charges expunged if the offenses occurred within the same 12-month period of time or if the charges are dismissed or findings are made at the same term of court. Unless circumstances otherwise clearly provide, the phrase "term of court" shall mean one week for superior court and one day for district court. There is no requirement that the multiple offenses arise out of the same transaction or occurrence or that the multiple offenses were consolidated for judgment. The court shall hold a hearing on the application. If the court finds (i) that the person had not previously received an expungement under this subsection, or that any previous expungement received under this subsection occurred prior to October 1, 2005 and was for an offense that occurred within the same 12-month period of time, or was dismissed or findings made at the same term of court, as the offenses that are the subject of the current application, (ii) that the person had not previously received an expungement under G.S. 15A-145, 15A-145.1, 15A-145.2, 15A-145.3, 15A-145.4, or 15A-145.5, and (iii) that the person had not previously been convicted of any felony under the laws of the United States, this State, or any other state, the court shall order the expunction. No person as to whom such an order has been entered shall be held thereafter under any provision of any law to be guilty of perjury, or to be guilty of otherwise giving a false statement or response to any inquiry made for any purpose, by reason of his failure to recite or acknowledge any expunged entries concerning apprehension or trial.

(b) The court may also order that the said entries, including civil revocations of drivers licenses as a result of the underlying charge, shall be expunged from the records of the court, and direct all law-enforcement agencies, the Division of Adult Correction of the Department of Public Safety, the Division of Motor Vehicles, and any other State or local government agencies identified by the petitioner as bearing record of the same to expunge their records of the entries, including civil revocations of drivers licenses as a result of the underlying charge being expunged. This subsection does not apply to civil or criminal charges based upon the civil revocation, or to civil revocations under G.S. 20-16.2. The clerk shall notify State and local agencies of the court's order as provided in G.S. 15A-150. The clerk shall forward a certified copy of the order to the Division of Motor Vehicles for the expunction of a civil revocation provided the underlying criminal charge is also expunged. The civil revocation of a drivers license shall not be expunged prior to a final disposition of any pending civil or criminal charge based upon the civil revocation. The costs of expunging the records, as required under G.S. 15A-150, shall not be taxed against the petitioner.

(b1) Any person entitled to expungement under this section may also apply to the court for an order expunging DNA records when the person's case has been dismissed by the trial court and the person's DNA record or profile has been included in the State DNA Database and the person's DNA sample is stored in the State DNA Databank. A copy of the application for expungement of the DNA record or DNA sample shall be served on the district attorney for the judicial district in which the felony charges were brought not less than 20 days prior to the date of the hearing on the application. If the application for expungement is granted, a certified copy of the trial court's order dismissing the charges shall be attached to an order of expungement. The order of expungement shall include the name and address of the defendant and the defendant's attorney and shall direct the North Carolina State Crime Laboratory to send a letter documenting expungement as required by subsection (b2) of this section.

(b2) Upon receiving an order of expungement entered pursuant to subsection (b1) of this section, the North Carolina State Crime Laboratory shall purge the DNA record and all other identifying information from the State DNA Database and the DNA sample stored in the State DNA Databank covered by the order, except that the order shall not apply to other offenses committed by the individual that qualify for inclusion in the State DNA Database and the State DNA Databank. A letter documenting expungement of the DNA record and destruction of the DNA sample shall be sent by the North Carolina State Crime

Laboratory to the defendant and the defendant's attorney at the address specified by the court in the order of expungement.

(c)   The clerk shall notify State and local agencies of the court's order as provided in G.S. 15A-150.

(d)   A person charged with a crime that is dismissed pursuant to compliance with a deferred prosecution agreement and who files a petition for expunction of a criminal record under this section must pay the clerk of superior court a fee of one hundred seventy-five dollars ($175.00) at the time the petition is filed. Fees collected under this subsection are payable to the Administrative Office of the Courts. The clerk of superior court shall remit one hundred twenty-two dollars and fifty cents ($122.50) of each fee to the North Carolina Department of Justice for the costs of criminal record checks performed in connection with processing petitions for expunctions under this section. The remaining fifty-two dollars and fifty cents ($52.50) of each fee shall be retained by the Administrative Office of the Courts and used to pay the costs of processing petitions for expunctions under this section. This subsection does not apply to petitions filed by an indigent. (1979, c. 61; 1985, c. 636, ss. 1-7; 1991, c. 326, s. 1; 1997-138, s. 1; 1999-406, s. 9; 2001-108, s. 2; 2001-282, s. 1; 2002-126, s. 29A.5(c); 2005-452, s. 1; 2007-509, s. 2; 2009-510, s. 5(a), (b); 2009-577, ss. 3.1, 8, 9; 2011-145, s. 19.1(h); 2012-191, s. 4; 2013-360, ss. 17.6(e), 18B.16(f).)

§ 15A-147. Expunction of records when charges are dismissed or there are findings of not guilty as a result of identity theft.

(a)   If any person is named in a charge for an infraction or a crime, either a misdemeanor or a felony, as a result of another person using the identifying information of the named person and the charge against the named person is dismissed, a finding of not guilty is entered, or the conviction is set aside, the named person may apply by petition or written motion to the court where the charge was last pending on a form approved by the Administrative Office of the Courts supplied by the clerk of court for an order to expunge from all official records any entries relating to the person's apprehension, charge, or trial. The court, after notice to the district attorney, shall hold a hearing on the motion or petition and, upon finding that the person's identity was used without permission and the charges were dismissed or the person was found not guilty, the court shall order the expunction.

(b)   No person as to whom such an order has been entered under this section shall be held thereafter under any provision of any law to be guilty of perjury, or to be guilty of otherwise giving a false statement or response to any inquiry made for any purpose, by reason of the person's failure to recite or acknowledge any expunged entries concerning apprehension, charge, or trial.

(c) The court shall also order that the said entries shall be expunged from the records of the court and direct all law enforcement agencies, the Division of Adult Correction of the Department of Public Safety, the Division of Motor Vehicles, or any other State or local government agencies identified by the petitioner as bearing record of the same to expunge their records of the entries. The clerk shall notify State and local agencies of the court's order as provided in G.S. 15A-150. The costs of expunging the records, as required under G.S. 15A-150, shall not be taxed against the petitioner.

(d) The Division of Motor Vehicles shall expunge from its records entries made as a result of the charge or conviction ordered expunged under this section. The Division of Motor Vehicles shall also reverse any administrative actions taken against a person whose record is expunged under this section as a result of the charges or convictions expunged, including the assessment of drivers license points and drivers license suspension or revocation. Notwithstanding any other provision of this Chapter, the Division of Motor Vehicles shall provide to the person whose motor vehicle record is expunged under this section a certified corrected driver history at no cost and shall reinstate at no cost any drivers license suspended or revoked as a result of a charge or conviction expunged under this section.

(e) The Division of Adult Correction of the Department of Public Safety and any other applicable State or local government agency shall expunge its records as provided in G.S. 15A-150. The agency shall also reverse any administrative actions taken against a person whose record is expunged under this section as a result of the charges or convictions expunged. Notwithstanding any other provision of law, the normal fee for any reinstatement of a license or privilege resulting under this section shall be waived.

(f) Any insurance company that charged any additional premium based on insurance points assessed against a policyholder as a result of a charge or conviction that was expunged under this section shall refund those additional premiums to the policyholder upon notification of the expungement. (2001-108, s. 1; 2005-414, s. 8; 2009-510, s. 6; 2011-145, s. 19.1(h).)

§ 15A-148. Expunction of DNA records when charges are dismissed on appeal or pardon of innocence is granted.

(a)   Upon a motion by the defendant following the issuance of a final order by an appellate court reversing and dismissing a conviction of an offense for which a DNA analysis was done in accordance with Article 13 of Chapter 15A of the General Statutes, or upon receipt of a pardon of innocence with respect to any such offense, the court shall issue an order of expungement of the DNA record and samples in accordance with subsection (b) of this section. The order of expungement shall include the name and address of the defendant and the defendant's attorney and shall direct the North Carolina State Crime Laboratory to send a letter documenting expungement as required by subsection (b) of this section.

(b)   When an order of expungement has been issued pursuant to subsection (a) of this section, the order of expungement, together with a certified copy of the final appellate court order reversing and dismissing the conviction or a certified copy of the instrument granting the pardon of innocence, shall be provided to the North Carolina State Crime Laboratory by the clerk of court. Upon receiving an order of expungement for an individual whose DNA record or profile has been included in the State DNA Database and whose DNA sample is stored in the State DNA Databank, the DNA profile shall be expunged and the DNA sample destroyed by the North Carolina State Crime Laboratory, except that the order shall not apply to other offenses committed by the individual that qualify for inclusion in the State DNA Database and the State DNA Databank. A letter documenting expungement of the DNA record and destruction of the DNA sample shall be sent by the North Carolina State Crime Laboratory to the defendant and the defendant's attorney at the address specified by the court in the order of expungement. The North Carolina State Crime Laboratory shall adopt procedures to comply with this subsection. (2001-282, s. 2; 2013-360, s. 17.6(e).)

§ 15A-149. Expunction of records when pardon of innocence is granted.

(a)   If any person is convicted of a crime and receives a pardon of innocence, the person may apply by petition or written motion to the court in which the person was convicted on a form approved by the Administrative Office of the Courts supplied by the clerk of court for an order to expunge from all official records any entries relating to the person's apprehension, charge, or trial.

Upon receipt of the petition or written motion, the clerk of court shall verify that an attested copy of the warrant and return granting a pardon of innocence has been filed with the court in accordance with G.S. 147-25. Upon verification by the clerk that the warrant and return have been filed, the court shall issue an order of expunction.

(b)   The order of expunction shall include an instruction that any entries relating to the person's apprehension, charge, or trial shall be expunged from the records of the court and direct all law enforcement agencies, the Division of Adult Correction of the Department of Public Safety, the Division of Motor Vehicles, or any other State or local government agencies identified by the petitioner as bearing record of the same to expunge their records of the entries. The clerk shall notify State and local agencies of the court's order as provided in G.S. 15A-150. The costs of expunging the records, as required under G.S. 15A-150, shall not be taxed against the petitioner.

(c)   No person as to whom such an order has been entered under this section shall be held thereafter under any provision of any law to be guilty of perjury, or to be guilty of otherwise giving a false statement or response to any inquiry made for any purpose, by reason of the person's failure to recite or acknowledge any expunged entries concerning apprehension, charge, or trial. (2005-319, s. 1; 2009-510, s. 7; 2011-145, s. 19.1(h).)

§ 15A-150. Notification requirements.

(a)   Notification to AOC. - The clerk of superior court in each county in North Carolina shall, as soon as practicable after each term of court, file with the Administrative Office of the Courts the names of the following:

(1)   Persons granted an expunction under this Article.

(2)   Persons granted a conditional discharge under G.S. 14-50.29.

(3)   Persons granted a conditional discharge under G.S. 90-96 or G.S. 90-113.14.

(4)   Repealed by Session Laws 2010-174, s. 7, effective October 1, 2010.

(5)   Persons granted a conditional discharge under G.S. 14-204.

(b) Notification to Other State and Local Agencies. - The clerk of superior court in each county in North Carolina shall send a certified copy of an order granting an expunction to a person named in subsection (a) of this section to all of the agencies listed in this subsection. An agency receiving an order under this subsection shall expunge from its records all entries made as a result of the charge or conviction ordered expunged, except as provided in G.S. 15A-151.

(1) The sheriff, chief of police, or other arresting agency.

(2) When applicable, the Division of Motor Vehicles and the Division of Adult Correction of the Department of Public Safety.

(3) Any State or local agency identified by the petition as bearing record of the offense that has been expunged.

(c) Notification to SBI and FBI. - An arresting agency that receives a certified copy of an order under this section shall forward a copy of the order with the form supplied by the State Bureau of Investigation to the State Bureau of Investigation. The State Bureau of Investigation shall forward the order to the Federal Bureau of Investigation.

(d) Notification to Private Entities. - A State agency that receives a certified copy of an order under this section shall notify any private entity with which it has a licensing agreement for bulk extracts of data from the agency criminal record database to delete the record in question. The private entity shall notify any other entity to which it subsequently provides in a bulk extract data from the agency criminal database to delete the record in question from its database. (2009-510, s. 1; 2010-174, s. 7; 2011-145, s. 19.1(h); 2013-368, s. 12.)

§ 15A-151. Confidential agency files; exceptions to expunction.

(a) The Administrative Office of the Courts shall maintain a confidential file containing the names of those people for whom it received a notice under G.S. 15A-150. The information contained in the file may be disclosed only as follows:

(1) To a judge of the General Court of Justice of North Carolina for the purpose of ascertaining whether a person charged with an offense has been previously granted a discharge or an expunction.

(2) To a person requesting confirmation of the person's own discharge or expunction, as provided in G.S. 15A-152.

(3) To the General Court of Justice of North Carolina in response to a subpoena or other court order issued pursuant to a civil action under G.S. 15A-152.

(4) If the criminal record was expunged pursuant to G.S. 15A-145.4 or G.S. 15A-145.5, to State and local law enforcement agencies for employment purposes only.

(5) If the criminal record was expunged pursuant to G.S. 15A-145.4, 15A-145.5, or [15A-]145.6, to the North Carolina Criminal Justice Education and Training Standards Commission for certification purposes only.

(6) If the criminal record was expunged pursuant to G.S. 15A-145.4, 15A-145.5, or 15A-145.6, to the North Carolina Sheriffs' Education and Training Standards Commission for certification purposes only.

(b) All agencies required under G.S. 15A-150 to expunge from records all entries made as a result of a charge or conviction ordered expunged who maintain a licensing agreement to provide record information to a private entity shall maintain a confidential file containing information verifying the expunction and subsequent notification to private entities as required by G.S. 15A-150(d). The information contained in the file shall be disclosed only to a person requesting confirmation of expunction of the record of the person's own discharge or expunction, as provided in G.S. 15A-152.

(c) The Division of Motor Vehicles shall not be required to expunge a record if the expunction of the record is expressly prohibited by the federal Commercial Motor Vehicle Safety Act of 1986, the federal Motor Carrier Safety Improvement Act of 1999, or regulations adopted pursuant to either act. (2009-510, s. 1; 2010-174, s. 8; 2011-278, s. 2; 2012-191, s. 5; 2013-368, s. 13.)

§ 15A-152. Civil liability for dissemination of certain criminal history information.

(a) Duty to Delete Record. - A private entity that holds itself out as being in the business of compiling and disseminating criminal history record information for compensation shall destroy and shall not disseminate any information in the possession of the entity with respect to which the entity has received a notice to delete the record in question. The private entity shall delete the record within the specified time and pursuant to the terms of the licensing agreement with the State agency. If the license does not specify a time for deletion, or if no license agreement exists between the private entity and state agency, the private entity shall delete the record within 10 business days of receiving notice to delete the record in question.

(b)   Dissemination of Information. - Unless the entity is regulated by the federal Fair Credit Reporting, Act 15 U.S.C. § 1681, et seq. or the Gramm-Leach-Bliley Act 15 U.S.C. §§ 6801-6809, a private entity described by subsection (a) of this section that is licensed to access a State agency's criminal history record database may disseminate that information only if, within the 90-day period preceding the date of dissemination, the entity originally obtained the information or received the information as an updated record information to its database. The private entity must notify the State agency from which it receives the information of any other entity to which it subsequently provides a bulk extract of the information.

(c)   Civil Liability. - A private entity subject to the provisions of this section that disseminates information in violation of this section is liable for any damages that are sustained as a result of the violation by the person who is the subject of that information. A person who prevails in an action brought under this section is also entitled to recover court costs and reasonable attorneys' fees. This subsection does not apply to an entity regulated by and subject to the civil liability remedies of the federal Fair Credit Reporting Act, 15 U.S.C. § 1681, et seq., or the Gramm Leach-Bliley Act, 15 U.S.C. 6801-6809, et seq.

(d)   Certificate of Verification. - Prior to filing an action under this section, a person who is the subject of a record that has been expunged may apply to the Administrative Office of the Courts for a certificate verifying that the person is the subject of a record that has been expunged and that notice of the expunction was made in accordance with G.S. 15A-150. The application must include a sworn affidavit attesting, under penalty of perjury, that the applicant is the person who was the subject of the record in question and identifying the specific case expunged. A notary or official taking an acknowledgment, oath, or affirmation of an applicant's affidavit under this subsection may not disclose the nature or content of the application, except as required in a court action related to the application. Unless made part of the record of a subsequent court proceeding, a certificate of verification and an application for the certificate are not public records under G.S. 132-1. The Administrative Office of the Courts may establish procedures pertaining to the application for and issuance of certificates of verification.

(e) Notice of Record Removal. - Prior to filing an action under this section, a person who is the subject of a record that has been expunged may request a notice of record removal of the expunction and subsequent notification to private entities as required by G.S. 15A-150(d) from an agency required under G.S. 15A-150 to expunge that person's record who maintains a licensing agreement to provide record information to a private entity. The application must include a sworn affidavit attesting, under penalty of perjury, that the applicant is the person who was the subject of the record in question and identifying the specific case expunged. A notary or official taking an acknowledgment, oath, or affirmation of an applicant's affidavit under this subsection may not disclose the nature or content of the application, except as required in a court action related to the application. Unless made part of the record of a subsequent court proceeding, a notice of record removal and an application for the notice are not public records under G.S. 132-1. State and local agencies may establish procedures pertaining to the application for and issuance of notices of record removal. (2009-510, s. 1; 2010-174, s. 9.)

§ 15A-153. Effect of expunction; prohibited practices by employers, educational institutions, agencies of State and local governments.

(a) Purpose. - The purpose of this section is to clear the public record of any entry of any arrest, criminal charge, or criminal conviction that has been expunged so that (i) the person who is entitled to and obtains the expunction may omit reference to the charges or convictions to potential employers and others and (ii) a records check for prior arrests and convictions will not disclose the expunged entries. Nothing in this section shall be construed to prohibit an employer from asking a job applicant about criminal charges or convictions that have not been expunged and are part of the public record.

(b) [Nondisclosure Protected. -] No person as to whom an order of expunction has been entered pursuant to this Article shall be held thereafter under any provision of any laws to be guilty of perjury or otherwise giving a false statement by reason of that person's failure to recite or acknowledge any expunged arrest, apprehension, charge, indictment, information, trial, or conviction in response to any inquiry made of him or her for any purpose other than as provided in subsection (e) of this section.

(c)   Employer or Educational Institution Inquiry Regarding Disclosure of Expunged Arrest, Criminal Charge, or Conviction. - An employer or educational institution shall not, in any application, interview, or otherwise, require an applicant for employment or admission to disclose information concerning any arrest, criminal charge, or criminal conviction of the applicant that has been expunged and shall not knowingly and willingly inquire about any arrest, charge, or conviction that they know to have been expunged. An applicant need not, in answer to any question concerning any arrest or criminal charge that has not resulted in a conviction, include a reference to or information concerning arrests, charges, or convictions that have been expunged. This subsection does not apply to State or local law enforcement agencies authorized pursuant to G.S. 15A-151 to obtain confidential information for employment purposes.

(d)   State or Local Government Agency, Official, and Employee Inquiry Regarding Disclosure of Expunged Arrest, Criminal Charge, or Conviction. - Agencies, officials, and employees of the State and local governments who request disclosure of information concerning any arrest, criminal charge, or criminal conviction of the applicant shall first advise the applicant that State law allows the applicant to not refer to any arrest, charge, or conviction that has been expunged. An applicant need not, in answer to any question concerning any arrest or criminal charge that has not resulted in a conviction, include a reference to or information concerning charges or convictions that have been expunged. Such application shall not be denied solely because of the applicant's refusal or failure to disclose information concerning any arrest, criminal charge, or criminal conviction of the applicant that has been expunged.

(e)   [Exceptions. -] The provisions of subsection (d) of this section do not apply to any applicant or licensee seeking or holding any certification issued by the North Carolina Criminal Justice Education and Training Standards Commission pursuant to Chapter 17C of the General Statutes or the North Carolina Sheriffs Education and Training Standards Commission pursuant to Chapter 17E of the General Statutes:

(1)   Convictions expunged pursuant to G.S. 15A-145.4. - Persons pursuing certification under the provisions of Chapter 17C or 17E of the General Statutes shall disclose any and all felony convictions to the certifying Commission regardless of whether or not the felony convictions were expunged pursuant to the provisions of G.S. 15A-145.4.

(2)   Convictions expunged pursuant to G.S. 15A-145.5. - Persons pursuing certification under the provisions of Chapter 17C or 17E of the General Statutes

shall disclose any and all convictions to the certifying Commission regardless of whether or not the convictions were expunged pursuant to the provisions of G.S. 15A-145.5.

(f) (See note) Penalty for Violation. - Upon investigation by the Commissioner of Labor or the Commissioner's authorized representative, any employer found to be in violation of subsection (c) of this section shall be issued a written warning for a first violation and shall be subject to a civil penalty of up to five hundred dollars ($500.00) for each additional violation occurring after receipt of the written warning. In determining the amount of any penalty ordered under authority of this section, the Commissioner shall give due consideration to the appropriateness of the penalty with respect to the size of the business of the person being charged, the gravity of the violation, the good faith of the person, and the record of previous violations. The determination of the amount of the penalty by the Commissioner shall be final, unless within 15 days after receipt of notice thereof by certified mail with return receipt, by signature confirmation as provided by the U.S. Postal Service, by a designated delivery service authorized pursuant to 26 U.S.C. § 7502(f)(2) with delivery receipt, or via hand delivery, the person charged with the violation takes exception to the determination in which event the final determination of the penalty shall be made in an administrative proceeding and in a judicial proceeding pursuant to Chapter 150B of the General Statutes, the Administrative Procedure Act. The Commissioner of Labor may adopt, modify, or revoke such rules as are necessary for carrying out the provisions of this subsection.

Nothing in this section shall be construed to create a private cause of action against any employer or its agents or employees, any educational institutions or their agents or employees, or any State or local government agencies, officials, or employees. (2013-53, s. 3.)

§ 15A-154: Reserved for future codification purposes.

§ 15A-155: Reserved for future codification purposes.

§ 15A-156: Reserved for future codification purposes.

§ 15A-157: Reserved for future codification purposes.

§ 15A-158: Reserved for future codification purposes.

§ 15A-159: Reserved for future codification purposes.

§ 15A-160. Reporting requirement.

The Department of Justice and the Administrative Office of the Courts shall report jointly to the Chairs of the Joint Legislative Oversight Committee on Justice and Public Safety Oversight by September 1 of each year regarding expunctions. The report shall include all of the following information:

(1)   The number and types of expunctions granted during the fiscal year in which the report is made.

(2)   The number and type of expunctions granted each fiscal year for the five fiscal years preceding the date of the report.

(3)   A full accounting of how the agencies have spent the receipts generated by the expunction fees received during the fiscal year in which the report is made and for the five preceding fiscal years. (2013-360, s. 18B.16(h).)

§ 15A-161: Reserved for future codification purposes.

§ 15A-162: Reserved for future codification purposes.

§ 15A-163: Reserved for future codification purposes.

§ 15A-164: Reserved for future codification purposes.

§ 15A-165: Reserved for future codification purposes.

§ 15A-166: Reserved for future codification purposes.

§ 15A-167: Reserved for future codification purposes.

§ 15A-168: Reserved for future codification purposes.

§ 15A-169: Reserved for future codification purposes.

§ 15A-170: Reserved for future codification purposes.

§ 15A-171: Reserved for future codification purposes.

§ 15A-172: Reserved for future codification purposes.

§ 15A-173: Reserved for future codification purposes.

Article 6.

Certificate of Relief.

§ 15A-173.1. Definitions.

The following definitions apply in this Article:

(1)   Collateral consequence. - A collateral sanction or a disqualification.

(2)   Collateral sanction. - A penalty, disability, or disadvantage, however denominated, imposed on an individual as a result of the individual's conviction of an offense which applies by operation of law, whether or not the penalty, disability, or disadvantage is included in the judgment or sentence. The term does not include imprisonment, probation, parole, post-release supervision, forfeiture, restitution, fine, assessment, or costs of prosecution.

(3)   Disqualification. - A penalty, disability, or disadvantage, however denominated, that an administrative agency, governmental official, or court in a civil proceeding may impose on an individual on grounds relating to the individual's conviction of an offense.

(4)   District attorney. - The office of the district attorney that prosecuted the offense giving rise to the collateral consequence from which relief is sought. (2011-265, s. 1.)

§ 15A-173.2. Certificate of Relief.

(a)   An individual who is convicted of no more than two Class G, H, or I felonies or misdemeanors in one session of court, and who has no other convictions for a felony or misdemeanor other than a traffic violation, may petition the court where the individual was convicted for a Certificate of Relief relieving collateral consequences as permitted by this Article. Except as otherwise provided in this subsection, the petition shall be heard by the senior resident superior court judge if the convictions were in superior court, or the chief district court judge if the convictions were in district court. The senior resident superior court judge and chief district court judge in each district may delegate their authority to hold hearings and issue, modify, or revoke Certificates of Relief to judges, clerks, or magistrates in that district.

(b)   Except as otherwise provided in G.S. 15A-173.3, the court may issue a Certificate of Relief if, after reviewing the petition, the individual's criminal history, any information provided by a victim under G.S. 15A-173.6 or the district attorney, and any other relevant evidence, it finds the individual has established by a preponderance of the evidence all of the following:

(1)   Twelve months have passed since the individual has completed his or her sentence. For purposes of this subdivision, an individual has not completed his or her sentence until the individual has served all of the active time, if any, imposed for each offense and has also completed any period of probation, post-release supervision, and parole related to the offense that is required by State law or court order.

(2)   The individual is engaged in, or seeking to engage in, a lawful occupation or activity, including employment, training, education, or rehabilitative programs, or the individual otherwise has a lawful source of support.

(3)   The individual has complied with all requirements of the individual's sentence, including any terms of probation, that may include substance abuse treatment, anger management, and educational requirements.

(4)   The individual is not in violation of the terms of any criminal sentence, or that any failure to comply is justified, excused, involuntary, or insubstantial.

(5)   A criminal charge is not pending against the individual.

(6)   Granting the petition would not pose an unreasonable risk to the safety or welfare of the public or any individual.

(c)   The Certificate of Relief shall specify any restriction imposed and collateral sanction or disqualification from which relief has not been granted under G.S. 15A-173.4(a).

(d) A Certificate of Relief relieves all collateral sanctions, except those listed in G.S. 15A-173.3, those sanctions imposed by the North Carolina Constitution or federal law, and any others specifically excluded in the certificate. A Certificate of Relief does not automatically relieve a disqualification; however, an administrative agency, governmental official, or court in a civil proceeding may consider a Certificate of Relief favorably in determining whether a conviction should result in disqualification.

(e) A Certificate of Relief issued under this Article does not result in the expunction of any criminal history record information, nor does it constitute a pardon.

(f) A Certificate of Relief may be revoked pursuant to G.S. 15A-173.4(b) if the individual is subsequently convicted of a felony or misdemeanor other than a traffic violation or is found to have made any material misrepresentation in his or her petition.

(g) The denial of a petition for a Certificate of Relief shall state the reasons for the denial, and the petitioner may file a subsequent petition 12 months from the denial and shall demonstrate that the petitioner has remedied the defects in the previous petition and has complied with any conditions for reapplication set by the court pursuant to G.S. 15A-173.4(a) in order to have the petition granted. (2011-265, s. 1.)

§ 15A-173.3. Collateral sanctions not subject to order of limited relief or Certificate of Relief.

A Certificate of Relief shall not be issued to relieve any of the following collateral sanctions:

(1) Requirements imposed by, and any statutory requirements or prohibitions imposed as a result of registration pursuant to, Article 27A of Chapter 14 of the General Statutes.

(2) Prohibitions on possession of firearms imposed by Articles 54A and 54B of Chapter 14 of the General Statutes.

(3) A motor vehicle license suspension, revocation, limitation, or ineligibility imposed pursuant to Chapter 20 of the General Statutes.

(4) Ineligibility for certification pursuant to Chapter 17C or 17E of the General Statutes.

(5) Ineligibility for employment as any of the following if the ineligibility is a sanction imposed by a statute or session law of North Carolina.

a. A corrections or probation officer.

b. A prosecutor or investigator in either the Department of Justice or in the office of a district attorney. For purposes of this subdivision, the term district attorney shall include any district attorney authorized pursuant to G.S. 7A-60. (2011-265, s. 1.)

§ 15A-173.4. Issuance, modification, and revocation of Certificate of Relief.

(a) When a petition is filed under G.S. 15A-173.2, including a petition for enlargement of an existing Certificate of Relief, the court shall notify the district attorney at least three weeks before the hearing on the matter. The court may issue a Certificate of Relief subject to restriction, condition, or additional requirement. When issuing, denying, modifying, or revoking a Certificate of Relief, the court may impose conditions for reapplication.

(b) The court may modify or revoke a Certificate of Relief it issued if it finds just cause by a preponderance of the evidence. Just cause includes subsequent conviction of a felony or misdemeanor other than a traffic violation in this State, or of an offense in another jurisdiction that is deemed a felony or misdemeanor other than a traffic violation in this State, or material misrepresentation by the petitioner in the petition for Certificate of Relief. A motion for modification or revocation of a Certificate of Relief may be initiated by the court on its own motion, or upon motion of the district attorney. The individual for whom the Certificate of Relief has been issued, and the district attorney, shall be given notice of the motion at least three weeks before any hearing on the matter. A hearing on the motion shall be held if requested by either the individual for whom the Certificate of Relief has been issued, or the district attorney.

(c) The district attorney shall have the right to appear and be heard at any proceeding relating to the issuance, modification, or revocation of the Certificate of Relief.

(d)   The court is authorized to call upon a probation officer for any additional investigation or verification of the individual's conduct it reasonably believes necessary to its decision to issue, modify, or revoke a Certificate of Relief. If there are material disputed issues of fact or law, the individual and the district attorney may submit evidence and be heard on those issues.

(e)   The issuance, modification, and revocation of Certificates of Relief shall be a public record. (2011-265, s. 1.)

§ 15A-173.5. Reliance on order or Certificate of Relief as evidence of due care.

In a judicial or administrative proceeding alleging negligence, a Certificate of Relief is a bar to any action alleging lack of due care in hiring, retaining, licensing, leasing to, admitting to a school or program, or otherwise transacting business or engaging in activity with the individual to whom the Certificate of Relief was issued, if the person against whom the judicial or administrative proceeding is brought knew of the Certificate of Relief at the time of the alleged negligence. (2011-265, s. 1.)

§ 15A-173.6. Victim's rights.

The victim of the underlying offense for which a Certificate of Relief is sought may appear and be heard, or may file a statement for consideration by the court, in a proceeding for issuance, modification, or revocation of the Certificate of Relief. Notification to the victim shall be made through the Victim Witness Coordinator in the office of the district attorney. (2011-265, s. 1.)

§ 15A-174: Reserved for future codification purposes.

§ 15A-175: Reserved for future codification purposes.

§ 15A-176: Reserved for future codification purposes.

§ 15A-177: Reserved for future codification purposes.

§ 15A-178: Reserved for future codification purposes.

§ 15A-179: Reserved for future codification purposes.

§ 15A-180: Reserved for future codification purposes.

§ 15A-181: Reserved for future codification purposes.

§ 15A-182: Reserved for future codification purposes.

§ 15A-183: Reserved for future codification purposes.

§ 15A-184: Reserved for future codification purposes.

§ 15A-185: Reserved for future codification purposes.

§ 15A-186: Reserved for future codification purposes.

§ 15A-187: Reserved for future codification purposes.

§ 15A-188: Reserved for future codification purposes.

§ 15A-189: Reserved for future codification purposes.

§ 15A-190: Reserved for future codification purposes.

§ 15A-191: Reserved for future codification purposes.

§ 15A-192: Reserved for future codification purposes.

§ 15A-193: Reserved for future codification purposes.

§ 15A-194: Reserved for future codification purposes.

§ 15A-195: Reserved for future codification purposes.

§ 15A-196: Reserved for future codification purposes.

§ 15A-197: Reserved for future codification purposes.

§ 15A-198: Reserved for future codification purposes.

§ 15A-199: Reserved for future codification purposes.

§ 15A-200: Reserved for future codification purposes.

SUBCHAPTER II. LAW-ENFORCEMENT AND INVESTIGATIVE PROCEDURES.

Article 7.

§§ 15A-201 through 15A-210. Reserved for future codification purposes.

Article 8.

Electronic Recording of Interrogations.

§ 15A-211. Electronic recording of interrogations.

(a)   Purpose. - The purpose of this Article is to require the creation of an electronic record of an entire custodial interrogation in order to eliminate disputes about interrogations, thereby improving prosecution of the guilty while affording protection to the innocent and increasing court efficiency.

(b)   Application. - The provisions of this Article shall apply to all custodial interrogations of juveniles in criminal investigations conducted at any place of detention. The provisions of this Article shall also apply to any custodial interrogation of any person in a criminal investigation conducted at any place of detention if the investigation is related to any of the following crimes: any Class A, B1, or B2 felony, and any Class C felony of rape, sex offense, or assault with a deadly weapon with intent to kill inflicting serious injury.

(c)   Definitions. - The following definitions apply in this Article:

(1)   Electronic recording. - An audio recording that is an authentic, accurate, unaltered record; or a visual recording that is an authentic, accurate, unaltered record. A visual and audio recording shall be simultaneously produced whenever reasonably feasible, provided that a defendant may not raise this as grounds for suppression of evidence.

(2)   In its entirety. - An uninterrupted record that begins with and includes a law enforcement officer's advice to the person in custody of that person's

constitutional rights, ends when the interview has completely finished, and clearly shows both the interrogator and the person in custody throughout. If the record is a visual recording, the camera recording the custodial interrogation must be placed so that the camera films both the interrogator and the suspect. Brief periods of recess, upon request by the person in custody or the law enforcement officer, do not constitute an "interruption" of the record. The record will reflect the starting time of the recess and the resumption of the interrogation.

(3)   Place of detention. - A jail, police or sheriff's station, correctional or detention facility, holding facility for prisoners, or other facility where persons are held in custody in connection with criminal charges.

(d)   Electronic Recording of Interrogations Required. - Any law enforcement officer conducting a custodial interrogation in an investigation of a juvenile shall make an electronic recording of the interrogation in its entirety. Any law enforcement officer conducting a custodial interrogation in an investigation relating to any of the following crimes shall make an electronic recording of the interrogation in its entirety: any Class A, B1, or B2 felony; and any Class C felony of rape, sex offense, or assault with a deadly weapon with intent to kill inflicting serious injury.

(e)   Admissibility of Electronic Recordings. - During the prosecution of any offense to which this Article applies, an oral, written, nonverbal, or sign language statement of a defendant made in the course of a custodial interrogation may be presented as evidence against the defendant if an electronic recording was made of the custodial interrogation in its entirety and the statement is otherwise admissible. If the court finds that the defendant was subjected to a custodial interrogation that was not electronically recorded in its entirety, any statements made by the defendant after that non-electronically recorded custodial interrogation, even if made during an interrogation that is otherwise in compliance with this section, may be questioned with regard to the voluntariness and reliability of the statement. The State may establish through clear and convincing evidence that the statement was both voluntary and reliable and that law enforcement officers had good cause for failing to electronically record the interrogation in its entirety. Good cause shall include, but not be limited to, the following:

(1)   The accused refused to have the interrogation electronically recorded, and the refusal itself was electronically recorded.

(2) The failure to electronically record an interrogation in its entirety was the result of unforeseeable equipment failure, and obtaining replacement equipment was not feasible.

(f) Remedies for Compliance or Noncompliance. - All of the following remedies shall be granted as relief for compliance or noncompliance with the requirements of this section:

(1) Failure to comply with any of the requirements of this section shall be considered by the court in adjudicating motions to suppress a statement of the defendant made during or after a custodial interrogation.

(2) Failure to comply with any of the requirements of this section shall be admissible in support of claims that the defendant's statement was involuntary or is unreliable, provided the evidence is otherwise admissible.

(3) When evidence of compliance or noncompliance with the requirements of this section has been presented at trial, the jury shall be instructed that it may consider credible evidence of compliance or noncompliance to determine whether the defendant's statement was voluntary and reliable.

(g) Article Does Not Preclude Admission of Certain Statements. - Nothing in this Article precludes the admission of any of the following:

(1) A statement made by the accused in open court during trial, before a grand jury, or at a preliminary hearing.

(2) A spontaneous statement that is not made in response to a question.

(3) A statement made during arrest processing in response to a routine question.

(4) A statement made during a custodial interrogation that is conducted in another state by law enforcement officers of that state.

(5) A statement obtained by a federal law enforcement officer.

(6) A statement given at a time when the interrogators are unaware that the person is suspected of an offense to which this Article applies.

(7) A statement used only for impeachment purposes and not as substantive evidence.

(h) Destruction or Modification of Recording After Appeals Exhausted. - The State shall not destroy or alter any electronic recording of a custodial interrogation of a defendant convicted of any offense related to the interrogation until one year after the completion of all State and federal appeals of the conviction, including the exhaustion of any appeal of any motion for appropriate relief or habeas corpus proceedings. Every electronic recording should be clearly identified and catalogued by law enforcement personnel. (2007-434, s. 1; 2011-329, s. 2.)

§ 15A-212. Reserved for future codification purposes.

§ 15A-213. Reserved for future codification purposes.

§ 15A-214. Reserved for future codification purposes.

§ 15A-215. Reserved for future codification purposes.

§ 15A-216. Reserved for future codification purposes.

§ 15A-217. Reserved for future codification purposes.

§ 15A-218. Reserved for future codification purposes.

§ 15A-219. Reserved for future codification purposes.

§ 15A-220. Reserved for future codification purposes.

Article 9.

Search and Seizure by Consent.

§ 15A-221. General authorization; definition of "consent".

(a) Authority to Search and Seize Pursuant to Consent. - Subject to the limitations in the other provisions of this Article, a law-enforcement officer may conduct a search and make seizures, without a search warrant or other authorization, if consent to the search is given.

(b) Definition of "Consent". - As used in this Article, "consent" means a statement to the officer, made voluntarily and in accordance with the requirements of G.S. 15A-222, giving the officer permission to make a search. (1973, c. 1286, s. 1.)

§ 15A-222. Person from whom effective consent may be obtained.

The consent needed to justify a search and seizure under G.S. 15A-221 must be given:

(1) By the person to be searched;

(2) By the registered owner of a vehicle to be searched or by the person in apparent control of its operation and contents at the time the consent is given;

(3) By a person who by ownership or otherwise is reasonably apparently entitled to give or withhold consent to a search of premises. (1973, c. 1286, s. 1.)

§ 15A-223. Permissible scope of consent search and seizure.

(a) Search Limited by Scope of Consent. - A search conducted pursuant to the provisions of this Article may not exceed, in duration or physical scope, the limits of the consent given.

(b) Items Seizable as Result of Consent Search. - The things subject to seizure in the course of a search pursuant to this Article are the same as those specified in G.S. 15A-242. Upon completion of the search, the officer must make a list of the things seized, and must deliver a receipt embodying the list to the person who consented to the search and, if known, to the owner of the vehicle or premises searched. (1973, c. 1286, s. 1.)

§§ 15A-224 through 15A-230. Reserved for future codification purposes.

Article 10.

Other Searches and Seizures.

§ 15A-231. Other searches and seizures.

Constitutionally permissible searches and seizures which are not regulated by the General Statutes of North Carolina are not prohibited. (1973, c. 1286, s. 1.)

§§ 15A-232 through 15A-240. Reserved for future codification purposes.

Article 11.

Search Warrants.

§ 15A-241. Definition of search warrant.

A search warrant is a court order and process directing a law-enforcement officer to search designated premises, vehicles, or persons for the purpose of seizing designated items and accounting for any items so obtained to the court which issued the warrant. (1868-9, c. 178, subch. 3, s. 38; Code, s. 1171; Rev., s. 3163; C.S., s. 4529; 1941, c. 53; 1949, c. 1179; 1955, c. 7; 1965, c. 377; 1969, c. 869, s. 8; 1973, c. 1286, s. 1.)

§ 15A-242. Items subject to seizure under a search warrant.

An item is subject to seizure pursuant to a search warrant if there is probable cause to believe that it:

(1)   Is stolen or embezzled; or

(2)   Is contraband or otherwise unlawfully possessed; or

(3)   Has been used or is possessed for the purpose of being used to commit or conceal the commission of a crime; or

(4)   Constitutes evidence of an offense or the identity of a person participating in an offense. (1868-9, c. 178, subch. 3, s. 38; Code, s. 1171; Rev., s. 3163; C.S., s. 4529; 1941, c. 53; 1949, c. 1179; 1955, c. 7; 1965, c. 377; 1969, c. 869, s. 8; 1973, c. 1286, s. 1.)

§ 15A-243. Who may issue a search warrant.

(a)   A search warrant valid throughout the State may be issued by:

(1)   A Justice of the Supreme Court.

(2)   A judge of the Court of Appeals.

(3)   A judge of the superior court.

(b)   Other search warrants may be issued by:

(1)   A judge of the district court as provided in G.S. 7A-291.

(2)	A clerk as provided in G.S. 7A-180 and 7A-181.

(3)	A magistrate as provided in G.S. 7A-273. (1868-9, c. 178, subch. 3, s. 38; Code, s. 1171; Rev., s. 3163; C.S., s. 4529; 1941, c. 53; 1949, c. 1179; 1955, c. 7; 1965, c. 377; 1969, c. 869, s. 8; 1973, c. 1286, s. 1.)

§ 15A-244. Contents of the application for a search warrant.

Each application for a search warrant must be made in writing upon oath or affirmation. All applications must contain:

(1)	The name and title of the applicant; and

(2)	A statement that there is probable cause to believe that items subject to seizure under G.S. 15A-242 may be found in or upon a designated or described place, vehicle, or person; and

(3)	Allegations of fact supporting the statement. The statements must be supported by one or more affidavits particularly setting forth the facts and circumstances establishing probable cause to believe that the items are in the places or in the possession of the individuals to be searched; and

(4)	A request that the court issue a search warrant directing a search for and the seizure of the items in question. (1973, c. 1286, s. 1.)

§ 15A-245. Basis for issuance of a search warrant; duty of the issuing official.

(a)	Before acting on the application, the issuing official may examine on oath the applicant or any other person who may possess pertinent information, but information other than that contained in the affidavit may not be considered by the issuing official in determining whether probable cause exists for the issuance of the warrant unless the information is either recorded or contemporaneously summarized in the record or on the face of the warrant by the issuing official. The information must be shown by one or more of the following:

(1)	Affidavit; or

(2)   Oral testimony under oath or affirmation before the issuing official; or

(3)   Oral testimony under oath or affirmation presented by a sworn law enforcement officer to the issuing official by means of an audio and video transmission in which both parties can see and hear each other. Prior to the use of audio and video transmission pursuant to this subdivision, the procedures and type of equipment for audio and video transmission shall be submitted to the Administrative Office of the Courts by the senior regular resident superior court judge and the chief district court judge for a judicial district or set of districts and approved by the Administrative Office of the Courts.

(b)   If the issuing official finds that the application meets the requirements of this Article and finds there is probable cause to believe that the search will discover items specified in the application which are subject to seizure under G.S. 15A-242, he must issue a search warrant in accordance with the requirements of this Article. The issuing official must retain a copy of the warrant and warrant application and must promptly file them with the clerk. If he does not so find, the official must deny the application. (1973, c. 1286, s. 1; 2005-334, s. 1.)

§ 15A-246. Form and content of the search warrant.

A search warrant must contain:

(1)   The name and signature of the issuing official with the time and date of issuance above his signature; and

(2)   The name of a specific officer or the classification of officers to whom the warrant is addressed; and

(3)   The names of the applicant and of all persons whose affidavits or testimony were given in support of the application; and

(4)   A designation sufficient to establish with reasonable certainty the premises, vehicles, or persons to be searched; and

(5)   A description or a designation of the items constituting the object of the search and authorized to be seized. (1868-9, c. 178, subch. 3, s. 39; Code, s.

1172; Rev., s. 3164; C.S., s. 4530; 1961, c. 1069; 1969, c. 869, s. 8; 1973, c. 1286, s. 1.)

§ 15A-247. Who may execute a search warrant.

A search warrant may be executed by any law-enforcement officer acting within his territorial jurisdiction, whose investigative authority encompasses the crime or crimes involved. (1868-9, c. 178, subch. 3, s. 38; Code, s. 1171; Rev., s. 3163; C.S., s. 4529; 1941, c. 53; 1949, c. 1179; 1955, c. 7; 1965, c. 377; 1969, c. 869, s. 8; 1973, c. 1286, s. 1.)

§ 15A-248. Time of execution of a search warrant.

A search warrant must be executed within 48 hours from the time of issuance. Any warrant not executed within that time limit is void and must be marked "not executed" and returned without unnecessary delay to the clerk of the issuing court. (1973, c. 1286, s. 1.)

§ 15A-249. Officer to give notice of identity and purpose.

The officer executing a search warrant must, before entering the premises, give appropriate notice of his identity and purpose to the person to be searched, or the person in apparent control of the premises to be searched. If it is unclear whether anyone is present at the premises to be searched, he must give the notice in a manner likely to be heard by anyone who is present. (1973, c. 1286, s. 1.)

§ 15A-250. Reserved for future codification purposes.

§ 15A-251. Entry by force.

An officer may break and enter any premises or vehicle when necessary to the execution of the warrant if:

(1) The officer has previously announced his identity and purpose as required by G.S. 15A-249 and reasonably believes either that admittance is being denied or unreasonably delayed or that the premises or vehicle is unoccupied; or

(2) The officer has probable cause to believe that the giving of notice would endanger the life or safety of any person. (1973, c. 1286, s. 1.)

§ 15A-252. Service of a search warrant.

Before undertaking any search or seizure pursuant to the warrant, the officer must read the warrant and give a copy of the warrant application and affidavit to the person to be searched, or the person in apparent control of the premises or vehicle to be searched. If no one in apparent and responsible control is occupying the premises or vehicle, the officer must leave a copy of the warrant affixed to the premises or vehicle. (1973, c. 1286, s. 1.)

§ 15A-253. Scope of the search; seizure of items not named in the warrant.

The scope of the search may be only such as is authorized by the warrant and is reasonably necessary to discover the items specified therein. Upon discovery of the items specified, the officer must take possession or custody of them. If in the course of the search the officer inadvertently discovers items not specified in the warrant which are subject to seizure under G.S. 15A-242, he may also take possession of the items so discovered. (1973, c. 1286, s. 1.)

§ 15A-254. List of items seized.

Upon seizing items pursuant to a search warrant, an officer must write and sign a receipt itemizing the items taken and containing the name of the court by which the warrant was issued. If the items were taken from a person, the receipt must be given to the person. If items are taken from a place or vehicle, the receipt must be given to the owner, or person in apparent control of the premises or vehicle if the person is present; or if he is not, the officer must leave the receipt in the premises or vehicle from which the items were taken. (1973, c. 1286, s. 1.)

§ 15A-255. Frisk of persons present in premises or vehicle to be searched.

An officer executing a warrant directing a search of premises or of a vehicle may, if the officer reasonably believes that his safety or the safety of others then present so requires, search for any dangerous weapons by an external patting of the clothing of those present. If in the course of such a frisk he feels an object which he reasonably believes to be a dangerous weapon, he may take possession of the object. (1973, c. 1286, s. 1.)

§ 15A-256. Detention and search of persons present in private premises or vehicle to be searched.

An officer executing a warrant directing a search of premises not generally open to the public or of a vehicle other than a common carrier may detain any person present for such time as is reasonably necessary to execute the warrant. If the search of such premises or vehicle and of any persons designated as objects of the search in the warrant fails to produce the items named in the warrant, the officer may then search any person present at the time of the officer's entry to the extent reasonably necessary to find property particularly described in the warrant which may be concealed upon the person, but no property of a different type from that particularly described in the warrant may be seized or may be the basis for prosecution of any person so searched. For the purpose of this section, all controlled substances are the same type of property. (1973, c. 1286, s. 1.)

§ 15A-257. Return of the executed warrant.

An officer who has executed a search warrant must, without unnecessary delay, return to the clerk of the issuing court the warrant together with a written inventory of items seized. The inventory, if any, and return must be signed and sworn to by the officer who executed the warrant. (1973, c. 1286, s. 1.)

§ 15A-258. Disposition of seized property.

Property seized shall be held in the custody of the person who applied for the warrant, or of the officer who executed it, or of the agency or department by which the officer is employed, or of any other law-enforcement agency or person for purposes of evaluation or analysis, upon condition that upon order of the court the items may be retained by the court or delivered to another court. (1973, c. 1286, s. 1.)

§ 15A-259. Application of Article to all warrants; exception as to inspection warrants and special riot situations.

The requirements of this Article apply to search warrants issued for any purpose, except that the contents of and procedure relating to inspection warrants are to be governed by the provisions of Article 4A of Chapter 15 and warrants to inspect vehicles in riot areas or approaching municipalities during emergencies are subject to the special procedures set out in G.S. 14-288.11. Nothing in this Article is intended to alter or affect the emergency search doctrine. (1957, c. 496; 1969, c. 869, s. 8; 1971, c. 872, s. 4; 1973, c. 1286, s. 1.)

Article 12.

Pen Registers; Trap and Trace Devices.

§ 15A-260. Definitions.

As used in this Article:

(1) "Electronic communication," "electronic communication service," and "wire communication" shall have the meaning as set forth in Section 2510 of Title 18 of the United States Code;

(2) "Pen register" means a device which records or decodes electronic or other impulses which identify numbers dialed or otherwise transmitted on the telephone line to which such device is attached, but the term does not include any device used by a provider or customer of a wire or electronic service for billing, or recording as an incident to billing, for communication services provided by the provider or any device used by a provider or customer of a wire communication service for cost accounting or other like purposes in the ordinary course of its business, nor shall the term include any device which allows the listening or recording of communications transmitted on the telephone line to which the device is attached.

(3) "Trap and trace device" means a device which captures the incoming electronic or other impulses which identify the originating number of an instrument or device from which a wire or electronic communication was transmitted. (1987 (Reg. Sess., 1988), c. 1104, s. 1.)

§ 15A-261. Prohibition and exceptions.

(a) In General. - Except as provided in subsection (b) of this section, no person may install or use a pen register or a trap and trace device without first obtaining a court order as provided in this Article.

(b) Exception. - The prohibition of subsection (a) of this section does not apply to the use of a pen register or a trap and trace device by a provider of wire or electronic communication service:

(1) Relating to the operation, maintenance, or testing of a wire or electronic communication service or to the protection of the rights or property of the provider, or to the protection of users of that service from abuse of service or unlawful use of service; or

(2) To record the fact that a wire or electronic communication was initiated or completed in order to protect the provider, another provider furnishing service toward the completion of the wire communication, or a user of that service, from fraudulent, unlawful or abusive use of service; or

(3) With the consent of the user of that service.

(c) Penalty. - A person who willfully and knowingly violates subsection (a) of this section is guilty of a Class 1 misdemeanor. (1987 (Reg. Sess., 1988), c. 1104, s. 1; 1993, c. 539, s. 297; 1994, Ex. Sess., c. 24, s. 14(c).)

§ 15A-262. Application for order for pen register or trap and trace device.

(a) Application. - A law enforcement officer may make an application for an order or an extension of an order under G.S. 15A-263 authorizing or approving the installation and use of a pen register or a trap and trace device, in writing under oath or affirmation, to a superior court judge.

(b) Contents of application. - An application under subsection (a) of this section shall include:

(1) The identity of the law enforcement officer making the application and the identity of the law enforcement agency conducting the investigation; and

(2) A certification by the applicant that the information likely to be obtained is relevant to an ongoing criminal investigation being conducted by that agency. (1987 (Reg. Sess., 1988), c. 1104, s. 1.)

§ 15A-263. Issuance of order for pen register or trap and trace device.

(a) In General. - Following application made under G.S. 15A-262, a superior court judge may enter an ex parte order authorizing the installation and use of a pen register or a trap and trace device within the State if the judge finds:

(1) That there is reasonable suspicion to believe that a felony offense, or a Class A1 or Class 1 misdemeanor offense has been committed;

(2) That there are reasonable grounds to suspect that the person named or described in the affidavit committed the offense, if that person is known and can be named or described; and

(3) That the results of procedures involving pen registers or trap and trace devices will be of material aid in determining whether the person named in the affidavit committed the offense.

(b) Contents of Order. - An order issued under this section:

(1) Shall specify:

a. The identity, if known, of the person to whom is leased or in whose name is listed the telephone line to which the pen register or trap and trace device is to be attached;

b. The identity, if known, of the person who is the subject of the criminal investigation;

c. The number and, if known, physical location of the telephone line to which the pen register or trap and trace device is to be attached and, in the case of a trap and trace device, the geographic limits of the trap and trace order; and

d. The offense to which the information likely to be obtained by the pen register or trap and trace device relates; and

(2) Shall direct, upon request of the applicant, the furnishing of information, facilities, or technical assistance necessary to accomplish the installation of the pen register or trap and trace device under G.S. 15A-264.

(c) Time Period and Extension.

(1) An order issued under this section shall authorize the installation and use of a pen register or a trap and trace device for a period not to exceed 60 days.

(2) An extension of an order issued under this section may be granted, but only upon an application for an order under G.S. 15A-262 and upon the judicial finding required by subsection (a) of this section. The period of extension shall not exceed 60 days.

(d) Nondisclosure of Existence of Pen Register or a Trap and Trace Device. - An order authorizing or approving the installation and use of a pen register or a trap and trace device shall direct that:

(1) The order be sealed until otherwise ordered by the judge; and

(2) The person owning or leasing the line to which the pen register or a trap and trace device is attached, or who has been ordered by the judge to provide

assistance to the applicant, not disclose the existence of the pen register or trap and trace device or the existence of the investigation to the listed subscriber, or to any person, unless otherwise ordered by the judge.

The provisions of G.S. 15A-903 and 15A-904 shall apply to this Article. (1987 (Reg. Sess., 1988), c. 1104, s. 1; 1997-80, s. 13.)

§ 15A-264. Assistance in installation and use of a pen register or a trap and trace device.

(a)   Pen Registers. - Upon the request of a law enforcement officer authorized to install and use a pen register under this Article, a provider of wire or electronic communication service, a landlord, a custodian, or other person shall furnish the officer promptly with all information, facilities, or technical assistance necessary to accomplish the installation of the pen register unobtrusively and with a minimum of interference with the communication services, if the assistance is directed by a court order as provided in G.S. 15A-263(b)(2).

(b)   Trap and Trace Devices. - Upon the request of a law enforcement officer authorized to receive the results of a trap and trace device under this Article, a provider of a wire or electronic communication service, a landlord, a custodian, or other person shall install the device immediately on the appropriate line and shall furnish the officer all additional information, facilities, or technical assistance, including installation and operation of the device unobtrusively and with a minimum of interference with the communication services, if the installation and assistance are directed by court order as provided in G.S. 15A-263(b)(2). Unless otherwise ordered by the judge, the results of the trap and trace device shall be furnished to the law enforcement officer designated in the court order at reasonable intervals during regular business hours for the duration of the order.

(c)   Compensation. - A provider of a wire or electronic communication service, a landlord, a custodian, or other person who furnishes facilities or technical assistance pursuant to this section shall be compensated for the reasonable expenses incurred in providing the facilities and assistance.

(d)   No Cause of Action Against a Provider Giving Information or Assistance Under this Article. - No cause of action shall be allowed in any court against any provider of a wire or electronic communication service, its officers, employees, agents, or other specified persons for providing information, facilities, or assistance in accordance with the terms of a court order under this Article.

(e)   Defense. - A good faith reliance on a court order or a statutory authorization is a complete defense against any civil or criminal action brought under this Article or any other law. (1987 (Reg. Sess., 1988), c. 1104, s. 1.)

§ 15A-265. Reserved for future codification purposes.

Article 13.

DNA Database and Databank.

§ 15A-266. Short title.

This Article may be cited as the DNA Database and Databank Act of 1993. (1993, c. 401, s. 1.)

§ 15A-266.1. Policy.

It is the policy of the State to assist federal, State, and local criminal justice and law enforcement agencies in the identification, detection, or exclusion of individuals who are subjects of the investigation or prosecution of felonies or violent crimes against the person. Identification, detection, and exclusion are facilitated by the analysis of biological evidence that is often left by the perpetrator or is recovered from the crime scene. The analysis of biological evidence can also be used to identify missing persons and victims of mass disasters. (1993, c. 401, s. 1; 2003-376, s. 1; 2009-203, s. 1.)

§ 15A-266.2. Definitions.

As used in this Article, unless another meaning is specified or the context clearly requires otherwise, the following terms have the meanings specified:

(1) "Arrestee" means any person arrested for an offense in G.S. 15A-266.3A(f) or (g).

(1a) "CODIS" means the FBI's national DNA identification index system that allows the storage and exchange of DNA records submitted by federal, State and local forensic DNA laboratories. The term "CODIS" is derived from Combined DNA Index System (NDIS) administered and operated by the Federal Bureau of Investigation.

(1b) "Conviction" includes a conviction by a jury or a court, a guilty plea, a plea of nolo contendere, or a finding of not guilty by reason of insanity or mental disease or defect.

(1c) "Crime Laboratory" [means] the North Carolina State Crime Laboratory of the Department of Justice.

(1d) "Criminal Justice Agency" means an agency or institution of a federal, State, or local government, other than the office of the public defender, that performs as part of its principal function, activities relating to the apprehension, investigation, prosecution, adjudication, incarceration, supervision, or rehabilitation of criminal offenders.

(1e) "Custodial Agency" means the governmental entity in possession of evidence collected as part of a criminal investigation or prosecution.

(2) "DNA" means deoxyribonucleic acid. DNA is located in the cells and provides an individual's personal genetic blueprint. DNA encodes genetic information that is the basis of human heredity and forensic identification.

(3) "DNA Record" means DNA identification information stored in the State DNA Database or CODIS for the purpose of generating investigative leads or supporting statistical interpretation of DNA test results. The DNA record is the result obtained from the DNA analysis. The DNA record is comprised of the characteristics of a DNA sample which are of value in establishing the identity of individuals. The results of all DNA identification analyses on an individual's DNA sample are also collectively referred to as the DNA profile of an individual.

(4) "DNA Sample" means blood, cheek swabs, or any biological sample containing cells provided by any person with respect to offenses covered by this Article or submitted to the State Bureau of Investigation pursuant to this Article for analysis pursuant to a criminal investigation or storage or both.

(5) "FBI" means the Federal Bureau of Investigation.

(5a) "NDIS" means the National DNA Index System that is the national DNA database system of DNA records that meet federal quality assurance and privacy standards.

(6) Repealed by Session Laws 2013-360, s. 17.6(i), effective July 1, 2013.

(7) "State DNA Databank" means the repository of DNA samples collected under the provisions of this Article.

(8) "State DNA Database" means the Crime Laboratory's DNA identification record system to support law enforcement. It is administered by the Crime Laboratory and provides DNA records to the FBI for storage and maintenance in CODIS. The Crime Laboratory's DNA Database system is the collective capability provided by computer software and procedures administered by the Crime Laboratory to store and maintain DNA records related to: forensic casework; convicted offenders and arrestees required to provide a DNA sample under this Article; persons required to register as sex offenders under G.S. 14-208.7; unidentified persons or body parts; missing persons; relatives of missing persons; and anonymous DNA profiles used for forensic validation, forensic protocol development, or quality control purposes or establishment of a population statistics database for use by criminal justice agencies. (1993, c. 401, s. 1; 2009-203, s. 2; 2010-94, s. 2; 2011-19, s. 5; 2013-360, s. 17.6(i).)

§ 15A-266.3. Establishment of State DNA database and databank.

There is established under the administration of the Crime Laboratory, the State DNA Database and State DNA Databank. The Crime Laboratory shall provide DNA records to the FBI for the searching of DNA records nationwide and storage and maintenance by CODIS. The State DNA Databank shall serve as the repository for DNA samples obtained pursuant to this Article. The State DNA Database shall be compatible with the procedures specified by the FBI, including use of comparable test procedures, laboratory and computer equipment, supplies and computer platform and software. The State DNA Database shall have the capability provided by computer software and procedures administered by the Crime Laboratory to store and maintain DNA records related to all of the following:

(1)   Crime scene evidence and forensic casework.

(2)   Arrestees, offenders, and persons found not guilty by reason of insanity, who are required to provide a DNA sample under this Article.

(3)   Persons required to register as sex offenders under G.S. 14-208.7.

(4)   Unidentified persons or body parts.

(5)   Missing persons.

(6)   Relatives of missing persons.

(7)   Anonymous DNA profiles used for forensic validation, forensic protocol development, or quality control purposes or establishment of a population statistics database, for use by criminal justice agencies. (1993, c. 401, s. 1; 2010-94, s. 3; 2013-360, s. 17.6(f).)

§ 15A-266.3A. DNA sample required for DNA analysis upon arrest for certain offenses.

(a)   Unless a DNA sample has previously been obtained by lawful process and the DNA record stored in the State DNA Database, and that record and sample has not been expunged pursuant to any provision of law, a DNA sample for DNA analysis and testing shall be obtained from any person who is arrested for committing an offense described in subsection (f) or (g) of this section.

(b)   The arresting law enforcement officer shall obtain, or cause to be obtained, a DNA sample from an arrested person at the time of arrest, or when fingerprinted. However, if the person is arrested without a warrant, then the DNA sample shall not be taken until a probable cause determination has been made pursuant to G.S. 15A-511(c)(1). The DNA sample shall be by cheek swab unless a court order authorizes that a DNA blood sample be obtained. If a DNA blood sample is taken, it shall comply with the requirements of G.S. 15A-

266.6(b). The arresting law enforcement officer shall forward, or cause to be forwarded, the DNA sample to the appropriate laboratory for DNA analysis and testing.

(c)   At the time a DNA sample is taken pursuant to this section, the person obtaining the DNA sample shall record, on a form promulgated by the Crime Laboratory, the date and time the sample was taken, the name of the person taking the DNA sample, the name and address of the person from whom the sample was taken, and the offense or offenses for which the person was arrested. This record shall be maintained in the case file and shall be available to the prosecuting district attorney for the purpose of completing the requirements of subsection (j) of this section.

(d)   After taking a DNA sample from an arrested person required to provide a DNA sample pursuant to this section, the person taking the DNA sample shall provide the arrested person with a written notice of the procedures for seeking an expunction of the DNA sample pursuant to subsections (h), (i), (j), (k), and (l) of this section. The Department of Justice shall provide the written notice required by this subsection.

(e)   The DNA record of identification characteristics resulting from the DNA testing and the DNA sample itself shall be stored and maintained by the Crime Laboratory in the State DNA Databank pursuant to this Article.

(f)   This section shall apply to a person arrested for violating any one of the following offenses in Chapter 14 of the General Statutes:

(1)   G.S. 14-17, First and Second Degree Murder.

(2)   G.S. 14-18, Manslaughter.

(3)   Any offense in Article 7A, Rape and Other Sex Offenses.

(4)   G.S. 14-32, Felonious assault with deadly weapon with intent to kill or inflicting serious injury; G.S. 14-32.4(a), Assault inflicting serious bodily injury; G.S. 14-34.2, Assault with a firearm or other deadly weapon upon governmental officers or employees, company police officers, or campus police officers; G.S. 14-34.5, Assault with a firearm on a law enforcement, probation, or parole officer or on a person employed at a State or local detention facility; G.S. 14-34.6, Assault or affray on a firefighter, an emergency medical technician, medical responder, emergency department nurse, or emergency department

physician; and G.S. 14-34.7, Assault inflicting serious injury on a law enforcement, probation, or parole officer or on a person employed at a State or local detention facility.

(5)   Any offense in Article 10, Kidnapping and Abduction, or Article 10A, Human Trafficking.

(6)   G.S. 14-51, First and second degree burglary; G.S. 14-53, Breaking out of dwelling house burglary; G.S. 14-54.1, Breaking or entering a place of religious worship; and G.S. 14-57, Burglary with explosives.

(7)   Any offense in Article 15, Arson.

(8)   G.S. 14-87, Armed robbery.

(9)   Any offense which would require the person to register under the provisions of Article 27A of Chapter 14 of the General Statutes, Sex Offender and Public Protection Registration Programs.

(10)   G.S. 14-196.3, Cyberstalking.

(11)   G.S. 14-277.3A, Stalking.

(g)   This section shall also apply to a person arrested for attempting, solicitation of another to commit, conspiracy to commit, or aiding and abetting another to commit, any of the violations included in subsection (f) of this section.

(h)   The Crime Laboratory shall remove a person's DNA record, and destroy any DNA biological samples that may have been retained, from the State DNA Database and DNA Databank if both of the following are determined pursuant to subsection (i) of this section:

(1)   As to the charge, or all charges, resulting from the arrest upon which a DNA sample is required under this section, a court or the district attorney has taken action resulting in any one of the following:

a.   The charge has been dismissed.

b.   The person has been acquitted of the charge.

c. The defendant is convicted of a lesser-included misdemeanor offense that is not an offense included in subsection (f) or (g) of this section.

d. No charge was filed within the statute of limitations, if any.

e. No conviction has occurred, at least three years has passed since the date of arrest, and no active prosecution is occurring.

(2) The person's DNA record is not required to be in the State DNA Database under some other provision of law, or is not required to be in the State DNA Database based upon an offense from a different transaction or occurrence from the one which was the basis for the person's arrest.

(i) Prior to June 1, 2012, upon the occurrence of one of the events in sub-subdivision d. or e. of subdivision (1) of subsection (h) of this section, the defendant or the defendant's counsel shall provide the prosecuting district attorney with a signed request form, promulgated by the Administrative Office of the Courts, requesting that the defendant's DNA record be expunged from the DNA Database and that any biological samples in the DNA Databank be destroyed. On or after June 1, 2012, upon the occurrence of one of the events in sub-subdivision d. or e. of subdivision (1) of subsection (h) of this section, no request form shall be required and the prosecuting district attorney shall initiate the procedure provided in subsection (j) of this section.

(j) Prior to June 1, 2012, within 30 days of the receipt of the form required by subsection (i) of this section or the occurrence of one of the events in sub-subdivision a., b., or c. of subdivision (1) of subsection (h) of this section; and on or after June 1, 2012, within 30 days of the occurrence of one of the events in subdivision (1) of subsection (h) of this section, the prosecuting district attorney shall determine if a DNA sample was taken pursuant to this section, and if so, shall:

(1) Verify and indicate the facts of the qualifying event on a verification form promulgated by the Administrative Office of the Courts.

(2) Include the last known address of the defendant, as reflected in the court files, on the verification form.

(3) Sign the verification form or, if the defendant was acquitted or the charges were dismissed by the court, obtain the signature of a judge.

(4) Transmit the verification form to the Crime Laboratory.

(k) Within 90 days of receipt of the verification form, the Crime Laboratory shall:

(1) Determine whether the requirement of subdivision (2) of subsection (h) of this section has been met.

(2) If the requirement has been met, remove the defendant's DNA record and samples as required by subsection (h) of this section.

(3) Mail to the defendant, at the address specified in the verification form, a notice doing either of the following:

a. Documenting expunction of the DNA record and destruction of the DNA sample.

b. Notifying the defendant that the DNA record and sample do not qualify for expunction pursuant to subsection (h) of this section.

(l) The defendant may file a motion with the court to review the denial of the defendant's request or the failure of either the district attorney or the Crime Laboratory to act within the prescribed time period.

(m) Any identification, warrant, probable cause to arrest, or arrest based upon a database match of the defendant's DNA sample which occurs after the expiration of the statutory periods prescribed for expunction of the defendant's DNA sample, shall be invalid and inadmissable in the prosecution of the defendant for any criminal offense.

(n) Notwithstanding subsection (h) of this section, the Crime Laboratory is not required to destroy or remove an item of physical evidence obtained from a sample if evidence relating to another person would thereby be destroyed.

(o) The Crime Laboratory shall adopt procedures to comply with this section. (2010-94, s. 4; 2013-171, s. 9; 2013-360, s. 17.6(f), (j).)

§ 15A-266.4. DNA sample required for DNA analysis upon conviction or finding of not guilty by reason of insanity.

(a) Unless a DNA sample has previously been obtained by lawful process and a record stored in the State DNA Database, and that record and sample have not been expunged pursuant to any provision of law, a person:

(1) Who is convicted of any of the crimes listed in subsection (b) of this section or who is found not guilty of any of these crimes by reason of insanity and committed to a mental health facility in accordance with G.S. 15A-1321, shall provide a DNA sample upon intake to jail, prison, or the mental health facility. In addition, every person convicted of any of these crimes, but who is not sentenced to a term of confinement, shall provide a DNA sample as a condition of the sentence.

(2) Who has been convicted and incarcerated as a result of a conviction of one or more of the crimes listed in subsection (b) of this section, or who was found not guilty of any of these crimes by reason of insanity and committed to a mental health facility in accordance with G.S. 15A-1321, shall provide a DNA sample before parole or release from the penal system or before release from the mental health facility.

(b) Crimes covered by this Article include all of the following:

(1) All felonies.

(2) G.S. 14-32.1 - Assaults on handicapped persons.

(3) Former G.S. 14-277.3 - Stalking.

(4) Repealed by Session Laws 2010-94, s. 5, effective February 1, 2011.

(5) All offenses described in G.S. 15A-266.3A. (1993, c. 401, s. 1; 2001-487, s. 46; 2003-376, s. 2; 2005-130, s. 2; 2009-58, s. 2; 2010-94, s. 5.)

§ 15A-266.5. Tests to be performed on DNA sample.

(a) The tests to be performed on each DNA sample are:

(1) To analyze and type only the genetic markers that are used for identification purposes contained in or derived from the DNA.

(2)   For law enforcement identification purposes.

(3)   For research and administrative purposes, including:

a.   Development of a population database when personal identifying information is removed.

b.   To support identification research and protocol development of forensic DNA analysis methods.

c.   For quality control purposes.

d.   To assist in the recovery or identification of human remains from mass disasters or for other humanitarian purposes, including identification of missing persons.

(b)   The DNA record of identification characteristics resulting from the DNA testing shall be stored and maintained by the Crime Laboratory in the State DNA Database. The DNA sample itself will be stored and maintained by the Crime Laboratory in the State DNA Databank.

(c)   The Crime Laboratory shall report annually to the Joint Legislative Commission on Governmental Operations and to the Joint Legislative Oversight Committee on Justice and Public Safety, on or before February 1, with information for the previous calendar year, which shall include: a summary of the operations and expenditures relating to the DNA Database and DNA Databank; the number of DNA records from arrestees entered; the number of DNA records from arrestees that have been expunged; and the number of DNA arrestee matches or hits that occurred with an unknown sample, and how many of those have led to an arrest and conviction; and how many letters notifying defendants that a record and sample have been expunged, along with the number of days it took to complete the expunction and notification process, from the date of the receipt of the verification form from the State.

(d)   The Department of Justice, in consultation with the Administrative Office of the Courts and the Conference of District Attorneys, shall study, develop, and recommend an automated procedure to facilitate the process of expunging DNA samples and records taken pursuant to G.S. 15A-266.3A, and shall report to the Joint Legislative Commission on Governmental Operations, the Joint Legislative Oversight Committee on Justice and Public Safety, and the Courts Commission, on or before February 1, 2011. (1993, c. 401, s. 1; 2010-94, s. 6; 2011-291, s. 2.3; 2013-360, s. 17.6(f).)

§ 15A-266.6. Procedures for obtaining DNA sample for analysis; refusal to provide sample.

(a) Each DNA sample provided pursuant to G.S. 15A-266.4 from persons who are incarcerated shall be obtained at the place of incarceration. DNA samples from persons who are not sentenced to a term of confinement shall be obtained immediately following sentencing. The sentencing court shall order any person not sentenced to a term of confinement, who has not previously provided a DNA sample pursuant to any provision of law requiring a sample and whose DNA record and sample have not been expunged pursuant to law, to report immediately following sentencing to the location designated by the sheriff. If the sample cannot be taken immediately, the sheriff shall inform the court of the date, time, and location at which the sample shall be taken, and the court shall enter that date, time, and location into its order. A copy of the court order indicating the date, time, and location the person is to appear to have a sample taken shall be given to the sheriff. If a person not sentenced to a term of confinement fails to appear immediately following sentencing or at the date, time, and location designated in the court order, the sheriff shall inform the court of the failure to appear and the court may issue an order to show cause pursuant to G.S. 5A-15 and may issue an order for arrest pursuant to G.S. 5A-16. The defendant shall continue to be subject to the court's order to provide a DNA sample until such time as his or her DNA sample is analyzed and a record is successfully entered into the State DNA Database.

(b) If, for any reason, the defendant provides a DNA blood sample instead of a cheek swab, only a correctional health nurse technician, physician, registered professional nurse, licensed practical nurse, laboratory technician, phlebotomist, or other health care worker with phlebotomy training shall draw the DNA blood sample to be submitted for analysis. No civil liability shall attach to any person authorized to draw blood by this section as a result of drawing blood from any person if the blood was drawn according to recognized medical procedures. No person shall be relieved from liability for negligence in obtaining a DNA sample by any method.

(c) The Crime Laboratory shall provide the materials, supplies, and postage prepaid envelopes necessary to obtain a DNA sample from a person required to provide a DNA sample pursuant to this Article and to forward the DNA sample to the appropriate laboratory for DNA analysis and testing. Any DNA sample obtained pursuant to this Article, other than a DNA sample obtained from a person who is incarcerated, shall be taken using the materials and supplies provided by the Crime Laboratory. (1993, c. 401, s. 1; 2003-376, s. 3; 2010-94, s. 7; 2013-360, s. 17.6(f).)

§ 15A-266.7. Procedures for conducting DNA analysis of DNA sample.

(a) The Crime Laboratory shall:

(1) Adopt procedures to be used in the collection, security, submission, identification, analysis, and storage of DNA samples and typing results of DNA samples submitted under this Article. These procedures shall also include quality assurance guidelines to insure that DNA identification records meet audit standards for laboratories which submit DNA records to the State DNA Database.

(2) Adopt Quality Assurance Guidelines for DNA Testing Laboratories and DNA Databasing Laboratories that meet or exceed the quality assurance guidelines established for such laboratories by the CODIS unit of the Federal Bureau of Investigation.

(b) DNA samples shall be securely stored in the State DNA Databank. The typing results shall be securely stored in the State DNA Database.

(c) Records of testing shall be retained on file at the Crime Laboratory. (1993, c. 401, s. 1; 2010-94, s. 8; 2013-360, s. 17.6(f).)

§ 15A-266.8. DNA database exchange.

(a) It shall be the duty of the Crime Laboratory to receive DNA samples, to store, to analyze or to contract out the DNA typing analysis to a qualified DNA laboratory that meets the guidelines as established by the Crime Laboratory, classify, and file the DNA record of identification characteristic profiles of DNA samples submitted pursuant to this Article and to make such information available as provided in this section. The Crime Laboratory may contract out

DNA typing analysis to a qualified DNA laboratory that meets guidelines as established by the Crime Laboratory. The results of the DNA profile of individuals in the State Database shall be made available to local, State, or federal law enforcement agencies, approved crime laboratories which serve these agencies, or the district attorney's office upon written or electronic request and in furtherance of an official investigation of a criminal offense. These records shall also be available upon receipt of a valid court order directing the Crime Laboratory to release these results to appropriate parties not listed above, when the court order is signed by a superior court judge after a hearing. The Crime Laboratory shall maintain a file of such court orders.

(b) The Crime Laboratory shall adopt rules governing the methods of obtaining information from the State Database and CODIS and procedures for verification of the identity and authority of the requester.

(c) The Crime Laboratory shall create a separate population database comprised of DNA samples obtained under this Article, after all personal identification is removed. Nothing shall prohibit the Crime Laboratory from sharing or disseminating population databases with other law enforcement agencies, crime laboratories that serve them, or other third parties the Crime Laboratory deems necessary to assist the Crime Laboratory with statistical analysis of the Crime Laboratory's population databases. The population database may be made available to and searched by other agencies participating in the CODIS system. (1993, c. 401, s. 1; 2010-94, s. 9; 2013-360, s. 17.6(f).)

§ 15A-266.9. Cancellation of authority to exchange DNA records.

The Crime Laboratory is authorized to revoke the right of a forensic DNA laboratory within the State to exchange DNA identification records with federal, State, or local criminal justice agencies if the required control and privacy standards specified by the Crime Laboratory for the State DNA Database are not met by these agencies. (1993, c. 401, s. 1; 2013-360, s. 17.6(f).)

§ 15A-266.10: Repealed by Session Laws 2001-282, s. 3.

§ 15A-266.11. Unauthorized uses of DNA Databank; penalties.

(a)　　Any person who has possession of, or access to, individually identifiable DNA information contained in the State DNA Database or Databank and who willfully discloses it in any manner to any person or agency not entitled to receive it is guilty of a Class H felony.

(b)　　Any person who, without authorization, willfully obtains individually identifiable DNA information from the State DNA Database or Databank is guilty of a Class H felony. (1993, c. 401, s. 1; 1994, Ex. Sess., c. 14, s. 15; 2010-94, s. 10.)

§ 15A-266.12. Confidentiality of records.

(a)　　All DNA profiles and samples submitted to the Crime Laboratory pursuant to this Article shall be treated as confidential and shall not be disclosed to or shared with any person or agency except as provided in G.S. 15A-266.8.

(b)　　Only DNA records and samples that directly relate to the identification of individuals shall be collected and stored. These records and samples shall solely be used as a part of the criminal justice system for the purpose of facilitating the personal identification of the perpetrator of a criminal offense; provided that in appropriate circumstances such records may be used to identify potential victims of mass disasters or missing persons.

(c)　　DNA records and DNA samples submitted to the Crime Laboratory pursuant to this Article are not a public record as defined by G.S. 132-1.

(d)　　In the case of a criminal proceeding, requests to access a person's DNA record shall be in accordance with the rules for criminal discovery as defined in G.S. 15A-902. The Crime Laboratory shall not be required to provide the State DNA Database for criminal discovery purposes.

(e)　　DNA records and DNA samples submitted to the Crime Laboratory may only be released for the following authorized purposes:

(1)　　For law enforcement identification purposes, including the identification of human remains, to federal, State, or local criminal justice agencies.

(2) For criminal defense and appeal purposes, to a defendant who shall have access to samples and analyses performed in connection with the case in which such defendant is charged or was convicted.

(3) If personally identifiable information is removed to local, State, or federal law enforcement agencies for forensic validation studies, forensic protocol development or quality control purposes, and for establishment or maintenance of a population statistics database.

(f) In order to maintain the computer system security of the Crime Laboratory DNA database program, the computer software and database structures used by the Crime Laboratory to implement this Article are confidential. (1993, c. 401, s. 1; 2003-376, s. 4; 2010-94, s. 11; 2013-360, s. 17.6(f).)

§ 15A-267. Access to DNA samples from crime scene.

(a) A criminal defendant shall have access before trial to the following:

(1) Any DNA analyses performed in connection with the case in which the defendant is charged.

(2) Any biological material, that has not been DNA tested, that was collected from the crime scene, the defendant's residence, or the defendant's property.

(3) A complete inventory of all physical evidence collected in connection with the investigation.

(b) Access as provided for in subsection (a) of this section shall be governed by G.S. 15A-902 and G.S. 15A-952.

(c) Upon a defendant's motion made before trial in accordance with G.S. 15A-952, the court shall order the Crime Laboratory or any approved vendor that meets Crime Laboratory contracting standards to perform DNA testing and, if the data meets NDIS criteria, order the Crime Laboratory to search and/or upload to CODIS any profiles obtained from the testing upon a showing of all of the following:

(1) That the biological material is relevant to the investigation.

(2) That the biological material was not previously DNA tested or that more accurate testing procedures are now available that were not available at the time of previous testing and there is a reasonable possibility that the result would have been different.

(3) That the testing is material to the defendant's defense.

(d) The defendant shall be responsible for bearing the cost of any further testing and comparison of the biological materials, including any costs associated with the testing and comparison by the Crime Laboratory in accordance with this section, unless the court has determined the defendant is indigent, in which event the State shall bear the costs. (2001-282, s. 4; 2007-539, s. 1; 2009-203, s. 3; 2013-360, s. 17.6(f).)

§ 15A-268. Preservation of biological evidence.

(a) As used in this section, the term "biological evidence" includes the contents of a sexual assault examination kit or any item that contains blood, semen, hair, saliva, skin tissue, fingerprints, or other identifiable human biological material that may reasonably be used to incriminate or exculpate any person in the criminal investigation, whether that material is catalogued separately on a slide or swab, in a test tube, or some other similar method, or is present on clothing, ligatures, bedding, other household materials, drinking cups, cigarettes, or any other item of evidence.

(a1) Notwithstanding any other provision of law and subject to subsection (b) of this section, a custodial agency shall preserve any physical evidence, regardless of the date of collection, that is reasonably likely to contain any biological evidence collected in the course of a criminal investigation or prosecution. Evidence shall be preserved in a manner reasonably calculated to prevent contamination or degradation of any biological evidence that might be present, subject to a continuous chain of custody, and securely retained with sufficient official documentation to locate the evidence.

(a2) The Crime Laboratory shall promulgate and publish minimum guidelines that meet the requirements for retention and preservation of biological evidence under subsection (a1) of this section. Guidelines shall be published no later than January 1, 2010, and shall be reviewed and updated biennially thereafter. Law enforcement agencies and the Conference of Clerks of Superior Court shall ensure the guidelines are distributed to all employees with responsibility for maintaining custody of evidence.

(a3) When physical evidence is offered or admitted into evidence in a criminal proceeding of the General Court of Justice, the presiding judge shall inquire of the State and defendant as to the identity of the collecting agency of the evidence and whether the evidence in question is reasonably likely to contain biological evidence and if that biological evidence is relevant to establishing the identity of the perpetrator in the case. If either party asserts that the evidence in question may have biological evidentiary value, and the court so finds, the court shall instruct that the evidence be so designated in the court's records and that the evidence be preserved pursuant to the requirements of this section.

(a4) If evidence has been designated by the court as biological evidence pursuant to subsection (a3) of this section, the clerk of superior court that takes custody of evidence pursuant to the rules of practice and procedure for the superior and district courts as adopted by the Supreme Court pursuant to G.S. 7A-34 shall preserve such evidence consistent with subsection (a1) of this section. Upon conclusion of the clerk's role as custodian, as provided in the applicable rules of practice, the clerk shall return such evidence to the collecting agency, as determined in subsection (a3) of this section, in a manner that ensures the chain of custody is maintained and documented.

(a5) The duty to preserve may not be waived knowingly and voluntarily by a defendant, without a court proceeding.

(a6) The evidence described by subsection (a1) of this section shall be preserved for the following period:

(1) For conviction resulting in a sentence of death, until execution.

(2) For conviction resulting in a sentence of life without parole, until the death of the convicted person.

(3) For conviction of any homicide, sex offense, assault, kidnapping, burglary, robbery, arson or burning, for which a Class B1-E felony punishment is imposed, the evidence shall be preserved during the period of incarceration and mandatory supervised release, including sex offender registration pursuant to Article 27A of Chapter 14 of the General Statutes, except in cases where the person convicted entered and was convicted on a plea of guilty, in which case

the evidence shall be preserved for the earlier of three years from the date of conviction or until released.

(4)   Biological evidence collected as part of a criminal investigation of any homicide or rape, in which no charges are filed, shall be preserved for the period of time that the crime remains unsolved.

(5)   A custodial agency in custody of biological evidence unrelated to a criminal investigation or prosecution referenced by subdivision (1), (2), (3), or (4) of this subsection may dispose of the evidence in accordance with the rules of the agency.

(a7)   Upon written request by the defendant, the custodial agency shall prepare an inventory of biological evidence relevant to the defendant's case that is in the custodial agency's custody. If the evidence was destroyed through court order or other written directive, the custodial agency shall provide the defendant with a copy of the court order or written directive.

(b)   The custodial agency required to preserve evidence pursuant to subsection (a1) of this section may dispose of the evidence prior to the expiration of the period of time described in subsection (a6) of this section if all of the following conditions are met:

(1)   The custodial agency sent notice of its intent to dispose of the evidence to the district attorney in the county in which the conviction was obtained.

(1a)   The custodial agency has determined that it has no duty to preserve the evidence under G.S. 15A-1471.

(2)   The district attorney gave to each of the following persons written notification of the intent of the custodial agency to dispose of the evidence: any defendant convicted of a felony who is currently incarcerated in connection with the case, the defendant's counsel of record for that case, and the Office of Indigent Defense Services. The notice shall be consistent with the provisions of this section, and the district attorney shall send a copy of the notice to the custodial agency. Delivery of written notification from the district attorney to the defendant was effectuated by the district attorney transmitting the written notification to the superintendent of the correctional facility where the defendant was assigned at the time and the superintendent's personal delivery of the written notification to the defendant. Certification of delivery by the

superintendent to the defendant in accordance with this subdivision was in accordance with subsection (c) of this section.

(3) The written notification from the district attorney specified the following:

a. That the custodial agency would destroy the evidence collected in connection with the case unless the custodial agency received a written request that the evidence not be destroyed.

b. The address of the custodial agency where the written request was to be sent.

c. That the written request from the defendant, or his or her representative, must be received by the custodial agency within 90 days of the date of receipt by the defendant of the district attorney's written notification.

d. That the written request must ask that the evidence not be destroyed or disposed of for one of the following reasons:

1. The case is currently on appeal.

2. The case is currently in postconviction proceedings.

3. The defendant will file a motion for DNA testing pursuant to G.S. 15A-269 within 180 days of the postmark of the defendant's response to the district attorney's written notification of the custodial agency's intent to dispose of the evidence, unless a request for extension is requested by the defendant and agreed to by the custodial agency.

4. The case has been referred to the North Carolina Innocence Inquiry Commission pursuant to Article 92 of Chapter 15A of the General Statutes.

(4) The custodial agency did not receive a written request in compliance with the conditions set forth in sub-subdivision (3)d. of this subsection within 90 days of the date of receipt by the defendant of the district attorney's written notification.

(c) Upon receiving a written notification from a district attorney in accordance with subdivision (b)(3) of this section, the superintendent shall personally deliver the written notification to the defendant. Upon effectuating personal delivery on the defendant, the superintendent shall sign a sworn written certification that the written notification had been delivered to the defendant in compliance with this subsection indicating the date the delivery was made. The superintendent's certification shall be sent by the superintendent to the custodial agency that intends to dispose of the sample of evidence. The custodial agency may rely on the superintendent's certification as evidence of the date of receipt by the defendant of the district attorney's written notification.

(d) After a hearing held in response to a defendant's written request that the evidence not be destroyed in response to notice pursuant to subsection (b) of this section, the court may enter an order authorizing the custodial agency to dispose of the evidence if the court determines by the preponderance of the evidence that the evidence:

(1) Has no significant value for biological analysis and should be returned to its rightful owner, destroyed, used for training purposes, or otherwise disposed of as provided by law; or

(2) Repealed by Session Laws 2009-203, s. 4, effective December 1, 2009.

(3) May have value for biological analysis but is of a size, bulk, or physical character as to render retention impracticable or should be returned to its rightful owner.

(e) The court order allowing the disposition of the evidence pursuant to subdivision (d)(3) of this section shall require the custodial agency to return such evidence to the collecting agency. The collecting agency shall take reasonable measures to remove or preserve portions of evidence likely to contain biological evidence related to the offense through cuttings, swabs, or other means consistent with Crime Laboratory minimum guidelines in a quantity sufficient to permit DNA testing before returning or disposing of the evidence. The court may provide the defendant an opportunity to take reasonable measures to preserve the evidence.

(f) An order regarding the disposition of evidence pursuant to this section shall be a final and appealable order. The defendant shall have 30 days from the entry of the order to file notice of appeal. The custodial agency shall not dispose of the evidence while the appeal is pending.

(g) If an entity is asked to produce evidence that is required to be preserved under the provisions of this section and cannot produce the evidence, the chief evidence custodian of the custodial agency shall provide an affidavit in which he or she describes, under penalty of perjury, the efforts taken to locate the evidence and affirms that the evidence could not be located. If the evidence that is required to be preserved pursuant to this section has been destroyed, the court may conduct a hearing to determine whether obstruction of justice and contempt proceedings are in order. If the court finds the destruction violated the defendant's due process rights, the court shall order an appropriate remedy, which may include dismissal of charges.

(h) All records documenting the possession, control, storage, and destruction of evidence related to a criminal investigation or prosecution of an offense referenced in subdivision (1), (2), (3), or (4) of subsection (a6) of this section shall be retained.

(i) Whoever knowingly and intentionally destroys, alters, conceals, or tampers with evidence that is required to be preserved under this section, with the intent to impair the integrity of that evidence, prevent that evidence from being subjected to DNA testing, or prevent production or use of that evidence in an official proceeding, shall be punished as follows:

(1) If the evidence is for a noncapital crime, then a violation of this subsection is a Class I felony.

(2) If the evidence is for a crime of first degree murder, then a violation of this subsection is a Class H felony. (2001-282, s. 4.; 2007-539, s. 2; 2009-203, s. 4; 2009-570, s. 30(a), (b); 2012-7, ss. 1-3; 2013-360, s. 17.6(f).)

§ 15A-269. Request for postconviction DNA testing.

(a) A defendant may make a motion before the trial court that entered the judgment of conviction against the defendant for performance of DNA testing and, if testing complies with FBI requirements and the data meets NDIS criteria, profiles obtained from the testing shall be searched and/or uploaded to CODIS if the biological evidence meets all of the following conditions:

(1) Is material to the defendant's defense.

(2) Is related to the investigation or prosecution that resulted in the judgment.

(3) Meets either of the following conditions:

a. It was not DNA tested previously.

b. It was tested previously, but the requested DNA test would provide results that are significantly more accurate and probative of the identity of the perpetrator or accomplice or have a reasonable probability of contradicting prior test results.

(b) The court shall grant the motion for DNA testing and, if testing complies with FBI requirements, the run of any profiles obtained from the testing, upon its determination that:

(1) The conditions set forth in subdivisions (1), (2), and (3) of subsection (a) of this section have been met;

(2) If the DNA testing being requested had been conducted on the evidence, there exists a reasonable probability that the verdict would have been more favorable to the defendant; and

(3) The defendant has signed a sworn affidavit of innocence.

(b1) If the court orders DNA testing, such testing shall be conducted by a Crime Laboratory-approved testing facility, mutually agreed upon by the petitioner and the State and approved by the court. If the parties cannot agree, the court shall designate the testing facility and provide the parties with reasonable opportunity to be heard on the issue.

(c) In accordance with rules adopted by the Office of Indigent Defense Services, the court shall appoint counsel for the person who brings a motion under this section if that person is indigent. If the petitioner has filed pro se, the court shall appoint counsel for the petitioner in accordance with rules adopted by the Office of Indigent Defense Services upon a showing that the DNA testing may be material to the petitioner's claim of wrongful conviction.

(d) The defendant shall be responsible for bearing the cost of any DNA testing ordered under this section unless the court determines the defendant is indigent, in which event the State shall bear the costs.

(e) DNA testing ordered by the court pursuant to this section shall be done as soon as practicable. However, if the court finds that a miscarriage of justice will otherwise occur and that DNA testing is necessary in the interests of justice, the court shall order a delay of the proceedings or execution of the sentence pending the DNA testing.

(f)   Upon receipt of a motion for postconviction DNA testing, the custodial agency shall inventory the evidence pertaining to that case and provide the inventory list, as well as any documents, notes, logs, or reports relating to the items of physical evidence, to the prosecution, the petitioner, and the court.

(g)   Upon receipt of a motion for postconviction DNA testing, the State shall, upon request, reactivate any victim services for the victim of the crime being investigated during the reinvestigation of the case and pendency of the proceedings.

(h)   Nothing in this Article shall prohibit a convicted person and the State from consenting to and conducting postconviction DNA testing by agreement of the parties, without filing a motion for postconviction testing under this Article. (2001-282, s. 4; 2007-539, s. 3; 2009-203, s. 5; 2011-326, s. 12(d); 2013-360, s. 17.6(k).)

§ 15A-270. Post-test procedures.

(a)   Notwithstanding any other provision of law, upon receiving the results of the DNA testing conducted under G.S. 15A-269, the court shall conduct a hearing to evaluate the results and to determine if the results are unfavorable or favorable to the defendant.

(b)   If the results of DNA testing conducted under this section are unfavorable to the defendant, the court shall dismiss the motion and, in the case of a defendant who is not indigent, shall assess the defendant for the cost of the testing.

(c)   If the results of DNA testing conducted under this section are favorable to the defendant, the court shall enter any order that serves the interests of justice, including an order that does any of the following:

(1)   Vacates and sets aside the judgment.

(2)   Discharges the defendant, if the defendant is in custody.

(3) Resentences the defendant.

(4) Grants a new trial. (2001-282, s. 4.)

§ 15A-270.1. Right to appeal denial of defendant's motion for DNA testing.

The defendant may appeal an order denying the defendant's motion for DNA testing under this Article, including by an interlocutory appeal. The court shall appoint counsel in accordance with rules adopted by the Office of Indigent Defense Services upon a finding of indigency. (2007-539, s. 4; 2009-203, s. 6; 2011-326, s. 12(e).)

Article 14.

Nontestimonial Identification.

§ 15A-271. Authority to issue order.

A nontestimonial identification order authorized by this Article may be issued by any judge upon request of a prosecutor. As used in this Article, "nontestimonial identification" means identification by fingerprints, palm prints, footprints, measurements, blood specimens, urine specimens, saliva samples, hair samples, or other reasonable physical examination, handwriting exemplars, voice samples, photographs, and lineups or similar identification procedures requiring the presence of a suspect. (1973, c. 1286, s. 1; 1975, c. 166, s. 27.)

§ 15A-272. Time of application; additional investigative procedures not precluded.

A request for a nontestimonial identification order may be made prior to the arrest of a suspect or after arrest and prior to trial. Nothing in this Article shall preclude such additional investigative procedures as are otherwise permitted by law. (1973, c. 1286, s. 1.)

§ 15A-273. Basis for order.

An order may issue only on an affidavit or affidavits sworn to before the judge and establishing the following grounds for the order:

(1)   That there is probable cause to believe that a felony offense, or a Class A1 or Class 1 misdemeanor offense has been committed;

(2)   That there are reasonable grounds to suspect that the person named or described in the affidavit committed the offense; and

(3)   That the results of specific nontestimonial identification procedures will be of material aid in determining whether the person named in the affidavit committed the offense. (1973, c. 1286, s. 1; 1997-80, s. 14.)

§ 15A-274. Issuance of order.

Upon a showing that the grounds specified in G.S. 15A-273 exist, the judge may issue an order requiring the person named or described with reasonable certainty in the affidavit to appear at a designated time and place and to submit to designated nontestimonial identification procedures. Unless the nature of the evidence sought makes it likely that delay will adversely affect its probative value, or when it appears likely that the person named in the order may destroy, alter, or modify the evidence sought or may not appear, the order must be served at least 72 hours before the time designated for the nontestimonial identification procedure. (1973, c. 1286, s. 1; 1977, c. 832, s. 1.)

§ 15A-275. Modification of order.

At the request of a person ordered to appear, the judge may modify the order with respect to time and place of appearance whenever it appears reasonable under the circumstances to do so. (1973, c. 1286, s. 1.)

§ 15A-276. Failure to appear.

Any person who fails without adequate excuse to obey an order to appear served upon him pursuant to this Article may be held in contempt of the court which issued the order. (1973, c. 1286, s. 1.)

§ 15A-277. Service of order.

An order to appear pursuant to this Article may be served by a law-enforcement officer. The order must be served upon the person named or described in the affidavit by delivery of a copy to him personally. The order must be served at least 72 hours in advance of the time of compliance, unless the judge issuing the order has determined, in accordance with G.S. 15A-274, that delay will adversely affect the probative value of the evidence sought or when it appears likely that the person named in the order may destroy, alter, or modify the evidence sought, or may not appear. (1973, c. 1286, s. 1; 1977, c. 832, s. 2.)

§ 15A-278. Contents of order.

An order to appear must be signed by the judge and must state:

(1)   That the presence of the person named or described in the affidavit is required for the purpose of permitting nontestimonial identification procedures in order to aid in the investigation of the offense specified therein;

(2)   The time and place of the required appearance;

(3)   The nontestimonial identification procedures to be conducted, the methods to be used, and the approximate length of time such procedures will require;

(4)   The grounds to suspect that the person named or described in the affidavit committed the offense specified therein;

(5)   That the person is entitled to be represented by counsel at the procedure, and to the appointment of counsel if he cannot afford to retain one;

(6) That the person will not be subjected to any interrogation or asked to make any statement during the period of his appearance except that required for voice identification;

(7) That the person may request the judge to make a reasonable modification of the order with respect to time and place of appearance, including a request to have any nontestimonial identification procedure other than a lineup conducted at his place of residence; and

(8) That the person, if he fails to appear, may be held in contempt of court. (1973, c. 1286, s. 1.)

§ 15A-279. Implementation of order.

(a) Nontestimonial identification procedures may be conducted by any law-enforcement officer or other person designated by the judge issuing the order. The extraction of any bodily fluid must be conducted by a qualified member of the health professions and the judge may require medical supervision for any other test ordered pursuant to this Article when he considers such supervision necessary.

(b) In conducting authorized identification procedures, no unreasonable or unnecessary force may be used.

(c) No person who appears under an order of appearance issued under this Article may be detained longer than is reasonably necessary to conduct the specified nontestimonial identification procedures, and in no event for longer than six hours, unless he is arrested for an offense.

(d) Any such person is entitled to have counsel present and must be advised prior to being subjected to any nontestimonial identification procedures of his right to have counsel present during any nontestimonial identification procedure and to the appointment of counsel if he cannot afford to retain counsel. Appointment of counsel shall be in accordance with rules adopted by the Office of Indigent Defense Services. No statement made during nontestimonial identification procedures by the subject of the procedures shall be admissible in any criminal proceeding against him, unless his counsel was present at the time the statement was made.

(e) Any person who resists compliance with the authorized nontestimonial identification procedures may be held in contempt of the court which issued the order pursuant to the provisions of G.S. 5A-12(a) and G.S. 5A-21(b).

(f) A nontestimonial identification order may not be issued against a person previously subject to a nontestimonial identification order unless it is based on different evidence which was not reasonably available when the previous order was issued.

(g) Resisting compliance with a nontestimonial identification order is not itself grounds for finding probable cause to arrest the suspect, but it may be considered with other evidence in making the determination whether probable cause exists. (1973, c. 1286, s. 1; 1977, c. 711, s. 20; 2000-144, s. 28.)

§ 15A-280. Return.

Within 90 days after the nontestimonial identification procedure, a return must be made to the judge who issued the order or to a judge designated in the order setting forth an inventory of the products of the nontestimonial identification procedures obtained from the person named in the affidavit. If, at the time of the return, probable cause does not exist to believe that the person has committed the offense named in the affidavit or any other offense, the person named in the affidavit is entitled to move that the authorized judge issue an order directing that the products and reports of the nontestimonial identification procedures, and all copies thereof, be destroyed. The motion must, except for good cause shown, be granted. (1973, c. 1286, s. 1.)

§ 15A-281. Nontestimonial identification order at request of defendant.

A person arrested for or charged with a felony offense, or a Class A1 or Class 1 misdemeanor offense may request that nontestimonial identification procedures be conducted upon himself. If it appears that the results of specific nontestimonial identification procedures will be of material aid in determining whether the defendant committed the offense, the judge to whom the request was directed must order the State to conduct the identification procedures. (1973, c. 1286, s. 1; 1997-80, s. 15.)

§ 15A-282. Copy of results to person involved.

A person who has been the subject of nontestimonial identification procedures or his attorney must be provided with a copy of any reports of test results as soon as the reports are available. (1973, c. 1286, s. 1.)

§§ 15A-283 through 15A-284.49 Reserved for future codification purposes.

Article 14A.

Eyewitness Identification Reform Act.

§ 15A-284.50. Short title.

This Article shall be called the "Eyewitness Identification Reform Act." (2007-421, s. 1.)

§ 15A-284.51. Purpose.

The purpose of this Article is to help solve crime, convict the guilty, and exonerate the innocent in criminal proceedings by improving procedures for eyewitness identification of suspects. (2007-421, s. 1.)

§ 15A-284.52. Eyewitness identification reform.

(a) Definitions. - The following definitions apply in this Article:

(1) Eyewitness. - A person whose identification by sight of another person may be relevant in a criminal proceeding.

(2) Filler. - A person or a photograph of a person who is not suspected of an offense and is included in a lineup.

(3) Independent administrator. - A lineup administrator who is not participating in the investigation of the criminal offense and is unaware of which person in the lineup is the suspect.

(4) Lineup. - A photo lineup or live lineup.

(5) Lineup administrator. - The person who conducts a lineup.

(6) Live lineup. - A procedure in which a group of people is displayed to an eyewitness for the purpose of determining if the eyewitness is able to identify the perpetrator of a crime.

(7) Photo lineup. - A procedure in which an array of photographs is displayed to an eyewitness for the purpose of determining if the eyewitness is able to identify the perpetrator of a crime.

(b) Eyewitness Identification Procedures. - Lineups conducted by State, county, and other local law enforcement officers shall meet all of the following requirements:

(1) A lineup shall be conducted by an independent administrator or by an alternative method as provided by subsection (c) of this section.

(2) Individuals or photos shall be presented to witnesses sequentially, with each individual or photo presented to the witness separately, in a previously determined order, and removed after it is viewed before the next individual or photo is presented.

(3) Before a lineup, the eyewitness shall be instructed that:

a. The perpetrator might or might not be presented in the lineup,

b. The lineup administrator does not know the suspect's identity,

c. The eyewitness should not feel compelled to make an identification,

d. It is as important to exclude innocent persons as it is to identify the perpetrator, and

e. The investigation will continue whether or not an identification is made.

The eyewitness shall acknowledge the receipt of the instructions in writing. If the eyewitness refuses to sign, the lineup administrator shall note the refusal of the eyewitness to sign the acknowledgement and shall also sign the acknowledgement.

(4) In a photo lineup, the photograph of the suspect shall be contemporary and, to the extent practicable, shall resemble the suspect's appearance at the time of the offense.

(5) The lineup shall be composed so that the fillers generally resemble the eyewitness's description of the perpetrator, while ensuring that the suspect does not unduly stand out from the fillers. In addition:

a. All fillers selected shall resemble, as much as practicable, the eyewitness's description of the perpetrator in significant features, including any unique or unusual features.

b. At least five fillers shall be included in a photo lineup, in addition to the suspect.

c. At least five fillers shall be included in a live lineup, in addition to the suspect.

d. If the eyewitness has previously viewed a photo lineup or live lineup in connection with the identification of another person suspected of involvement in the offense, the fillers in the lineup in which the current suspect participates shall be different from the fillers used in any prior lineups.

(6) If there are multiple eyewitnesses, the suspect shall be placed in a different position in the lineup or photo array for each eyewitness.

(7) In a lineup, no writings or information concerning any previous arrest, indictment, or conviction of the suspect shall be visible or made known to the eyewitness.

(8) In a live lineup, any identifying actions, such as speech, gestures, or other movements, shall be performed by all lineup participants.

(9) In a live lineup, all lineup participants must be out of view of the eyewitness prior to the lineup.

(10) Only one suspect shall be included in a lineup.

(11) Nothing shall be said to the eyewitness regarding the suspect's position in the lineup or regarding anything that might influence the eyewitness's identification.

(12) The lineup administrator shall seek and document a clear statement from the eyewitness, at the time of the identification and in the eyewitness's own words, as to the eyewitness's confidence level that the person identified in a given lineup is the perpetrator. The lineup administrator shall separate all witnesses in order to discourage witnesses from conferring with one another before or during the procedure. Each witness shall be given instructions regarding the identification procedures without other witnesses present.

(13) If the eyewitness identifies a person as the perpetrator, the eyewitness shall not be provided any information concerning the person before the lineup administrator obtains the eyewitness's confidence statement about the selection. There shall not be anyone present during the live lineup or photographic identification procedures who knows the suspect's identity, except the eyewitness and counsel as required by law.

(14) Unless it is not practical, a video record of live identification procedures shall be made. If a video record is not practical, the reasons shall be documented, and an audio record shall be made. If neither a video nor audio record are practical, the reasons shall be documented, and the lineup administrator shall make a written record of the lineup.

(15) Whether video, audio, or in writing, the record shall include all of the following information:

a. All identification and nonidentification results obtained during the identification procedure, signed by the eyewitness, including the eyewitness's confidence statement. If the eyewitness refuses to sign, the lineup administrator shall note the refusal of the eyewitness to sign the results and shall also sign the notation.

b. The names of all persons present at the lineup.

c. The date, time, and location of the lineup.

d. The words used by the eyewitness in any identification, including words that describe the eyewitness's certainty of identification.

e. Whether it was a photo lineup or live lineup and how many photos or individuals were presented in the lineup.

f. The sources of all photographs or persons used.

g. In a photo lineup, the photographs themselves.

h. In a live lineup, a photo or other visual recording of the lineup that includes all persons who participated in the lineup.

(c) Alternative Methods for Identification if Independent Administrator Is Not Used. - In lieu of using an independent administrator, a photo lineup eyewitness identification procedure may be conducted using an alternative method specified and approved by the North Carolina Criminal Justice Education and Training Standards Commission. Any alternative method shall be carefully structured to achieve neutral administration and to prevent the administrator from knowing which photograph is being presented to the eyewitness during the identification procedure. Alternative methods may include any of the following:

(1) Automated computer programs that can automatically administer the photo lineup directly to an eyewitness and prevent the administrator from seeing which photo the witness is viewing until after the procedure is completed.

(2) A procedure in which photographs are placed in folders, randomly numbered, and shuffled and then presented to an eyewitness such that the administrator cannot see or track which photograph is being presented to the witness until after the procedure is completed.

(3) Any other procedures that achieve neutral administration.

(d) Remedies. - All of the following shall be available as consequences of compliance or noncompliance with the requirements of this section:

(1) Failure to comply with any of the requirements of this section shall be considered by the court in adjudicating motions to suppress eyewitness identification.

(2) Failure to comply with any of the requirements of this section shall be admissible in support of claims of eyewitness misidentification, as long as such evidence is otherwise admissible.

(3) When evidence of compliance or noncompliance with the requirements of this section has been presented at trial, the jury shall be instructed that it may consider credible evidence of compliance or noncompliance to determine the reliability of eyewitness identifications. (2007-421, s. 1.)

§ 15A-284.53. Training of law enforcement officers.

Pursuant to its authority under G.S. 17C-6 and G.S. 17E-4, the North Carolina Criminal Justice Education and Training Standards Commission and the North Carolina Sheriffs' Education and Training Standards Commission, in consultation with the Department of Justice, shall create educational materials and conduct training programs on how to conduct lineups in compliance with this Article. (2007-421, s. 1.)

Article 15.

Urgent Necessity.

§ 15A-285. Non-law-enforcement actions when urgently necessary.

When an officer reasonably believes that doing so is urgently necessary to save life, prevent serious bodily harm, or avert or control public catastrophe, the officer may take one or more of the following actions:

(1) Enter buildings, vehicles, and other premises.

(2) Limit or restrict the presence of persons in premises or areas.

(3) Exercise control over the property of others.

An action taken to enforce the law or to seize a person or evidence cannot be justified by authority of this section. (1973, c. 1286, s. 1.)

Article 16.

Electronic Surveillance.

§ 15A-286. Definitions.

As used in this Article, unless the context requires otherwise:

(1) "Aggrieved person" means a person who was a party to any intercepted wire, oral, or electronic communication or a person against whom the interception was directed.

(2) "Attorney General" means the Attorney General of the State of North Carolina, unless otherwise specified.

(3) "Aural transfer" means a transfer containing the human voice at any point between and including the point of origin and the point of reception.

(4) "Chapter 119 of the United States Code" means Chapter 119 of Part I of Title 18, United States Code, being Public Law 90-351, the Omnibus Crime Control and Safe Streets Act of 1968, as amended by the Electronic Communications Privacy Act of 1986.

(5) "Communications common carrier" shall have the same meaning which is given the term "common carrier" by section 153(h) of Title 47 of the United States Code.

(6) "Contents" when used with respect to any wire, oral, or electronic communication means and includes any information concerning the substance, purport, or meaning of that communication.

(7) "Electronic, mechanical, or other device" means any device or apparatus which can be used to intercept a wire, oral, or electronic communication other than:

a. Any telephone or telegraph instrument, equipment, or facility, or any component thereof:

1. Furnished to the subscriber or user by a provider of wire or electronic communication service in the ordinary course of its business and being used by the subscriber or user in the ordinary course of its business or furnished by the

subscriber or user for connection to the facilities of such service and used in the ordinary course of its business; or

2. Being used by a provider of wire or electronic communication service in the ordinary course of its business or by an investigative or law enforcement officer in the ordinary course of the officer's duties.

b. A hearing aid or similar device being used to correct subnormal hearing to not better than normal.

(8) "Electronic communication" means any transfer of signs, signals, writing, images, sounds, data, or intelligence of any nature transmitted in whole or in part by a wire, radio, electromagnetic, photoelectronic, or photooptical system that affects interstate or foreign commerce but does not include:

a. Any wire or oral communication;

b. Any communication made through a tone-only paging device; or

c. Any communication from a tracking device (as defined in section 3117 of Title 18 of the United States Code).

(9) "Electronic communication service" means any service which provides to users thereof the ability to send or receive wire or electronic communications.

(10) "Electronic communication system" means any wire, radio, electronic, magnetic, photooptical, or photoelectronic facilities for the transmission of electronic communications, and any computer facilities or related electronic equipment for the storage of such communications.

(11) "Electronic surveillance" means the interception of wire, oral, or electronic communications as provided by this Article.

(12) "Electronic storage" means:

a. Any temporary, intermediate storage of a wire or electronic communication incidental to the electronic transmission thereof; and

b. Any storage of such communication by an electronic communication service for the purposes of backup protection of the communication.

(13) "Intercept" means the aural or other acquisition of the contents of any wire, oral, or electronic communication through the use of any electronic, mechanical, or other device.

(14) "Investigative or law enforcement officer" means any officer of the State of North Carolina or any political subdivision thereof, who is empowered by the laws of this State to conduct investigations of or to make arrests for offenses enumerated in G.S. 15A-290, and any attorney authorized by the laws of this State to prosecute or participate in the prosecution of those offenses, including the Attorney General of North Carolina.

(15) "Judge" means any judge of the trial divisions of the General Court of Justice.

(16) "Judicial review panel" means a three-judge body, composed of such judges as may be assigned by the Chief Justice of the Supreme Court of North Carolina, which shall review applications for electronic surveillance orders and may issue orders valid throughout the State authorizing such surveillance as provided by this Article, and which shall submit a report of its decision to the Chief Justice.

(17) "Oral communication" means any oral communication uttered by a person exhibiting an expectation that such communication is not subject to interception under circumstances justifying such expectation, but the term does not include any electronic communication.

(18) "Person" means any employee or agent of the United States or any state or any political subdivision thereof, and any individual, partnership, association, joint stock company, trust, or corporation.

(19) "Readily accessible to the general public" means, with respect to a radio communication, that the communication is not:

a. Scrambled or encrypted;

b. Transmitted using modulation techniques whose essential parameters have been withheld from the public with the intention of preserving the privacy of the communication;

c. Carried on a subcarrier or other signal subsidiary to a radio transmission;

d. Transmitted over a communications system provided by a common carrier, unless the communication is a tone-only paging system communication; or

e. Transmitted on frequencies allocated under Part 25, Subpart D, E, or F or Part 94 of the Rules of the Federal Communications Commission as provided by 18 U.S.C. § 2510(16)(E).

(20) "User" means any person or entity who:

a. Uses an electronic communications service; and

b. Is duly authorized by the provider of the service to engage in the use.

(21) "Wire communication" means any aural transfer made in whole or in part through the use of facilities for the transmission of communications by the aid of wire, cable, or other like connection between the point of origin and the point of reception (including the use of such connection in a switching station) furnished or operated by any person engaged in providing or operating such facilities for the transmission of interstate or foreign communications or communications affecting interstate or foreign commerce and the term includes any electronic storage of such communication. (1995, c. 407, s. 1; 1997-435, s. 1.)

§ 15A-287. Interception and disclosure of wire, oral, or electronic communications prohibited.

(a) Except as otherwise specifically provided in this Article, a person is guilty of a Class H felony if, without the consent of at least one party to the communication, the person:

(1) Willfully intercepts, endeavors to intercept, or procures any other person to intercept or endeavor to intercept, any wire, oral, or electronic communication.

(2) Willfully uses, endeavors to use, or procures any other person to use or endeavor to use any electronic, mechanical, or other device to intercept any oral communication when:

a. The device is affixed to, or otherwise transmits a signal through, a wire, cable, or other like connection used in wire communications; or

b. The device transmits communications by radio, or interferes with the transmission of such communications.

(3) Willfully discloses, or endeavors to disclose, to any other person the contents of any wire, oral, or electronic communication, knowing or having reason to know that the information was obtained through violation of this Article; or

(4) Willfully uses, or endeavors to use, the contents of any wire or oral communication, knowing or having reason to know that the information was obtained through the interception of a wire or oral communication in violation of this Article.

(b) It is not unlawful under this Article for any person to:

(1) Intercept or access an electronic communication made through an electronic communication system that is configured so that the electronic communication is readily accessible to the general public;

(2) Intercept any radio communication which is transmitted:

a. For use by the general public, or that relates to ships, aircraft, vehicles, or persons in distress;

b. By any governmental, law enforcement, civil defense, private land mobile, or public safety communication system, including police and fire, readily available to the general public;

c. By a station operating on any authorized band within the bands allocated to the amateur, citizens band, or general mobile radio services; or

d. By any marine or aeronautical communication system; or

(3) Intercept any communication in a manner otherwise allowed by Chapter 119 of the United States Code.

(c) It is not unlawful under this Article for an operator of a switchboard, or an officer, employee, or agent of a provider of electronic communication service, whose facilities are used in the transmission of a wire or electronic communication, to intercept, disclose, or use that communication in the normal course of employment while engaged in any activity that is a necessary incident to the rendition of his or her service or to the protection of the rights or property of the provider of that service, provided that a provider of wire or electronic communication service may not utilize service observing or random monitoring except for mechanical or service quality control checks.

(d) It is not unlawful under this Article for an officer, employee, or agent of the Federal Communications Commission, in the normal course of his employment and in discharge of the monitoring responsibilities exercised by the Commission in the enforcement of Chapter 5 of Title 47 of the United States Code, to intercept a wire or electronic communication, or oral communication transmitted by radio, or to disclose or use the information thereby obtained.

(e) Any person who, as a result of the person's official position or employment, has obtained knowledge of the contents of any wire, oral, or electronic communication lawfully intercepted pursuant to an electronic surveillance order or of the pendency or existence of or implementation of an electronic surveillance order who shall knowingly and willfully disclose such information for the purpose of hindering or thwarting any investigation or prosecution relating to the subject matter of the electronic surveillance order, except as is necessary for the proper and lawful performance of the duties of his position or employment or as shall be required or allowed by law, shall be guilty of a Class G felony.

(f) Any person who shall, knowingly or with gross negligence, divulge the existence of or contents of any electronic surveillance order in a way likely to hinder or thwart any investigation or prosecution relating to the subject matter of the electronic surveillance order or anyone who shall, knowingly or with gross negligence, release the contents of any wire, oral, or electronic communication intercepted under an electronic surveillance order, except as is necessary for the proper and lawful performance of the duties of his position or employment or as is required or allowed by law, shall be guilty of a Class 1 misdemeanor.

(g) Any public officer who shall violate subsection (a) or (d) of this section or who shall knowingly violate subsection (e) of this section shall be removed from any public office he may hold and shall thereafter be ineligible to hold any public office, whether elective or appointed. (1995, c. 407, s. 1.)

§ 15A-288. Manufacture, distribution, possession, and advertising of wire, oral, or electronic communication intercepting devices prohibited.

(a)   Except as otherwise specifically provided in this Article, a person is guilty of a Class H felony if the person:

(1)   Manufactures, assembles, possesses, purchases, or sells any electronic, mechanical, or other device, knowing or having reason to know that the design of the device renders it primarily useful for the purpose of the surreptitious interception of wire, oral, or electronic communications; or

(2)   Places in any newspaper, magazine, handbill, or other publication, any advertisement of:

a.   Any electronic, mechanical, or other device knowing or having reason to know that the design of the device renders it primarily useful for the purpose of the surreptitious interception of wire, oral, or electronic communications; or

b.   Any other electronic, mechanical, or other device where the advertisement promotes the use of the device for the purpose of the surreptitious interception of wire, oral, or electronic communications.

(b)   It is not unlawful under this section for the following persons to manufacture, assemble, possess, purchase, or sell any electronic, mechanical, or other device, knowing or having reason to know that the design of the device renders it primarily useful for the purpose of the surreptitious interception of wire, oral, or electronic communications:

(1)   A communications common carrier or an officer, agent, or employee of, or a person under contract with, a communications common carrier, acting in the normal course of the communications common carrier's business, or

(2)   An officer, agent, or employee of, or a person under contract with, the State, acting in the course of the activities of the State, and with the written authorization of the Attorney General.

(c)   An officer, agent, or employee of, or a person whose normal and customary business is to design, manufacture, assemble, advertise and sell electronic, mechanical and other devices primarily useful for the purpose of the surreptitious interceptions of wire, oral, or electronic communications, exclusively for and restricted to State and federal investigative or law enforcement agencies and departments. (1995, c. 407, s. 1.)

§ 15A-289. Confiscation of wire, oral, or electronic communication interception devices.

Any electronic, mechanical, or other device used, sent, carried, manufactured, assembled, possessed, sold, or advertised in violation of G.S. 15A-288 may be seized and forfeited to this State. (1995, c. 407, s. 1.)

§ 15A-290. Offenses for which orders for electronic surveillance may be granted.

(a) Orders authorizing or approving the interception of wire, oral, or electronic communications may be granted, subject to the provisions of this Article and Chapter 119 of the United States Code, when the interception:

(1) May provide or has provided evidence of the commission of, or any conspiracy to commit:

a. Any of the drug-trafficking violations listed in G.S. 90-95(h); or

b. A continuing criminal enterprise in violation of G.S. 90-95.1.

(2) May expedite the apprehension of persons indicted for the commission of, or any conspiracy to commit, an offense listed in subdivision (1) of this subsection.

(b) Orders authorizing or approving the interception of wire, oral, or electronic communications may be granted, subject to the provisions of this Article and Chapter 119 of the United States Code, when the interception may provide, or has provided, evidence of any offense that involves the commission of, or any conspiracy to commit, murder, kidnapping, hostage taking, robbery, extortion, bribery, rape, or any sexual offense, or when the interception may expedite the apprehension of persons indicted for the commission of these offenses.

(c) Orders authorizing or approving the interception of wire, oral, or electronic communications may be granted, subject to the provisions of this

Article and Chapter 119 of the United States Code, when the interception may provide, or has provided, evidence of any of the following offenses, or any conspiracy to commit these offenses, or when the interception may expedite the apprehension of persons indicted for the commission of these offenses:

(1)   Any felony offense against a minor, including any violation of G.S. 14-27.7 (Intercourse and sexual offenses with certain victims; consent no defense), G.S. 14-41 (Abduction of children), G.S. 14-43.11 (Human trafficking), G.S. 14-43.12 (Involuntary servitude), G.S. 14-43.13 (Sexual servitude), G.S. 14-190.16 (First degree sexual exploitation of a minor), G.S. 14-190.17 (Second degree sexual exploitation of a minor), G.S. 14-202.1 (Taking indecent liberties with children), G.S. 14-205.2(c) or (d) (Patronizing a prostitute who is a minor or a mentally disabled person), or G.S. 14-205.3(b) (Promoting prostitution of a minor or a mentally disabled person).

(2)   Any felony obstruction of a criminal investigation, including any violation of G.S. 14-221.1 (Altering, destroying, or stealing evidence of criminal conduct).

(3)   Any felony offense involving interference with, or harassment or intimidation of, jurors or witnesses, including any violation of G.S. 14-225.2 or G.S. 14-226.

(4)   Any felony offense involving assault or threats against any executive or legislative officer in violation of Article 5A of Chapter 14 of the General Statutes or assault with a firearm or other deadly weapon upon governmental officers or employees in violation of G.S. 14-34.2.

(5)   Any offense involving the manufacture, assembly, possession, storage, transportation, sale, purchase, delivery, or acquisition of weapons of mass death or destruction in violation of G.S. 14-288.8 or the adulteration or misbranding of food, drugs, cosmetics, etc., with the intent to cause serious injury in violation of G.S. 14-34.4.

(d)   When an investigative or law enforcement officer, while engaged in intercepting wire, oral, or electronic communications in the manner authorized, intercepts wire, electronic, or oral communications relating to offenses other than those specified in the order of authorization or approval, the contents thereof, and evidence derived therefrom, may be disclosed or used as provided in G.S. 15A-294(a) and (b). Such contents and any evidence derived therefrom may be used in accordance with G.S. 15A-294(c) when authorized or approved by a judicial review panel where the panel finds, on subsequent application made as soon as practicable, that the contents were otherwise intercepted in accordance with this Article or Chapter 119 of the United States Code.

(e) No otherwise privileged wire, oral, or electronic communication intercepted in accordance with, or in violation of, the provisions of this Article or Chapter 119 of the United States Code, shall lose its privileged character. (1995, c. 407, s. 1; 2013-368, s. 6.)

§ 15A-291. Application for electronic surveillance order; judicial review panel.

(a) The Attorney General or the Attorney General's designee may, pursuant to the provisions of section 2516(2) of Chapter 119 of the United States Code, apply to a judicial review panel for an order authorizing or approving the interception of wire, oral, or electronic communications by investigative or law enforcement officers having responsibility for the investigation of the offenses as to which the application is made, and for such offenses and causes as are enumerated in G.S. 15A-290. A judicial review panel shall be composed of such judges as may be assigned by the Chief Justice of the Supreme Court of North Carolina or an Associate Justice acting as the Chief Justice's designee, which shall review applications for electronic surveillance orders and may issue orders valid throughout the State authorizing such surveillance as provided by this Article, and which shall submit a report of its decision to the Chief Justice. A judicial review panel may be appointed by the Chief Justice or an Associate Justice acting as the Chief Justice's designee upon the notification of the Attorney General's Office of the intent to apply for an electronic surveillance order.

(b) A judicial review panel is hereby authorized to grant orders valid throughout the State for the interception of wire, oral, or electronic communications. Applications for such orders may be made by the Attorney General or the Attorney General's designee. The Attorney General or the Attorney General's designee in applying for such orders, and a judicial review panel in granting such orders, shall comply with all procedural requirements of section 2518 of Chapter 119 of the United States Code. The Attorney General or the Attorney General's designee may make emergency applications as provided by section 2518 of Chapter 119 of the United States Code. In applying section 2518 the word "judge" in that section shall be construed to refer to the judicial review panel, unless the context otherwise indicates. The judicial review panel may stipulate any special conditions it feels necessary to assure compliance with the terms of this act.

(c) No judge who sits as a member of a judicial review panel shall preside at any trial or proceeding resulting from or in any manner related to information gained pursuant to a lawful electronic surveillance order issued by that panel.

(d) Each application for an order authorizing or approving the interception of a wire, oral, or electronic communication must be made in writing upon oath or affirmation to the judicial review panel. Each application must include the following information:

(1) The identity of the office requesting the application;

(2) A full and complete statement of the facts and circumstances relied upon by the applicant, to justify his belief that an order should be issued, including:

a. Details as to the particular offense that has been, or is being committed;

b. Except as provided in G.S. 15A-294(i), a particular description of the nature and location of the facilities from which or the place where the communication is to be intercepted;

c. A particular description of the type of communications sought to be intercepted; and

d. The identity of the person, if known, committing the offense and whose communications are to be intercepted;

(3) A full and complete statement as to whether or not other investigative procedures have been tried and failed or why they reasonably appear to be unlikely to succeed if tried or to be too dangerous;

(4) A statement of the period of time for which the interception is required to be maintained. If the nature of the investigation is such that the authorization for interception should not automatically terminate when the described type of communication has been obtained, a particular description of facts establishing probable cause to believe that additional communications of the same type will occur thereafter must be added;

(5) A full and complete statement of the facts concerning all previous applications known to the individual authorizing and making adjudication, made to a judicial review panel for authorization to intercept, or for approval of interceptions of wire, oral, or electronic communications involving any of the same persons, facilities, or places specified in the application, and the action taken by that judicial review panel on each such application; and

(6) Where the application is for the extension of an order, a statement setting forth the results thus far obtained from the interception, or a reasonable explanation of the failure to obtain such results.

(e) Before acting on the application, the judicial review panel may examine on oath the person requesting the application or any other person who may possess pertinent information, but information other than that contained in the affidavit may not be considered by the panel in determining whether probable cause exists for the issuance of the order unless the information is either recorded or contemporaneously summarized in the record or on the face of the order by the panel. (1995, c. 407, s. 1; 1997-435, s. 2; 2005-207, s. 1.)

§ 15A-292. Request for application for electronic surveillance order.

(a) The head of any municipal, county, or State law enforcement agency or any district attorney may submit a written request to the Attorney General that the Attorney General apply to a judicial review panel for an electronic surveillance order to be executed within the requesting agency's jurisdiction. The written requests shall be on a form approved by the Attorney General and shall provide sufficient information to form the basis for an application for an electronic surveillance order. The head of a law enforcement agency shall also submit a copy of the request to the district attorney, who shall review the request and forward it to the Attorney General along with any comments he may wish to include. The Attorney General is authorized to review the request and decide whether it is appropriate to submit an application to a judicial review panel for an electronic surveillance order. If a request for an application is deemed inappropriate, the Attorney General shall send a signed, written statement to the person submitting the request, and to the district attorney, summarizing the reasons for failing to make an application. If the Attorney General decides to submit an application to a judicial review panel, he shall so notify the requesting agency head, the district attorney, and the head of the local law enforcement agency which has the primary responsibility for enforcing the criminal laws in the location in which it is anticipated the majority of the surveillance will take place, if not the same as the requesting agency head, unless the Attorney General has probable cause to believe that the latter notifications should substantially jeopardize the success of the surveillance or the investigation in general. If a judicial review panel grants an electronic surveillance order, a copy of such order shall be sent to the requesting agency head and the district attorney, and a summary of the order shall be sent to the head of the local law enforcement agency with primary responsibility for enforcing the criminal laws in the jurisdiction where the majority of the surveillance will take place, if not the same as the requesting agency head, unless the judicial review panel finds probable cause to believe that the latter notifications would substantially jeopardize the success of the surveillance or the investigation.

(b)   This Article does not limit the authority of the Attorney General to apply for electronic surveillance orders independent of, or contrary to, the requests of law enforcement agency heads, nor does it limit the discretion of the Attorney General in determining whether an application is appropriate under any given circumstances.

(c)   The Chief Justice of the North Carolina Supreme Court shall receive a report concerning each decision of a judicial review panel. (1995, c. 407, s. 1.)

§ 15A-293. Issuance of order for electronic surveillance; procedures for implementation.

(a)   Upon application by the Attorney General pursuant to the procedures in G.S. 15A-291, a judicial review panel may enter an ex parte order, as requested or as modified, authorizing the interception of wire, oral, or electronic communications, if the panel determines on the basis of the facts submitted by the applicant that:

(1)   There is probable cause for belief that an individual is committing, has committed, or is about to commit an offense set out in G.S. 15A-290;

(2)   There is probable cause for belief that particular communications concerning that offense will be obtained through such interception;

(3)   Normal investigative procedures have been tried and have failed or reasonably appear to be unlikely to succeed if tried or to be too dangerous; and

(4)   Except as provided in G.S. 15A-294(i), there is probable cause for belief that the facilities from which, or the place where, the wire, oral, or electronic

communications are to be intercepted are being used, or are about to be used, in connection with the commission of such offense, or are leased to, listed in the name of, or commonly used by the individual described in subdivision (1) of this subsection.

(b)   Each order authorizing the interception of any wire, oral, or electronic communications must specify:

(1)   The identity of the person, if known, whose communications are to be intercepted;

(2)   The nature and location of the communications facilities as to which, or the place where, authority to intercept is granted, and the means by which such interceptions may be made;

(3)   A particular description of the type of communication sought to be intercepted and a statement of the particular offense to which it relates;

(4)   The identity of the agency authorized to intercept the communications and of the person requesting the application; and

(5)   The period of time during which such interception is authorized, including a statement as to whether or not the interception automatically terminates when the described communication has been first obtained.

(c)   No order entered under this Article may authorize the interception of any wire, oral, or electronic communication for any period longer than is necessary to achieve the objective of the authorization, nor in any event longer than 30 days. Such 30-day period begins on the earlier of the day on which the investigative or law enforcement officer first begins to conduct an interception under the order or 10 days after the order is entered. Extensions of an order may be granted, but only upon application for an extension made in accordance with G.S. 15A-291 and the panel making the findings required by subsection (a) of this section. The period of extension shall be no longer than the panel determines to be necessary to achieve the purpose for which it was granted and in no event for longer than 30 days. Every order and extension thereof must contain a provision that the authorization to intercept be executed as soon as practicable, be conducted in such a way as to minimize the interception of communications not otherwise subject to interception under this Article, and terminate upon attainment of the authorized objective, or in any event in 30 days, as is appropriate. In the event the intercepted communication is in a code or foreign language, and an expert in that foreign language or code is not reasonably available during the interception period, minimization may be accomplished as soon as practicable after the interception. An interception under this Article may be conducted in whole or in part by State or federal government personnel, or by an individual operating under a contract with the State or federal government, acting under the supervision of an investigative or law enforcement officer authorized to conduct the interception.

(d) Whenever an order authorizing interception is entered pursuant to this Article, the order may require reports to be made to the issuing judicial review panel showing that progress has been made toward achievement of the authorized objective and the need for continued interception. Such reports must be made at such intervals as the panel may require.

(1) The contents of any wire, oral, or electronic communication intercepted by any means authorized by this Article must be recorded on tape, wire, or electronic or other comparable device. The recording of the contents of any wire, electronic, or oral communication under this subsection must be done in such way as will protect the recording from editing or other alterations. Immediately upon the expiration of the period of the order, or extensions thereof, the recordings must be made available to the judicial review panel and sealed under its direction. Custody of the recordings is wherever the panel orders. They may not be destroyed except upon an order of the issuing panel and in any event must be kept for 10 years. Duplicate recordings may be made for use or disclosure pursuant to the provisions of G.S. 15A-294(a) and (b) for investigations. The contents of any wire, oral, or electronic communication or evidence derived therefrom may not be disclosed or used under G.S. 15A-294(c) unless they have been kept sealed.

(2) Applications made and orders granted under this Article must be sealed by the panel. Custody of the applications and orders may be disclosed only upon a showing of good cause before the issuing panel and may not be destroyed except on its order and in any event must be kept for 10 years.

(3) Any violation of the provisions of this subsection may be punished as for contempt.

(e) The State Bureau of Investigation shall own or control and may operate any equipment used to implement electronic surveillance orders issued by a judicial review panel and may operate or use, in implementing any electronic surveillance order, electronic surveillance equipment in which a local government or any of its agencies has a property interest.

(f)   The Attorney General shall establish procedures for the use of electronic surveillance equipment in assisting local law enforcement agencies implementing electronic surveillance orders. The Attorney General shall supervise such assistance given to local law enforcement agencies and is authorized to conduct statewide training sessions for investigative and law enforcement officers regarding this Article. (1995, c. 407, s. 1; 1997-435, s. 2.1; 2005-207, ss. 2, 3.)

§ 15A-294. Authorization for disclosure and use of intercepted wire, oral, or electronic communications.

(a)   Any investigative or law enforcement officer who, by any means authorized by this Article or Chapter 119 of the United States Code, has obtained knowledge of the contents of any wire, oral, or electronic communication, or evidence derived therefrom, may disclose such contents to another investigative or law enforcement officer to the extent that such disclosure is appropriate to the proper performance of the official duties of the officer making or receiving the disclosure.

(b)   Any investigative or law enforcement officer, who by any means authorized by this Article or Chapter 119 of the United States Code, has obtained knowledge of the contents of any wire, oral, or electronic communication, or evidence derived therefrom, may use such contents to the extent such use is appropriate to the proper performance of the officers' official duties.

(c)   Any person who has received, by any means authorized by this Article or Chapter 119 of the United States Code, any information concerning a wire, oral, or electronic communication, or evidence derived therefrom, intercepted in accordance with the provisions of this Article, may disclose the contents of that communication or such derivative evidence while giving testimony under oath or affirmation in any proceeding in any court or before any grand jury in this State, or in any court of the United States or of any state, or in any federal or state grand jury proceeding.

(d) Within a reasonable time, but no later than 90 days after the filing of an application for an order or the termination of the period of an order or the extensions thereof, the issuing judicial review panel must cause to be served on the persons named in the order or the application and such other parties as the panel in its discretion may determine, an inventory that includes notice of:

(1) The fact of the entry of the order or the application;

(2) The date of the entry and the period of the authorized interception; and

(3) The fact that during the period wire, oral, or electronic communications were or were not intercepted.

(d1) The notification required pursuant to G.S. 15A-294(d) may be delayed if the judicial review panel has probable cause to believe that notification would substantially jeopardize the success of an electronic surveillance or a criminal investigation. Delay of notification shall be only by order of the judicial review panel. The period of delay shall be designated by the judicial review panel and may be extended from time to time until the jeopardy to the electronic surveillance or the criminal investigation dissipates.

(e) The issuing judicial review panel, upon the filing of a motion, may in its discretion, make available to such person or his counsel for inspection, such portions of the intercepted communications, applications, and orders as the panel determines to be required by law or in the interest of justice.

(f) The contents of any intercepted wire, oral, or electronic communication, or evidence derived therefrom, may not be received in evidence or otherwise disclosed in any trial, hearing, or other proceeding in any court of this State unless each party, not less than 20 working days before the trial, hearing, or other proceeding, has been furnished with a copy of the order and accompanying application, under which the interception was authorized.

(g) Any aggrieved person in any trial, hearing, or proceeding in or before any court, department, officer, agency, regulatory body, or other authority of this State, or a political subdivision thereof, may move to suppress the contents of any intercepted wire, oral, or electronic communication, or evidence derived therefrom, on the grounds that:

(1) The communication was unlawfully intercepted;

(2) The order of authorization under which it was intercepted is insufficient on its face; or

(3) The interception was not made in conformity with the order of authorization.

Such motion must be made before the trial, hearing, or proceeding unless there was no opportunity to make such motion or the person was not aware of the grounds of this motion. If the motion is granted, the contents of the intercepted wire, oral, or electronic communication, or evidence derived therefrom, must be treated as having been obtained in violation of this Article.

(h) In addition to any other right to appeal, the State may appeal:

(1) From an order granting a motion to suppress made under subdivision (1) of this subsection, if the district attorney certifies to the judge granting the motion that the appeal is not taken for purposes of delay. The appeal must be taken within 30 days after the date the order of suppression was entered and must be prosecuted as are other interlocutory appeals; or

(2) From an order denying an application for an order of authorization, and the appeal may be made ex parte and must be considered in camera and in preference to all other pending appeals.

(i) The requirements of G.S. 15A-293(b)(2) and G.S. 15A-293(a)(4) relating to the specification of the facilities from which, or the place where, the communication is to be intercepted do not apply if:

(1) In the case of an application with respect to the interception of an oral communication:

a. The application is by a State investigative or law enforcement officer and is approved by the Attorney General or his designee;

b. The application contains a full and complete statement as to why the specification is not practical and identifies the person committing the offense and whose communications are to be intercepted; and

c. The judicial review panel finds that the specification is not practical.

(2) In the case of an application with respect to a wire or electronic communication:

a. The application is by a State investigative or law enforcement officer and is approved by the Attorney General or his designee;

b. The application identifies the person believed to be committing the offense and whose communications are to be intercepted, and the applicant makes a showing that there is probable cause to believe that the person's actions could have the effect of thwarting interception from a specified facility;

c. The judicial review panel finds that the showing has been adequately made; and

d. The order authorizing or approving the interception is limited to interception only for such time as it is reasonable to presume that the person identified in the application is or was reasonably proximate to the instrument through which the communication will be or was transmitted.

(j) An interception of a communication under an order with respect to which the requirements of G.S. 15A-293(b)(2) and G.S. 15A-293(a)(4) do not apply by reason of subdivision (i)(1) of this section shall not begin until the place where the communication is to be intercepted is ascertained by the person implementing the interception order. A provider of wire or electronic communications service that has received an order as provided for in subdivision (i)(2) of this section may move the court to modify or quash the order on the grounds that its assistance with respect to the interception cannot be performed in a timely or reasonable fashion. The court, upon notice to the government, shall decide such a motion expeditiously. (1995, c. 407, s. 1; 1997-435, s. 3; 2005-207, s. 4.)

§ 15A-295. Reports concerning intercepted wire, oral, or electronic communications.

In January of each year, the Attorney General of this State must report to the Administrative Office of the United States Court the information required to be filed by section 2519 of Title 18 of the United States Code, as heretofore or hereafter amended, and file a copy of the report with the Administrative Office of the Courts of North Carolina. (1995, c. 407, s. 1.)

§ 15A-296. Recovery of civil damages authorized.

(a)   Any person whose wire, oral, or electronic communication is intercepted, disclosed, or used in violation of this Article, has a civil cause of action against any person who intercepts, discloses, uses, or procures any other person to intercept, disclose, or use such communications, and is entitled to recover from any other person:

(1)   Actual damages, but not less than liquidated damages, computed at the rate of one hundred dollars ($100.00) a day for each day of violation or one thousand dollars ($1,000), whichever is higher;

(2)   Punitive damages; and

(3)   A reasonable attorneys' fee and other litigation costs reasonably incurred.

(b)   Good faith reliance on a court order or on a representation made by the Attorney General or a district attorney is a complete defense to any civil or criminal action brought under this Article. (1995, c. 407, s. 1.)

§ 15A-297. Conformity to provisions of federal law.

It is the intent of this Article to conform the requirements of all interceptions of wire, oral, or electronic communications conducted by investigative or law enforcement officers in this State to provisions of Chapter 119 of the United States Code, except where the context indicates a purpose to provide safeguards even more protective of individual privacy and constitutional rights. (1995, c. 407, s. 1.)

§ 15A-298. Subpoena authority.

Pursuant to rules issued by the Attorney General, the Director of the State Bureau of Investigation or the Director's designee may issue an administrative subpoena to a communications common carrier or an electronic communications service to compel production of business records if the records:

(1) Disclose information concerning local or long-distance toll records or subscriber information; and

(2) Are material to an active criminal investigation being conducted by the State Bureau of Investigation. (1995, c. 407, s. 1; 1997-435, s. 4.)

Article 16A.

Discontinuation of Telecommunications Services.

§ 15A-299. Discontinuation of telecommunications services used for unlawful purposes.

(a) The legislature finds that some persons use telecommunications services to violate State or federal criminal law. The legislature further finds that some persons use telecommunications services or technology, such as call forwarding and cellular radio transmission, to avoid detection or arrest.

(b) A customer of a telecommunications company operating within the State may use telecommunications services only for lawful purposes.

(c) If a local, State, or federal law enforcement officer acting within the scope of the officer's duties obtains evidence that telecommunications services are being used or have been used by a customer or by the employee or agent of the customer to violate State or federal criminal law, the officer may request either the district attorney or the Attorney General as appropriate to apply to the district court of the county in which the suspected violation of State or federal criminal law occurred for an order requiring the telecommunications company to discontinue service to the customer. The court shall hold a hearing on the application as soon as possible, but no sooner than 48 hours after notice of the application for discontinuation of service is delivered to the address at which the telecommunications services are furnished or to the address to which bills for telecommunications services are mailed, according to the telecommunications company records. Notice must also be given to the registered agent for the service of process upon the telecommunications company at least 48 hours prior to the hearing. Notices required under this section shall be given pursuant to the provisions of Rule 4 of the North Carolina Rules of Civil Procedure. If the court finds clear and convincing evidence that the telecommunications services are being used or have been used to violate State or federal criminal law, the court may order the telecommunications company to discontinue such service immediately.

(d) Telecommunications services discontinued under this section may be reinstated only by court order, and call forwarding or message referrals, whether recorded or live, may not be provided until reinstatement of service is ordered by the court. The court may order reinstatement of telecommunications services if it finds that the customer is not likely to use the services to violate State or federal criminal law. The standard of proof shall be the same as that used for the disconnect order.

(e) A telecommunications company shall be held harmless from liability to any person when complying with any court order issued under this section. (1997-372, s. 1.)

§ 15A-300. Reserved for future codification purposes.

SUBCHAPTER III. CRIMINAL PROCESS.

Article 17.

Criminal Process.

§ 15A-301. Criminal process generally.

(a) Formal Requirements. -

(1) A record of each criminal process issued in the trial division of the General Court of Justice must be maintained in the office of the clerk in either paper form or in electronic form in the Electronic Repository as provided in G.S. 15A-301.1.

(2) Criminal process, other than a citation, must be signed and dated by the justice, judge, magistrate, or clerk who issues it. The citation must be signed and dated by the law-enforcement officer who issues it.

(b) To Whom Directed. - Warrants for arrest and orders for arrest must be directed to a particular officer, a class of officers, or a combination thereof, having authority and territorial jurisdiction to execute the process. A criminal summons must be directed to the person summoned to appear and must be delivered to and may be served by any law-enforcement officer having authority and territorial jurisdiction to make an arrest for the offense charged, except that in those instances where the defendant is called into a law-enforcement agency to receive a summons, any employee so designated by the agency's chief executive officer may serve a criminal summons at the agency's office. The citation must be directed to the person cited to appear.

(b1) (For effective date, see note) Approval by District Attorney; school personnel. - Notwithstanding any other provision of law, no warrant for arrest, order for arrest, criminal summons, or other criminal process shall be issued by a magistrate against a school employee, as defined in G.S. 14-33(c)(6), for an offense that occurred while the school employee was in the process of discharging his or her duties of employment, without the prior written approval of the district attorney or the district attorney's designee. For purposes of this subsection, the term "district attorney" means the person elected to the office of district attorney. This subsection does not apply if the offense is a traffic offense or if the offense occurred in the presence of a sworn law enforcement officer. The district attorney may decline to accept the authority set forth in this subsection; in such case, the procedure and review authority shall be as set forth in subsection (b2) of this section.

(b2) (For effective date, see note) Magistrate review; school personnel. - A district attorney may decline the authority provided under subsection (b1) of this section by transmitting a letter so indicating to the chief district court judge. Upon receipt of a letter from the district attorney declining the authority provided in subsection (b1) of this section, the chief district court judge shall appoint a magistrate or magistrates to review any application for a warrant for arrest, order for arrest, criminal summons, or other criminal process against a school employee, as defined in G.S. 14-33(c)(6), where the allegation is that the school employee committed a misdemeanor offense while discharging his or her duties of employment. The failure to comply with any of the requirements in this subsection shall not affect the validity of any warrant, order, summons, or other criminal process. The following exceptions apply to the requirements in this subsection:

(1) The offense is a traffic offense.

(2) The offense occurred in the presence of a sworn law enforcement officer.

(3) There is no appointed magistrate available to review the application.

(c) Service. -

(1) A law-enforcement officer or other employee designated as provided in subsection (b) receiving for service or execution a criminal process that was first created and exists only in paper form must note thereon the date and time of its receipt. A law enforcement officer receiving a copy of a criminal process that was printed in paper form as provided in G.S. 15A-301.1 shall cause the date of receipt to be recorded as provided in that section. Upon execution or service, a copy of the process must be delivered to the person arrested or served.

(2) A corporation may be served with criminal summons as provided in G.S. 15A-773.

(d) Return. -

(1) The officer or other employee designated as provided in subsection (b) who serves or executes a criminal process that was first created and exists only in paper form must enter the date and time of the service or execution on the process and return it to the clerk of court in the county in which issued. The officer or other employee designated as provided in subsection (b) of this section who serves or executes a copy of a criminal process that was printed in paper form as provided in G.S. 15A-301.1 shall promptly cause the date of the service or execution to be recorded as provided in that section.

(2) If criminal process that was created and exists only in paper form is not served or executed within a number of days indicated below, it must be returned to the clerk of court in the county in which it was issued, with a reason for the failure of service or execution noted thereon.

a. Warrant for arrest - 180 days.

b. Order for arrest - 180 days.

c. Criminal summons - 90 days or the date the defendant is directed to appear, whichever is earlier.

(3) Failure to return the process to the clerk as required by subdivision (2) of this subsection does not invalidate the process, nor does it invalidate service or execution made after the period specified in subdivision (2).

(4) The clerk to which return of a criminal process that was created and exists only in paper form is made may redeliver the process to a law-enforcement officer or other employee designated as provided in subsection (b) for further attempts at service. If the process is a criminal summons, he may reissue it only upon endorsement of a new designated time and date of appearance.

(e) Copies to Be Made by Clerk. -

(1) The clerk may make a certified copy of any criminal process that was created and exists only in paper form filed in his office pursuant to subsection (a) when the original process has been lost or when the process has been returned pursuant to subdivision (d)(2). The copy may be executed as effectively as the original process whether or not the original has been redelivered as provided in G.S. 15A-301(d)(4).

(2) When criminal process is returned to the clerk pursuant to subdivision (d)(1) and it appears that the appropriate venue is in another county, the clerk must make and retain a certified copy of the process and transmit the original process to the clerk in the appropriate county.

(3) Upon request of a defendant, the clerk must make and furnish to him without charge one copy of every criminal process filed against him.

(4) Nothing in this section prevents the making and retention of uncertified copies of process for information purposes under G.S. 15A-401(a)(2) or for any other lawful purpose.

(f) Protection of Process Server. - An officer or other employee designated as provided in subsection (b), and serving process as provided in subsection (b), receiving under this section or under G.S. 15A-301.1 criminal process which is complete and regular on its face may serve the process in accordance with its terms and need not inquire into its regularity or continued validity, nor does he incur criminal or civil liability for its due service.

(g) Recall of Process - Authority. - A criminal process that has not been served on the defendant, other than a citation, shall be recalled by a judicial official or by a person authorized to act on behalf of a judicial official as follows:

(1) A warrant or criminal summons shall be recalled by the issuing judicial official when that official determines that probable cause did not exist for its issuance.

(2) Any criminal process other than a warrant or criminal summons may be recalled for good cause by any judicial official of the trial division in which it was issued. Good cause includes, without limitation, the fact that:

a. A copy of the process has been served on the defendant.

b. All charges on which the process is based have been disposed.

c. The person named as the defendant in the process is not the person who committed the charged offense.

d. It has been determined that grounds for the issuance of an order for arrest did not exist, no longer exist or have been satisfied.

(3) The disposition of all charges on which a process is based shall effect the recall, without further action by the court, of that process and of all other outstanding process issued in connection with the charges, including all orders for arrest issued for the defendant's failure to appear to answer the charges.

When the process was first created and exists only in paper form, the recall shall promptly be communicated by any reasonable means to each law enforcement agency known to be in possession of the original or a copy of the process, and each agency shall promptly return the process to the court, unserved. When the process is in the Electronic Repository, the recall shall promptly be entered in the Electronic Repository, and no further copies of the process shall be printed in paper form. The recall shall also be communicated by any reasonable means to each agency that is known to be in possession of a copy of the process in paper form and that does not have remote electronic access to the Electronic Repository. (1868-9, c. 178, subch. 3, s. 4; Code, s. 1135; Rev., s. 3159; C.S., s. 4525; 1957, c. 346; 1969, c. 44, s. 28; 1973, c. 1286, s. 1; 1975, 2nd Sess., c. 983, ss. 136, 137; 1979, c. 725, ss. 1-3; 1989, c. 262, s. 3; 2002-64, s. 3; 2012-149, s. 5.)

§ 15A-301.1. Electronic Repository.

(a) The Administrative Office of the Courts shall create and maintain, in cooperation with State and local law enforcement agencies, an automated electronic repository for criminal process (hereinafter referred to as the Electronic Repository), which shall comprise a secure system of electronic data entry, storage, and retrieval that provides for creating, signing, issuing, entering, filing, and retaining criminal process in electronic form, and that provides for the following with regard to criminal process in electronic form:

(1) Tracking criminal process.

(2) Accessing criminal process through remote electronic means by all authorized judicial officials and employees and all authorized law enforcement officers and agencies that have compatible electronic access capacity.

(3) Printing any criminal process in paper form by any authorized judicial official or employee or any authorized law enforcement officer or agency.

The Administrative Office of the Courts shall assure that all electronic signatures effected through use of the system meet the requirements of G.S. 15A-101.1(5).

(b) Any criminal process may be created, signed, and issued in electronic form, filed electronically in the office of a clerk of superior court, and retained in electronic form in the Electronic Repository.

(c) Any process that was first created, signed, and issued in paper form may subsequently be filed in electronic form and entered in the Electronic Repository by the judicial official who issued the process or by any person authorized to enter it on behalf of the judicial official. All copies of the process in paper form are then subject to the provisions of subsections (i) and (k) of this section.

(d) Any criminal process in the Electronic Repository shall be part of the official records of the clerk of superior court of the county for which it was issued and shall be maintained in the office of that clerk as required by G.S. 15A-301(a).

(e) Any criminal process in the Electronic Repository may, at any time and at any place in this State, be printed in paper form and delivered to a law enforcement agency or officer by any judicial official, law enforcement officer, or other authorized person.

(f)   When printed in paper form pursuant to subsection (e) of this section, any copy of a criminal process in the Electronic Repository confers the same authority and has the same force and effect for all other purposes as the original of a criminal process that was created and exists only in paper form.

(g)   Service of any criminal process in the Electronic Repository may be effected by delivering to the person to be served a copy of the process that was printed in paper form pursuant to subsection (e) of this section.

(h)   The tracking information specified in subsection (i) of this section shall promptly be entered in the Electronic Repository when one or both of the following occurs:

(1)   A process is first created, signed, and issued in paper form and subsequently entered in electronic form in the Electronic Repository as provided in subsection (c) of this section.

(2)   A copy of a process in the Electronic Repository is printed in paper form pursuant to subsection (e) of this section.

(i)   The following tracking information shall be entered in the Electronic Repository in accordance with subsections (c) and (h) of this section:

(1)   The date and time when the process was printed in paper form.

(2)   The name of the law enforcement agency by or for which the process was printed in paper form.

(3)   If available, the name and identification number of the law enforcement officer to whom any copy of the process was delivered.

(j)   The service requirements set forth in subsection (k) of this section shall apply to:

(1)   Each copy of a criminal process that is first created in paper form and subsequently entered into the Electronic Repository as provided in subsection (c) of this section.

(2) Each copy of a criminal process in the Electronic Repository that is printed in paper form pursuant to subsection (e) of this section.

(k) Service Requirements for Process Entered in the Electronic Repository. - The copy of the process shall be served not later than 24 hours after it has been printed. The date, time, and place of service shall promptly be recorded in the Electronic Repository and shall be part of the official records of the court. If the process is not served within 24 hours, that fact shall promptly be recorded in the Electronic Repository and all copies of the process in paper form shall be destroyed. The process may again be printed in paper form at later times and at the same or other places. Subsection (f) of this section applies to each successively printed copy of the process. When service of the warrant is no longer being actively pursued, that fact shall be promptly recorded in the Electronic Repository.

(l) A law enforcement officer or agency that does not have compatible remote access to the Electronic Repository shall promptly communicate, by any reasonable means, the information required by subsection (k) of this section to the clerk of superior court of the county in which the process was issued or to any other person authorized to enter information into the Electronic Repository, and the information shall promptly be entered in the Electronic Repository.

(m) Failure to enter any information as required by subsection (i) or (k) of this section does not invalidate the process, nor does it invalidate service or execution made after the period specified in subsection (k) of this section.

(n) A warrant created and existing only in paper form is returned within the meaning of G.S. 132-1.4(k) when it is returned as provided in G.S. 15A-301(d). A warrant that exists only in electronic form in the Electronic Repository is returned within the meaning of G.S. 132-1.4(k), when it has been served or when service of the warrant is no longer being actively pursued, as either fact is entered in the Electronic Repository pursuant to subsection (k) of this section. (2002-64, s. 2.)

§ 15A-302. Citation.

(a) Definition. - A citation is a directive, issued by a law enforcement officer or other person authorized by statute, that a person appear in court and answer a misdemeanor or infraction charge or charges.

(b) When Issued. - An officer may issue a citation to any person who he has probable cause to believe has committed a misdemeanor or infraction.

(c) Contents. - The citation must:

(1) Identify the crime charged, including the date, and where material, identify the property and other persons involved,

(2) Contain the name and address of the person cited, or other identification if that cannot be ascertained,

(3) Identify the officer issuing the citation, and

(4) Cite the person to whom issued to appear in a designated court, at a designated time and date.

(d) Service. - A copy of the citation shall be delivered to the person cited who may sign a receipt on the original which shall thereafter be filed with the clerk by the officer. If the cited person refuses to sign, the officer shall certify delivery of the citation by signing the original, which shall thereafter be filed with the clerk. Failure of the person cited to sign the citation shall not constitute grounds for his arrest or the requirement that he post a bond. When a citation is issued for a parking offense, a copy shall be delivered to the operator of a vehicle who is present at the time of service, or shall be delivered to the registered owner of the vehicle if the operator is not present by affixing a copy of the citation to the vehicle in a conspicuous place.

(e) Dismissal by Prosecutor. - If the prosecutor finds that no crime or infraction is charged in the citation, or that there is insufficient evidence to warrant prosecution, he may dismiss the charge and so notify the person cited. An appropriate entry must be made in the records of the clerk. It is not necessary to enter the dismissal in open court or to obtain consent of the judge.

(f) Citation No Bar to Criminal Summons or Warrant. - If the offense is a misdemeanor, a criminal summons or a warrant may issue notwithstanding the prior issuance of a citation for the same offense. If a defendant fails to appear in court as directed by a citation that charges the defendant with a misdemeanor, an order for arrest for failure to appear may be issued by a judicial official.

(g) Preparation of Form. - The form and content of the citation is as prescribed by the Administrative Officer of the Courts. The form of citation used for violation of the motor vehicle laws must contain a notice that the driving privilege of the person cited may be revoked for failure to appear as cited, and must be prepared as provided in G.S. 7A-148(b). (1973, c. 1286, s. 1; 1975, c. 166, ss. 3, 27; 1983, c. 327, s. 4; 1985, c. 385; c. 764, s. 4; 1989, c. 243, s. 1; 2003-15, s. 1.)

§ 15A-303. Criminal summons.

(a) Definition. - A criminal summons consists of a statement of the crime or infraction of which the person to be summoned is accused, and an order directing that the person so accused appear and answer to the charges made against him. It is based upon a showing of probable cause supported by oath or affirmation.

(b) Statement of the Crime or Infraction. - The criminal summons must contain a statement of the crime or infraction of which the person summoned is accused. No criminal summons is invalid because of any technicality of pleading if the statement is sufficient to identify the crime or infraction.

(c) Showing of Probable Cause; Record. - The showing of probable cause for the issuance of a criminal summons, and the record thereof, is the same as provided in G.S. 15A-304(d) for the issuance of a warrant for arrest.

(d) Order to Appear. - The summons must order the person named to appear in a designated court at a designated time and date and answer to the charges made against him and advise him that he may be held in contempt of court for failure to appear. Except for cause noted in the criminal summons by the issuing official, an appearance date may not be set more than one month following the issuance or reissuance of the criminal summons.

(e) Enforcement. -

(1) If the offense charged is a criminal offense, a warrant for arrest, based upon the same or another showing of probable cause, may be issued by the same or another issuing official, notwithstanding the prior issuance of a criminal summons.

(2) If the offense charged is a criminal offense, an order for arrest, as provided in G.S. 15A-305, may issue for the arrest of any person who fails to appear as directed in a duly executed criminal summons.

(3) A person served with criminal summons who willfully fails to appear as directed may be punished for contempt as provided in G.S. 5A-11.

(4) Repealed by Session Laws 1975, c. 166, s. 4.

(f) Who May Issue. - A criminal summons, valid throughout the State, may be issued by any person authorized to issue warrants for arrest. (1973, c. 1286, s. 1; 1975, c. 166, ss. 4, 5; 1975, 2nd Sess., c. 983, s. 138; 1983, c. 294, s. 3; 1985, c. 764, s. 5.)

§ 15A-304. Warrant for arrest.

(a) Definition. - A warrant for arrest consists of a statement of the crime of which the person to be arrested is accused, and an order directing that the person so accused be arrested and held to answer to the charges made against him. It is based upon a showing of probable cause supported by oath or affirmation.

(b) When Issued. - A warrant for arrest may be issued, instead of or subsequent to a criminal summons, when it appears to the judicial official that the person named should be taken into custody. Circumstances to be considered in determining whether the person should be taken into custody may include, but are not limited to, failure to appear when previously summoned, facts making it apparent that a person summoned will fail to appear, danger that the person accused will escape, danger that there may be injury to person or property, or the seriousness of the offense.

(c) Statement of the Crime. - The warrant must contain a statement of the crime of which the person to be arrested is accused. No warrant for arrest, nor any arrest made pursuant thereto, is invalid because of any technicality of pleading if the statement is sufficient to identify the crime.

(d) Showing of Probable Cause. - A judicial official may issue a warrant for arrest only when he is supplied with sufficient information, supported by oath or affirmation, to make an independent judgment that there is probable cause to believe that a crime has been committed and that the person to be arrested committed it. The information must be shown by one or more of the following:

(1)   Affidavit;

(2)   Oral testimony under oath or affirmation before the issuing official; or

(3)   Oral testimony under oath or affirmation presented by a sworn law enforcement officer to the issuing official by means of an audio and video transmission in which both parties can see and hear each other. Prior to the use of audio and video transmission pursuant to this subdivision, the procedures and type of equipment for audio and video transmission shall be submitted to the Administrative Office of the Courts by the senior regular resident superior court judge and the chief district court judge for a judicial district or set of districts and approved by the Administrative Office of the Courts.

If the information is insufficient to show probable cause, the warrant may not be issued. A judicial official shall not refuse to issue a warrant for the arrest of a person solely because a prior warrant has been issued for the arrest of another person involved in the same matter.

(e)   Order for Arrest. - The order for arrest must direct that a law-enforcement officer take the defendant into custody and bring him without unnecessary delay before a judicial official to answer to the charges made against him.

(f)   Who May Issue. - A warrant for arrest, valid throughout the State, may be issued by:

(1)   A Justice of the Supreme Court.

(2)   A judge of the Court of Appeals.

(3)   A judge of the superior court.

(4)   A judge of the district court, as provided in G.S. 7A-291.

(5)   A clerk, as provided in G.S. 7A-180 and 7A-181.

(6)   A magistrate, as provided in G.S. 7A-273. (1868-9, c. 178, subch. 3, ss. 1-3; Code, ss. 1132-1134; 1901, c. 668; Rev., ss. 3156-3158; C.S., ss. 4522-

4524; 1955, c. 332; 1969, c. 44, s. 27; c. 1062, s. 1; 1973, c. 1286, s. 1; 1997-268, s. 2; 2004-186, s. 15.1.)

§ 15A-305. Order for arrest.

(a) Definition. - As used in this section, an order for arrest is an order issued by a justice, judge, clerk, or magistrate that a law-enforcement officer take a named person into custody.

(b) When Issued. - An order for arrest may be issued when:

(1) A grand jury has returned a true bill of indictment against a defendant who is not in custody and who has not been released from custody pursuant to Article 26 of this Chapter, Bail, to answer to the charges in the bill of indictment.

(2) A defendant who has been arrested and released from custody pursuant to Article 26 of this Chapter, Bail, fails to appear as required.

(3) The defendant has failed to appear as required by a duly executed criminal summons issued pursuant to G.S. 15A-303 or a citation issued by a law enforcement officer or other person authorized by statute pursuant to G.S. 15A-302 that charged the defendant with a misdemeanor.

(4) A defendant has violated the conditions of probation.

(5) In any criminal proceeding in which the defendant has become subject to the jurisdiction of the court, it becomes necessary to take the defendant into custody.

(6) It is authorized by G.S. 15A-803 in connection with material witness proceedings.

(7) The common-law writ of capias has heretofore been issuable.

(8) When a defendant fails to appear as required in a show cause order issued in a criminal proceeding.

(9) It is authorized by G.S. 5A-16 in connection with contempt proceedings.

(c) Statement of Cause and Order; Copy of Indictment. -

(1) The process must state the cause for its issuance and order an officer described in G.S. 15A-301(b) to take the person named therein into custody and bring him before the court. If the defendant is to be held without bail, the order must so provide.

(2) When the order is issued pursuant to subdivision (b)(1), a copy of the bill of indictment must be attached to each copy of the order for arrest.

(d) Who May Issue. - An order for arrest, valid throughout the State, may be issued by any person authorized to issue warrants for arrest. (1973, c. 1286, s. 1; 1975, c. 166, s. 6; 1977, c. 711, s. 21; 2003-15, s. 2.)

Article 18.

§§ 15A-306 through 15A-353. Reserved for future codification purposes.

Article 19.

§§ 15A-354 through 15A-400. Reserved for future codification purposes.

SUBCHAPTER IV. ARREST.

Article 20.

Arrest.

§ 15A-401. Arrest by law-enforcement officer.

(a) Arrest by Officer Pursuant to a Warrant. -

(1) Warrant in Possession of Officer. - An officer having a warrant for arrest in his possession may arrest the person named or described therein at any time and at any place within the officer's territorial jurisdiction.

(2) Warrant Not in Possession of Officer. - An officer who has knowledge that a warrant for arrest has been issued and has not been executed, but who does not have the warrant in his possession, may arrest the person named therein at any time. The officer must inform the person arrested that the warrant has been issued and serve the warrant upon him as soon as possible. This subdivision applies even though the arrest process has been returned to the clerk under G.S. 15A-301.

(b) Arrest by Officer Without a Warrant. -

(1) Offense in Presence of Officer. - An officer may arrest without a warrant any person who the officer has probable cause to believe has committed a criminal offense, or has violated a pretrial release order entered under G.S. 15A-534 or G.S. 15A-534.1(a)(2), in the officer's presence.

(2) Offense Out of Presence of Officer. - An officer may arrest without a warrant any person who the officer has probable cause to believe:

a. Has committed a felony; or

b. Has committed a misdemeanor, and:

1. Will not be apprehended unless immediately arrested, or

2. May cause physical injury to himself or others, or damage to property unless immediately arrested; or

c. Has committed a misdemeanor under G.S. 14-72.1, 14-134.3, 20-138.1, or 20-138.2; or

d. Has committed a misdemeanor under G.S. 14-33(a), 14-33(c)(1), 14-33(c)(2), or 14-34 when the offense was committed by a person with whom the alleged victim has a personal relationship as defined in G.S. 50B-1; or

e. Has committed a misdemeanor under G.S. 50B-4.1(a); or

f. Has violated a pretrial release order entered under G.S. 15A-534 or G.S. 15A-534.1(a)(2).

(3) Repealed by Session Laws 1991, c. 150.

(4) A law enforcement officer may detain an individual arrested for violation of an order limiting freedom of movement or access issued pursuant to G.S. 130A-475 or G.S. 130A-145 in the area designated by the State Health Director or local health director pursuant to such order. The person may be detained in such area until the initial appearance before a judicial official pursuant to G.S. 15A-511 and G.S. 15A-534.5.

(c) How Arrest Made. -

(1) An arrest is complete when:

a. The person submits to the control of the arresting officer who has indicated his intention to arrest, or

b. The arresting officer, with intent to make an arrest, takes a person into custody by the use of physical force.

(2) Upon making an arrest, a law-enforcement officer must:

a. Identify himself as a law-enforcement officer unless his identity is otherwise apparent,

b. Inform the arrested person that he is under arrest, and

c. As promptly as is reasonable under the circumstances, inform the arrested person of the cause of the arrest, unless the cause appears to be evident.

(d) Use of Force in Arrest. -

(1) Subject to the provisions of subdivision (2), a law-enforcement officer is justified in using force upon another person when and to the extent that he reasonably believes it necessary:

a. To prevent the escape from custody or to effect an arrest of a person who he reasonably believes has committed a criminal offense, unless he knows that the arrest is unauthorized; or

b. To defend himself or a third person from what he reasonably believes to be the use or imminent use of physical force while effecting or attempting to effect an arrest or while preventing or attempting to prevent an escape.

(2) A law-enforcement officer is justified in using deadly physical force upon another person for a purpose specified in subdivision (1) of this subsection only when it is or appears to be reasonably necessary thereby:

a. To defend himself or a third person from what he reasonably believes to be the use or imminent use of deadly physical force;

b. To effect an arrest or to prevent the escape from custody of a person who he reasonably believes is attempting to escape by means of a deadly weapon, or who by his conduct or any other means indicates that he presents an imminent threat of death or serious physical injury to others unless apprehended without delay; or

c. To prevent the escape of a person from custody imposed upon him as a result of conviction for a felony.

Nothing in this subdivision constitutes justification for willful, malicious or criminally negligent conduct by any person which injures or endangers any person or property, nor shall it be construed to excuse or justify the use of unreasonable or excessive force.

(e) Entry on Private Premises or Vehicle; Use of Force. -

(1) A law-enforcement officer may enter private premises or a vehicle to effect an arrest when:

a. The officer has in his possession a warrant or order or a copy of the warrant or order for the arrest of a person, provided that an officer may utilize a copy of a warrant or order only if the original warrant or order is in the possession of a member of a law enforcement agency located in the county where the officer is employed and the officer verifies with the agency that the warrant is current and valid; or the officer is authorized to arrest a person without a warrant or order having been issued,

b. The officer has reasonable cause to believe the person to be arrested is present, and

c. The officer has given, or made reasonable effort to give, notice of his authority and purpose to an occupant thereof, unless there is reasonable cause to believe that the giving of such notice would present a clear danger to human life.

(2) The law-enforcement officer may use force to enter the premises or vehicle if he reasonably believes that admittance is being denied or unreasonably delayed, or if he is authorized under subsection (e)(1)c to enter without giving notice of his authority and purpose.

(f) Use of Deadly Weapon or Deadly Force to Resist Arrest. -

(1) A person is not justified in using a deadly weapon or deadly force to resist an arrest by a law-enforcement officer using reasonable force, when the person knows or has reason to know that the officer is a law-enforcement officer and that the officer is effecting or attempting to effect an arrest.

(2) The fact that the arrest was not authorized under this section is no defense to an otherwise valid criminal charge arising out of the use of such deadly weapon or deadly force.

(3) Nothing contained in this subsection (f) shall be construed to excuse or justify the unreasonable or excessive force by an officer in effecting an arrest. Nothing contained in this subsection (f) shall be construed to bar or limit any civil action arising out of an arrest not authorized by this Article.

(g) Care of minor children. - When a law enforcement officer arrests an adult who is supervising minor children who are present at the time of the arrest, the minor children must be placed with a responsible adult approved by a parent or guardian of the minor children. If it is not possible to place the minor children with a responsible adult approved by a parent or guardian within a reasonable period of time, the law enforcement officer shall contact the county department of social services. (1868-9, c. 178, subch. 1, ss. 3, 5; Code, ss. 1126, 1128; Rev., ss. 3178, 3180; C.S., ss. 4544, 4546; 1955, c. 58; 1973, c. 1286, s. 1; 1979, c. 561, s. 3; c. 725, s. 4; 1983, c. 762, s. 1; 1985, c. 548; 1991, c. 150, s. 1; 1995, c. 506, s. 10; 1997-456, s. 3; 1999-23, s. 7; 1999-399, s. 1; 2002-179, s. 14; 2004-186, s. 13.1; 2009-544, s. 2; 2011-245, s. 1.)

§ 15A-402. Territorial jurisdiction of officers to make arrests.

(a) Territorial Jurisdiction of State Officers. - Law-enforcement officers of the State of North Carolina may arrest persons at any place within the State.

(b) Territorial Jurisdiction of County and City Officers. - Law-enforcement officers of cities and counties may arrest persons within their particular cities or counties and on any property and rights-of-way owned by the city or county outside its limits.

(c) City Officers, Outside Territory. - Law-enforcement officers of cities may arrest persons at any point which is one mile or less from the nearest point in the boundary of such city. Law enforcement officers of cities may transport a person in custody to or from any place within the State for the purpose of that person attending criminal court proceedings. While engaged in the transportation of persons for the purpose of attending criminal court proceedings, law enforcement officers of cities may arrest persons at any place within the State for offenses occurring in connection with and incident to the transportation of persons in custody.

(d) County and City Officers, Immediate and Continuous Flight. - Law-enforcement officers of cities and counties may arrest persons outside the territory described in subsections (b) and (c) when the person arrested has committed a criminal offense within that territory, for which the officer could have arrested the person within that territory, and the arrest is made during such person's immediate and continuous flight from that territory.

(e) County Officers, Outside Territory, for Felonies. - Law-enforcement officers of counties may arrest persons at any place in the State of North Carolina when the arrest is based upon a felony committed within the territory described in subsection (b). For purposes of this subsection, law enforcement officers of counties shall include all officers of consolidated county-city law enforcement agencies.

(f) Campus Police Officers, Immediate and Continuous Flight. - A campus police officer: (i) appointed by a campus law-enforcement agency established pursuant to G.S. 116-40.5(a); (ii) appointed by a campus law enforcement agency established under G.S. 115D-21.1(a); or (iii) commissioned by the Attorney General pursuant to Chapter 74E or Chapter 74G of the General Statutes and employed by a college or university which is licensed, or exempted from licensure, by G.S. 116-15 may arrest a person outside his territorial jurisdiction when the person arrested has committed a criminal offense within the territorial jurisdiction, for which the officer could have arrested the person within that territory, and the arrest is made during such person's immediate and continuous flight from that territory. (1935, c. 204; 1973, c. 1286, s. 1; 1987, c.

671, s. 3; 1989, c. 518, s. 4; 1991 (Reg. Sess., 1992), c. 1043, s. 3; 1995, c. 206, s. 1; 1999-68, s. 2; 2005-231, s. 7; 2007-45, s. 1.)

§ 15A-403. Arrest by officers from other states.

(a)   Any law-enforcement officer of a state contiguous to the State of North Carolina who enters this State in fresh pursuit and continues within this State in such fresh pursuit of a person who is in immediate and continuous flight from the commission of a criminal offense, has the same authority to arrest and hold in custody such person on the ground that he has committed a criminal offense in another state which is a criminal offense under the laws of the State of North Carolina as law-enforcement officers of this State have to arrest and hold in custody a person on the ground that he has committed a criminal offense in this State.

(b)   If an arrest is made in this State by a law-enforcement officer of another state in accordance with the provisions of subsection (a), he must, without unnecessary delay, take the person arrested before a judicial official of this State, who must conduct a hearing for the purpose of determining the lawfulness of the arrest. If the judicial official determines that the arrest was lawful, he must commit the person arrested to await a reasonable time for the issuance of an extradition warrant by the Governor of this State or release him pursuant to Article 26 of this Chapter, Bail. If the judicial official determines that the arrest was unlawful, he must discharge the person arrested.

(c)   This section applies only to law-enforcement officers of a state which by its laws has made similar provision for the arrest and custody of persons closely pursued within its territory. (1973, c. 1286, s. 1.)

§ 15A-404. Detention of offenders by private persons.

(a)   No Arrest; Detention Permitted. - No private person may arrest another person except as provided in G.S. 15A-405. A private person may detain another person as provided in this section.

(b) When Detention Permitted. - A private person may detain another person when he has probable cause to believe that the person detained has committed in his presence:

(1) A felony,

(2) A breach of the peace,

(3) A crime involving physical injury to another person, or

(4) A crime involving theft or destruction of property.

(c) Manner of Detention. - The detention must be in a reasonable manner considering the offense involved and the circumstances of the detention.

(d) Period of Detention. - The detention may be no longer than the time required for the earliest of the following:

(1) The determination that no offense has been committed.

(2) Surrender of the person detained to a law-enforcement officer as provided in subsection (e).

(e) Surrender to Officer. - A private person who detains another must immediately notify a law-enforcement officer and must, unless he releases the person earlier as required by subsection (d), surrender the person detained to the law-enforcement officer. (1973, c. 1286, s. 1.)

§ 15A-405. Assistance to law-enforcement officers by private persons to effect arrest or prevent escape; benefits for private persons.

(a) Assistance upon Request; Authority. - Private persons may assist law-enforcement officers in effecting arrests and preventing escapes from custody when requested to do so by the officer. When so requested, a private person has the same authority to effect an arrest or prevent escape from custody as the officer making the request. He does not incur civil or criminal liability for an invalid arrest unless he knows the arrest to be invalid. Nothing in this subsection constitutes justification for willful, malicious or criminally negligent conduct by such person which injures or endangers any person or property, nor shall it be construed to excuse or justify the use of unreasonable or excessive force.

(b) Benefits to Private Persons. - A private person assisting a law-enforcement officer pursuant to subsection (a) is:

(1) Repealed by Session Laws 1989, c. 290, s. 1.

(2) Entitled to the same benefits as a "law-enforcement officer" as that term is defined in G.S. 143-166.2(d) (Law-Enforcement Officers', Firemen's and Rescue Squad Workers' Death Benefit Act); and

(3) To be treated as an employee of the employer of the law-enforcement officer within the meaning of G.S. 97-2(2) (Workers' Compensation Act).

The Governor and the Council of State are authorized to allocate funds from the Contingency and Emergency Fund for the payment of benefits under subdivision (3) when no other source is available for the payment of such benefits and when they determine that such allocation is necessary and appropriate. (1868-9, c. 178, subch. 1, s. 2; Code, s. 1125; Rev., s. 3181; C.S., s. 4547; 1973, c. 1286, s. 1; 1979, c. 714, s. 2; 1989, c. 290, s. 1.)

§ 15A-406. Assistance by federal officers.

(a) For purposes of this section, "federal law enforcement officer" means any of the following persons who are employed as full-time law enforcement officers by the federal government and who are authorized to carry firearms in the performance of their duties:

(1) United States Secret Service special agents;

(2) Federal Bureau of Investigation special agents;

(3) Bureau of Alcohol, Tobacco and Firearms special agents;

(4) United States Naval Investigative Service special agents;

(5) Drug Enforcement Administration special agents;

(6)   United States Customs Service officers;

(7)   United States Postal Service inspectors;

(8)   Internal Revenue Service special agents;

(9)   United States Marshals Service marshals and deputies;

(10)   United States Forest Service officers;

(11)   National Park Service officers;

(12)   United States Fish and Wildlife Service officers;

(13)   Immigration and Naturalization Service officers;

(14)   Tennessee Valley Authority officers; and

(15)   Veterans Administration police officers.

(b)   A federal law enforcement officer is authorized under the following circumstances to enforce criminal laws anywhere within the State:

(1)   If the federal law enforcement officer is asked by the head of a state or local law enforcement agency, or his designee, to provide temporary assistance and the request is within the scope of the state or local law enforcement agency's subject matter and territorial jurisdiction; or

(2)   If the federal law enforcement officer is asked by a state or local law enforcement officer to provide temporary assistance when at the time of the request the state or local law enforcement officer is acting within the scope of his subject matter and territorial jurisdiction.

(c)   A federal law enforcement officer shall have the same powers as those invested by statute or common law in a North Carolina law enforcement officer, and shall have the same legal immunity from personal civil liability as a North Carolina law enforcement officer, while acting pursuant to this section.

(d)   A federal law enforcement officer who acts pursuant to this section shall not be considered an officer, employee, or agent of any state or local law enforcement agency.

(e) For purposes of the Federal Tort Claims Act, a federal law enforcement officer acts within the scope of his office or employment while acting pursuant to this section.

(f) Nothing in this section shall be construed to expand the authority of federal officers to initiate or conduct an independent investigation into violation of North Carolina law. (1991, c. 262, s. 1; 1991 (Reg. Sess., 1992), c. 1030, s. 8; 1993 (Reg. Sess., 1994), c. 571, s. 1; 2001-257, s. 1; 2003-36, s. 1.)

§§ 15A-407 through 15A-409. Reserved for future codification purposes.

Article 21.

§§ 15A-410 through 15A-453. Reserved for future codification purposes.

Article 22.

§§ 15A-454 through 15A-500: Reserved for future codification purposes.

SUBCHAPTER V. CUSTODY.

Article 23.

Police Processing and Duties upon Arrest.

§ 15A-501. Police processing and duties upon arrest generally.

Upon the arrest of a person, with or without a warrant, but not necessarily in the order hereinafter listed, a law-enforcement officer:

(1) Must inform the person arrested of the charge against him or the cause for his arrest.

(2) Must, with respect to any person arrested without a warrant and, for purpose of setting bail, with respect to any person arrested upon a warrant or order for arrest, take the person arrested before a judicial official without unnecessary delay.

(3)   May, prior to taking the person before a judicial official, take the person arrested to some other place if the person so requests.

(4)   May, prior to taking the person before a judicial official, take the person arrested to some other place if such action is reasonably necessary for the purpose of having that person identified.

(5)   Must without unnecessary delay advise the person arrested of his right to communicate with counsel and friends and must allow him reasonable time and reasonable opportunity to do so.

(6)   Must make available to the State on a timely basis all materials and information acquired in the course of all felony investigations. This responsibility is a continuing affirmative duty. (1868-9, c. 178, subch. 1, s. 7; Code, s. 1130; Rev., s. 3182; C.S., s. 4548; 1937, c. 257, ss. 1, 2; 1955, c. 889; 1969, c. 296; 1973, c. 1286, s. 1; 1975, c. 166, ss. 7, 8; 2004-154, s. 11.)

§ 15A-502. Photographs and fingerprints.

(a)   A person charged with the commission of a felony or a misdemeanor may be photographed and his fingerprints may be taken for law-enforcement records only when he has been:

(1)   Arrested or committed to a detention facility, or

(2)   Committed to imprisonment upon conviction of a crime, or

(3)   Convicted of a felony.

(a1)   It shall be the duty of the arresting law-enforcement agency to cause a person charged with the commission of a felony to be fingerprinted and to forward those fingerprints to the State Bureau of Investigation.

(a2)   If the person cannot be identified by a valid form of identification, it shall be the duty of the arresting law-enforcement agency to cause a person charged with the commission of:

(1)   Any offense involving impaired driving, as defined in G.S. 20-4.01(24a), or

(2)   Driving while license revoked if the revocation is for an Impaired Driving License Revocation as defined in G.S. 20-28.2

to be fingerprinted and photographed.

(b)   This section does not authorize the taking of photographs or fingerprints when the offense charged is a Class 2 or 3 misdemeanor under Chapter 20 of the General Statutes, "Motor Vehicles." Notwithstanding the prohibition in this subsection, a photograph may be taken of a person who operates a motor vehicle on a street or highway if:

(1)   The person is cited by a law enforcement officer for a motor vehicle moving violation, and

(2)   The person does not produce a valid drivers license upon the request of a law enforcement officer, and

(3)   The law enforcement officer has a reasonable suspicion concerning the true identity of the person.

As used in this subsection, the phrase "motor vehicle moving violation" does not include the offenses listed in the third paragraph of G.S. 20-16(c) for which no points are assessed, nor does it include equipment violations specified in Part 9 of Article 3 of Chapter 20 of the General Statutes.

(b1)   Any photograph authorized by subsection (b) of this section and taken by a law enforcement officer or agency:

(1)   Shall only be taken of the operator of the motor vehicle, and only from the neck up.

(2)   Shall be taken at either the location where the citation is issued, or at the jail if an arrest is made.

(3)   Shall be retained by the law enforcement officer or agency until the final disposition of the case.

(4)   Shall not be used for any purpose other than to confirm the identity of the alleged offender.

(5) Shall be destroyed by the law enforcement officer or agency upon a final disposition of the charge.

(c) This section does not authorize the taking of photographs or fingerprints of a juvenile alleged to be delinquent except under Article 21 of Chapter 7B of the General Statutes.

(d) This section does not prevent the taking of photographs, moving pictures, video or sound recordings, fingerprints, or the like to show a condition of intoxication or for other evidentiary use.

(e) Fingerprints or photographs taken pursuant to subsection (a), (a1), or (a2) of this section may be forwarded to the State Bureau of Investigation, the Federal Bureau of Investigation, or other law-enforcement agencies. (1973, c. 1286, s. 1; 1977, c. 711, s. 22; 1979, c. 850; 1981, c. 862, s. 3; 1993, c. 539, s. 298; 1994, Ex. Sess., c. 24, s. 14(c); 1996, 2nd Ex. Sess., c. 18, s. 23.2(b); 1998-202, s. 13(f); 2007-370, s. 1; 2007-534, s. 1.)

§ 15A-502.1. DNA sample upon arrest.

A DNA sample shall be obtained from any person arrested for an offense designated under G.S. 15A-266.3A, in accordance with the provisions contained in Article 13 of Chapter 15A of the General Statutes. (2010-94, s. 12.)

§ 15A-503. Police assistance to persons arrested while unconscious or semiconscious.

(a) Whenever a law-enforcement officer arrests a person who is unconscious, semiconscious, or otherwise apparently suffering from some disabling condition, and who is unable to provide information on the causes of the condition, the officer should make a reasonable effort to determine if the person arrested is wearing a bracelet or necklace containing the Medic Alert Foundation's emergency alert symbol to indicate that the person suffers from diabetes, epilepsy, a cardiac condition, or any other form of illness which would cause a loss of consciousness. If such a symbol is found indicating that the person being arrested suffers from one of those conditions, the officer must make a reasonable effort to have appropriate medical care provided.

(b) Failure of a law-enforcement officer to make a reasonable effort to discover an emergency alert symbol, as required by this section, does not by itself establish negligence of the officer, but may be considered along with other evidence to determine if the officer took reasonable precautions to ascertain the emergency medical needs of the person in his custody.

(c) A person who is provided medical care under the provisions of this section is liable for the reasonable costs of that care unless he is indigent.

(d) Repealed by Session Laws 1975, c. 818, s. 1. (1975, c. 306, s. 1; c. 818, s. 1.)

§ 15A-504. Return of released person.

(a) Upon a magistrate's finding under G.S. 15A-511(c)(2) of no probable cause for a warrantless arrest, a law-enforcement officer may return the person previously arrested and any other person accompanying him to the scene of the arrest.

(b) No officer acting pursuant to this section may be held to answer in any civil or criminal action for injury to any person or damage to any property when damage results, whether directly or indirectly, from the actions of the person so released or transported.

(c) Nothing in this section shall be construed to supersede the provisions of G.S. 122C-301. (1981, c. 928; 1987, c. 282, s. 3.)

§ 15A-505. Notification of parent and school.

(a) A law enforcement officer who charges a minor with a criminal offense shall notify the minor's parent or guardian of the charge, as soon as practicable, in person or by telephone. If the minor is taken into custody, the law enforcement officer or the officer's immediate superior shall notify a parent or guardian in writing that the minor is in custody within 24 hours of the minor's arrest. If the parent or guardian of the minor cannot be found, then the officer or the officer's immediate superior shall notify the minor's next-of-kin of the minor's arrest as soon as practicable.

(b)   The notification provided for by subsection (a) of this section shall not be required if:

(1)   The minor is emancipated;

(2)   The minor is not taken into custody and has been charged with a motor vehicle moving violation for which three or fewer points are assessed under G.S. 20-16(c), except an offense involving impaired driving, as defined in G.S. 20-4.01(24a); or

(3)   The minor has been charged with a motor vehicle offense that is not a moving violation.

(c)   A law enforcement officer who charges a person with a criminal offense that is a felony, except for a criminal offense under Chapter 20 of the General Statutes, shall notify the principal of any school the person attends of the charge as soon as practicable but at least within five days. The notification may be made in person or by telephone. If the person is taken into custody, the law enforcement officer or the officer's immediate supervisor shall notify the principal of any school the person attends. This notification shall be in writing and shall be made within five days of the person's arrest. If a principal receives notification under this subsection, a representative from the district attorney's office shall notify that principal of the final disposition at the trial court level. This notification shall be in writing and shall be made within five days of the disposition. As used in this subsection, the term "school" means any public or private school in the State that is authorized under Chapter 115C of the General Statutes. (1983, c. 681, s. 1; 1994, Ex. Sess., c. 26, s. 1; 1997-443, s. 8.29(g).)

§§ 15A-506 through 15A-510: Reserved for future codification purposes.

Article 24.

Initial Appearance.

§ 15A-511. Initial appearance.

(a)   Appearance before Magistrate. -

(1) A law-enforcement officer making an arrest with or without a warrant must take the arrested person without unnecessary delay before a magistrate as provided in G.S. 15A-501.

(2) The magistrate must proceed in accordance with this section, except in those cases in which he has the power to determine the matter pursuant to G.S. 7A-273. In those cases, if the arrest has been without a warrant, the magistrate must prepare a magistrate's order containing a statement of the crime with which the defendant is charged.

(3) If the defendant brought before a magistrate is so unruly as to disrupt and impede the proceedings, becomes unconscious, is grossly intoxicated, or is otherwise unable to understand the procedural rights afforded him by the initial appearance, upon order of the magistrate he may be confined or otherwise secured. If this is done, the magistrate's order must provide for an initial appearance within a reasonable time so as to make certain that the defendant has an opportunity to exercise his rights under this Chapter.

(a1) A proceeding for initial appearance in a noncapital case under this section may be conducted by an audio and video transmission between the magistrate or other authorized judicial official and the defendant in which the parties can see and hear each other. If the defendant has counsel, the defendant shall be allowed to communicate fully and confidentially with his attorney during the proceeding. Prior to the use of audio and video transmission pursuant to this subsection, the procedures and type of equipment for audio and video transmission shall be submitted to the Administrative Office of the Courts by the senior regular resident superior court judge and the chief district court judge for a judicial district or set of districts and approved by the Administrative Office of the Courts.

(b) Statement by the Magistrate. - The magistrate must inform the defendant of:

(1) The charges against him;

(2) His right to communicate with counsel and friends; and

(3) The general circumstances under which he may secure release under the provisions of Article 26, Bail.

(c) Procedure When Arrest Is without Warrant; Magistrate's Order. - If the person has been arrested, for a crime, without a warrant:

(1) The magistrate must determine whether there is probable cause to believe that a crime has been committed and that the person arrested committed it, and in the manner provided by G.S. 15A-304(d).

(2) If the magistrate determines that there is no probable cause the person must be released.

(3) If the magistrate determines that there is probable cause, he must issue a magistrate's order:

a. Containing a statement of the crime of which the person is accused in the same manner as is provided in G.S. 15A-304(c) for a warrant for arrest, and

b. Containing a finding that the defendant has been arrested without a warrant and that there is probable cause for his detention.

(4) Following the issuance of the magistrate's order, the magistrate must proceed in accordance with subsection (e) and must file the order with any supporting affidavits and records in the office of the clerk.

(d) Procedure When Arrest Is Pursuant to Warrant. - If the arrest is made pursuant to a warrant, the magistrate must proceed in accordance with subsection (e).

(e) Commitment or Bail. - If the person arrested is not released pursuant to subsection (c), the magistrate must release him in accordance with Article 26 of this Chapter, Bail, or commit him to an appropriate detention facility pursuant to G.S. 15A-521 pending further proceedings in the case.

(f) Powers Not Limited to Magistrate. - Any judge, justice, or clerk of the General Court of Justice may also conduct an initial appearance as provided in this section. (1868-9, c. 178, subch. 1, s. 7; Code, s. 1130; Rev., s. 3182; C.S., s. 4548; 1973, c. 1286, s. 1; 1975, c. 166, ss. 9-11; 1975, 2nd Sess., c. 983, s. 141; 1997-268, s. 1.)

§§ 15A-512 through 15A-520. Reserved for future codification purposes.

Article 25.

Commitment.

§ 15A-521. Commitment to detention facility pending trial.

(a) Commitment. - Every person charged with a crime and held in custody who has not been released pursuant to Article 26 of this Chapter, Bail, must be committed by a written order of the judicial official who conducted the initial appearance as provided in Article 24 to an appropriate detention facility as provided in this section.

(b) Order of Commitment; Modification. - The order of commitment must:

(1) State the name of the person charged or identify him if his name cannot be ascertained.

(2) Specify the offense charged.

(3) Designate the place of confinement.

(4) If release is authorized pursuant to Article 26 of this Chapter, Bail, state the conditions of release. If a separate order stating the conditions has been entered, the commitment may make reference to that order, a copy of which must be attached to the commitment.

(5) Subject to the provisions of subdivision (4), direct, as appropriate, that the defendant be:

a. Produced before a district court judge pursuant to Article 29 of this Chapter, First Appearance before District Court Judge,

b. Produced before a district court judge for a probable cause hearing as provided in Article 30 of this Chapter, Probable-Cause Hearing,

c. Produced for trial in the district or superior court, or

d. Held for other specified purposes.

(6) State the name and office of the judicial official making the order and be signed by him.

The order of commitment may be modified or continued by the same or another judicial official by supplemental order.

(c) Copies and Use of Order, Receipt of Prisoner. -

(1) The order of commitment must be delivered to a law-enforcement officer, who must deliver the order and the prisoner to the detention facility named therein.

(2) The jailer must receive the prisoner and the order of commitment, and note on the order of commitment the time and date of receipt. As used in this subdivision, "jailer" includes any person having control of a detention facility.

(3) Upon releasing the prisoner pursuant to the terms of the order, or upon delivering the prisoner to the court, the jailer must note the time and date on the order and return it to the clerk.

(4) Repealed by Session Laws 1975, 2nd Sess., c. 983, s. 142.

(d) Commitment of Witnesses. - If a court directs detention of a material witness pursuant to G.S. 15A-803, the court must enter an order in the manner provided in this section, except that the order must:

(1) State the reason for the detention in lieu of the description of the offense charged, and

(2) Direct that the witness be brought before the appropriate court when his testimony is required. (1868-9, c. 178, subch. 3, ss. 24, 32; Code, ss. 1155, 1163; Rev., ss. 3230, 3232; C.S., ss. 4597, 4599; 1973, c. 1286, s. 1; 1975, 2nd Sess., c. 983, s. 142.)

§§ 15A-522 through 15A-530. Reserved for future codification purposes.

Article 26.

Bail.

Part 1. General Provisions.

§ 15A-531. Definitions.

As used in this Article the following definitions apply unless the context clearly requires otherwise:

(1) "Accommodation bondsman" means a natural person who has reached the age of 18 years and is a bona fide resident of this State and who, aside from love and affection and release of the person concerned, receives no consideration for action as surety and who endorses the bail bond after providing satisfactory evidences of ownership, value, and marketability of real or personal property to the extent necessary to reasonably satisfy the official taking bond that such real or personal property will in all respects be sufficient to assure that the full principal sum of the bond will be realized in the event of breach of the conditions thereof. "Consideration" as used in this subdivision does not include the legal rights of a surety against a defendant by reason of breach of the conditions of a bail bond nor does it include collateral furnished to and securing the surety so long as the value of the surety's rights in the collateral do not exceed the defendant's liability to the surety by reason of a breach in the conditions of said bail bond.

(2) "Address of record" means:

a. For a defendant or an accommodation bondsman, the address entered on the bail bond under G.S. 15A-544.2, or any later address filed by that person with the clerk of superior court.

b. For an insurance company, the address of the insurance company as it appears on the power of appointment of the company's bail agent registered with the clerk of superior court under G.S. 58-71-140.

c. For a bail agent, the address shown on the bail agent's license from the Department of Insurance registered with the clerk of superior court under G.S. 58-71-140.

d. For a professional bondsman, the address shown on that bondsman's license from the Department of Insurance, as registered with the clerk of superior court under G.S. 58-71-140.

(3) "Bail agent" means any person who is licensed by the Commissioner as a surety bondsman under Article 71 of Chapter 58 of the General Statutes, is appointed by an insurance company by power of attorney to execute or countersign bail bonds for the insurance company in connection with judicial proceedings, and receives or is promised consideration for doing so.

(4) "Bail bond" means an undertaking by the defendant to appear in court as required upon penalty of forfeiting bail to the State in a stated amount. Bail bonds include an unsecured appearance bond, an appearance bond secured by a cash deposit of the full amount of the bond, an appearance bond secured by a mortgage under G.S. 58-74-5, and an appearance bond secured by at least one solvent surety. A bail bond signed by any surety, as defined in G.S. 15A-531(8)a. and b., is considered the same as a cash deposit for all purposes in this Article. Cash bonds set in child support contempt proceedings shall not be satisfied in any manner other than the deposit of cash.

(5) "Defendant" means a person obligated to appear in court as required upon penalty of forfeiting bail under a bail bond.

(5a) House arrest with electronic monitoring. - Pretrial release in which the offender is required to remain at his or her residence unless the court authorizes the offender to leave for the purpose of employment, counseling, a course of study, or vocational training. The offender shall be required to wear a device which permits the supervising agency to electronically monitor the offender's compliance with the condition.

(6) "Insurance company" means any domestic, foreign, or alien surety company which has qualified under Chapter 58 of the General Statutes generally to transact surety business and specifically to transact bail bond business in this State.

(7) "Professional bondsman" means any person who is approved and licensed by the Commissioner of Insurance under Article 71 of Chapter 58 of the General Statutes and who pledges cash or approved securities with the Commissioner as security for bail bonds written in connection with a judicial proceeding and receives or is promised money or other things of value therefor.

(8) "Surety" means:

    a. The insurance company, when a bail bond is executed by a bail agent on behalf of an insurance company.

b. The professional bondsman, when a bail bond is executed by a professional bondsman or by a runner on behalf of a professional bondsman.

c. The accommodation bondsman, when a bail bond is executed by an accommodation bondsman. (1973, c. 1286, s. 1; 1975, c. 166, s. 12; 1995, c. 290, s. 1; c. 503, s. 1; 2000-133, s. 1; 2009-547, s. 2; 2013-139, s. 1.)

§ 15A-532. Persons authorized to determine conditions for release; use of two-way audio and video transmission.

(a) Judicial officials may determine conditions for release of persons brought before them or as provided in subsection (b) of this section, in accordance with this Article.

(b) Any proceeding under this Article to determine, modify, or revoke conditions of pretrial release in a noncapital case may be conducted by an audio and video transmission between the judicial official and the defendant in which the parties can see and hear each other. If the defendant has counsel, the defendant shall be allowed to communicate fully and confidentially with his attorney during the proceeding. Upon motion of the defendant, the court may not use an audio and video transmission.

(c) Prior to the use of audio and video transmission pursuant to subsection (b) of this section, the procedures and type of equipment for audio and video transmission shall be submitted to the Administrative Office of the Courts by the senior regular resident superior court judge for a judicial district or set of districts and approved by the Administrative Office of the Courts. (1973, c. 1286, s. 1; 1993, c. 30, s. 1.)

§ 15A-533. Right to pretrial release in capital and noncapital cases.

(a) A defendant charged with any crime, whether capital or noncapital, who is alleged to have committed this crime while still residing in or subsequent to his escape or during an unauthorized absence from involuntary commitment in a mental health facility designated or licensed by the Department of Health and Human Services, and whose commitment is determined to be still valid by the judge or judicial officer authorized to determine pretrial release to be valid, has no right to pretrial release. In lieu of pretrial release, however, the individual shall be returned to the treatment facility in which he was residing at the time of the alleged crime or from which he escaped or absented himself for continuation of his treatment pending the additional proceedings on the criminal offense.

(b) A defendant charged with a noncapital offense must have conditions of pretrial release determined, in accordance with G.S. 15A-534.

(c) A judge may determine in his discretion whether a defendant charged with a capital offense may be released before trial. If he determines release is warranted, the judge must authorize release of the defendant in accordance with G.S. 15A-534.

(d) There shall be a rebuttable presumption that no condition of release will reasonably assure the appearance of the person as required and the safety of the community if a judicial official finds the following:

(1) There is reasonable cause to believe that the person committed an offense involving trafficking in a controlled substance;

(2) The drug trafficking offense was committed while the person was on pretrial release for another offense; and

(3) The person has been previously convicted of a Class A through E felony or an offense involving trafficking in a controlled substance and not more than five years has elapsed since the date of conviction or the person's release from prison for the offense, whichever is later.

(e) There shall be a rebuttable presumption that no condition of release will reasonably assure the appearance of the person as required and the safety of the community, if a judicial official finds the following:

(1) There is reasonable cause to believe that the person committed an offense for the benefit of, at the direction of, or in association with, any criminal street gang, as defined in G.S. 14-50.16;

(2) The offense described in subdivision (1) of this subsection was committed while the person was on pretrial release for another offense; and

(3) The person has been previously convicted of an offense described in G.S. 14-50.16 through G.S. 14-50.20, and not more than five years has elapsed

since the date of conviction or the person's release for the offense, whichever is later.

(f)   There shall be a rebuttable presumption that no condition of release will reasonably assure the appearance of the person as required and the safety of the community, if a judicial official finds there is reasonable cause to believe that the person committed a felony or Class A1 misdemeanor offense involving the illegal use, possession, or discharge of a firearm; and the judicial official also finds any of the following:

(1)   The offense was committed while the person was on pretrial release for another felony or Class A1 misdemeanor offense involving the illegal use, possession, or discharge of a firearm.

(2)   The person has previously been convicted of a felony or Class A1 misdemeanor offense involving the illegal use, possession, or discharge of a firearm and not more than five years have elapsed since the date of conviction or the person's release for the offense, whichever is later.

(g)   Persons who are considered for bond under the provisions of subsections (d), (e), and (f) of this section may only be released by a district or superior court judge upon a finding that there is a reasonable assurance that the person will appear and release does not pose an unreasonable risk of harm to the community. (1973, c. 1286, s. 1; 1981, c. 936, s. 2; 1997-443, s. 11A.118(a); 1998-208, s. 1; 2008-214, s. 4; 2013-298, s. 1.)

§ 15A-534. Procedure for determining conditions of pretrial release.

(a)   In determining conditions of pretrial release a judicial official must impose at least one of the following conditions:

(1)   Release the defendant on his written promise to appear.

(2)   Release the defendant upon his execution of an unsecured appearance bond in an amount specified by the judicial official.

(3)   Place the defendant in the custody of a designated person or organization agreeing to supervise him.

(4) Require the execution of an appearance bond in a specified amount secured by a cash deposit of the full amount of the bond, by a mortgage pursuant to G.S. 58-74-5, or by at least one solvent surety.

(5) House arrest with electronic monitoring.

If condition (5) is imposed, the defendant must execute a secured appearance bond under subdivision (4) of this subsection. If condition (3) is imposed, however, the defendant may elect to execute an appearance bond under subdivision (4). If the defendant is required to provide fingerprints pursuant to G.S. 15A-502(a1) or (a2), or a DNA sample pursuant to G.S. 15A-266.3A or G.S. 15A-266.4, and (i) the fingerprints or DNA sample have not yet been taken or (ii) the defendant has refused to provide the fingerprints or DNA sample, the judicial official shall make the collection of the fingerprints or DNA sample a condition of pretrial release. The judicial official may also place restrictions on the travel, associations, conduct, or place of abode of the defendant as conditions of pretrial release. The judicial official may include as a condition of pretrial release that the defendant abstain from alcohol consumption, as verified by the use of a continuous alcohol monitoring system, of a type approved by the Division of Adult Correction of the Department of Public Safety, and that any violation of this condition be reported by the monitoring provider to the district attorney.

(b) The judicial official in granting pretrial release must impose condition (1), (2), or (3) in subsection (a) above unless he determines that such release will not reasonably assure the appearance of the defendant as required; will pose a danger of injury to any person; or is likely to result in destruction of evidence, subornation of perjury, or intimidation of potential witnesses. Upon making the determination, the judicial official must then impose condition (4) or (5) in subsection (a) above instead of condition (1), (2), or (3), and must record the reasons for so doing in writing to the extent provided in the policies or requirements issued by the senior resident superior court judge pursuant to G.S. 15A-535(a).

(c) In determining which conditions of release to impose, the judicial official must, on the basis of available information, take into account the nature and circumstances of the offense charged; the weight of the evidence against the defendant; the defendant's family ties, employment, financial resources, character, and mental condition; whether the defendant is intoxicated to such a degree that he would be endangered by being released without supervision; the length of his residence in the community; his record of convictions; his history of flight to avoid prosecution or failure to appear at court proceedings; and any other evidence relevant to the issue of pretrial release.

(d) The judicial official authorizing pretrial release under this section must issue an appropriate order containing a statement of the conditions imposed, if any; inform the defendant in writing of the penalties applicable to violations of the conditions of his release; and advise him that his arrest will be ordered immediately upon any violation. The order of release must be filed with the clerk and a copy given the defendant.

(d1) When conditions of pretrial release are being imposed on a defendant who has failed on one or more prior occasions to appear to answer one or more of the charges to which the conditions apply, the judicial official shall at a minimum impose the conditions of pretrial release that are recommended in any order for the arrest of the defendant that was issued for the defendant's most recent failure to appear. If no conditions are recommended in that order for arrest, the judicial official shall require the execution of a secured appearance bond in an amount at least double the amount of the most recent previous secured or unsecured bond for the charges or, if no bond has yet been required for the charges, in the amount of at least one thousand dollars ($1,000). The judicial official shall also impose such restrictions on the travel, associations, conduct, or place of abode of the defendant as will assure that the defendant will not again fail to appear. The judicial official shall indicate on the release order that the defendant was arrested or surrendered after failing to appear as required under a prior release order. If the information available to the judicial official indicates that the defendant has failed on two or more prior occasions to appear to answer the charges, the judicial official shall indicate that fact on the release order.

(d2) When conditions of pretrial release are being determined for a defendant who is charged with a felony offense and the defendant is currently on probation for a prior offense, a judicial official shall determine whether the defendant poses a danger to the public prior to imposing conditions of pretrial release and must record that determination in writing. This subsection shall apply to any judicial official authorized to determine or review the defendant's eligibility for release under any proceeding authorized by this Chapter.

(1) If the judicial official determines that the defendant poses a danger to the public, the judicial official must impose condition (4) or (5) in subsection (a) of this section instead of condition (1), (2), or (3).

(2) If the judicial official finds that the defendant does not pose a danger to the public, then conditions of pretrial release shall be imposed as otherwise provided in this Article.

(3) If there is insufficient information to determine whether the defendant poses a danger to the public, then the defendant shall be retained in custody until a determination of pretrial release conditions is made pursuant to this subdivision. The judicial official that orders that the defendant be retained in custody shall set forth, in writing, the following at the time that the order is entered:

a. The defendant is being held pursuant to this subdivision.

b. The basis for the judicial official's decision that additional information is needed to determine whether the defendant poses a danger to the public and the nature of the necessary information.

c. A date, within 96 hours of the time of arrest, when the defendant shall be brought before a judge for a first appearance pursuant to Article 29 of this Chapter. If the necessary information is provided to the court at any time prior to the first appearance, the first available judicial official shall set the conditions of pretrial release. The judge who reviews the defendant's eligibility for release at the first appearance shall determine the conditions of pretrial release as provided in this Article.

(d3) When conditions of pretrial release are being determined for a defendant who is charged with an offense and the defendant is currently on pretrial release for a prior offense, the judicial official shall require the execution of a secured appearance bond in an amount at least double the amount of the most recent previous secured or unsecured bond for the charges or, if no bond has yet been required for the charges, in the amount of at least one thousand dollars ($1,000).

(e) A magistrate or a clerk may modify his pretrial release order at any time prior to the first appearance before the district court judge. At or after such first appearance, except when the conditions of pretrial release have been reviewed by the superior court pursuant to G.S. 15A-539, a district court judge may modify a pretrial release order of the magistrate or clerk or any pretrial release order entered by him at any time prior to:

(1)   In a misdemeanor case tried in the district court, the noting of an appeal; and

(2)   In a case in the original trial jurisdiction of the superior court, the binding of the defendant over to superior court after the holding, or waiver, of a probable-cause hearing.

After a case is before the superior court, a superior court judge may modify the pretrial release order of a magistrate, clerk, or district court judge, or any such order entered by him, at any time prior to the time set out in G.S. 15A-536(a).

(f)   For good cause shown any judge may at any time revoke an order of pretrial release. Upon application of any defendant whose order of pretrial release has been revoked, the judge must set new conditions of pretrial release in accordance with this Article.

(g)   In imposing conditions of pretrial release and in modifying and revoking orders of release under this section, the judicial official must take into account all evidence available to him which he considers reliable and is not strictly bound by the rules of evidence applicable to criminal trials.

(h)   A bail bond posted pursuant to this section is effective and binding upon the obligor throughout all stages of the proceeding in the trial division of the General Court of Justice until the entry of judgment in the district court from which no appeal is taken or the entry of judgment in the superior court. The obligation of an obligor, however, is terminated at an earlier time if:

(1)   A judge authorized to do so releases the obligor from his bond; or

(2)   The principal is surrendered by a surety in accordance with G.S. 15A-540; or

(3)   The proceeding is terminated by voluntary dismissal by the State before forfeiture is ordered under G.S. 15A-544.3; or

(4)   Prayer for judgment has been continued indefinitely in the district court.

(i)   Repealed by Session Laws 2012-146, s. 1(b), effective December 1, 2012. (1973, c. 1286, s. 1; 1975, c. 166, s. 13; 1977, 2nd Sess., c. 1134, s. 5; 1987, c. 481, s. 1; 1989, c. 259; 2001-487, s. 46.5(b); 2009-412, s. 1; 2009-547, ss. 3, 4, 4.1; 2010-94, s. 12.1; 2010-96, s. 3; 2011-191, s. 5; 2012-146, s. 1(a), (b); 2013-298, s. 2.)

§ 15A-534.1. Crimes of domestic violence; bail and pretrial release.

(a) In all cases in which the defendant is charged with assault on, stalking, communicating a threat to, or committing a felony provided in Articles 7A, 8, 10, or 15 of Chapter 14 of the General Statutes upon a spouse or former spouse or a person with whom the defendant lives or has lived as if married, with domestic criminal trespass, or with violation of an order entered pursuant to Chapter 50B, Domestic Violence, of the General Statutes, the judicial official who determines the conditions of pretrial release shall be a judge. The judge shall direct a law enforcement officer or a district attorney to provide a criminal history report for the defendant and shall consider the criminal history when setting conditions of release. After setting conditions of release, the judge shall return the report to the providing agency or department. No judge shall unreasonably delay the determination of conditions of pretrial release for the purpose of reviewing the defendant's criminal history report. The following provisions shall apply in addition to the provisions of G.S. 15A-534:

(1) Upon a determination by the judge that the immediate release of the defendant will pose a danger of injury to the alleged victim or to any other person or is likely to result in intimidation of the alleged victim and upon a determination that the execution of an appearance bond as required by G.S. 15A-534 will not reasonably assure that such injury or intimidation will not occur, a judge may retain the defendant in custody for a reasonable period of time while determining the conditions of pretrial release.

(2) A judge may impose the following conditions on pretrial release:

a. That the defendant stay away from the home, school, business or place of employment of the alleged victim.

b. That the defendant refrain from assaulting, beating, molesting, or wounding the alleged victim.

c. That the defendant refrain from removing, damaging or injuring specifically identified property.

d. That the defendant may visit his or her child or children at times and places provided by the terms of any existing order entered by a judge.

e. That the defendant abstain from alcohol consumption, as verified by the use of a continuous alcohol monitoring system, of a type approved by the Division of Adult Correction of the Department of Public Safety, and that any violation of this condition be reported by the monitoring provider to the district attorney.

The conditions set forth above may be imposed in addition to requiring that the defendant execute a secured appearance bond.

(3) Should the defendant be mentally ill and dangerous to himself or others or a substance abuser and dangerous to himself or others, the provisions of Article 5 of Chapter 122C of the General Statutes shall apply.

(b) A defendant may be retained in custody not more than 48 hours from the time of arrest without a determination being made under this section by a judge. If a judge has not acted pursuant to this section within 48 hours of arrest, the magistrate shall act under the provisions of this section. (1979, c. 561, s. 4; 1989, c. 290, s. 2; 1995, c. 527, s. 3; 2001-518, s. 2; 2007-14, s. 1; 2010-135, s. 1; 2012-146, s. 2.)

§ 15A-534.2. Detention of impaired drivers.

(a) A judicial official conducting an initial appearance for an offense involving impaired driving, as defined in G.S. 20-4.01(24a), must follow the procedure in G.S. 15A-511 except as modified by this section. This section may not be interpreted to impede a defendant's right to communicate with counsel and friends.

(b) If at the time of the initial appearance the judicial official finds by clear and convincing evidence that the impairment of the defendant's physical or mental faculties presents a danger, if he is released, of physical injury to himself or others or damage to property, the judicial official must order that the defendant be held in custody and inform the defendant that he will be held in custody until one of the requirements of subsection (c) is met; provided, however, that the judicial official must at this time determine the appropriate conditions of pretrial release in accordance with G.S. 15A-534.

(c)   A defendant subject to detention under this section has the right to pretrial release under G.S. 15A-534 when the judicial official determines either that:

(1)   The defendant's physical and mental faculties are no longer impaired to the extent that he presents a danger of physical injury to himself or others or of damage to property if he is released; or

(2)   A sober, responsible adult is willing and able to assume responsibility for the defendant until his physical and mental faculties are no longer impaired. If the defendant is released to the custody of another, the judicial official may impose any other condition of pretrial release authorized by G.S. 15A-534, including a requirement that the defendant execute a secured appearance bond.

The defendant may be denied pretrial release under this section for a period no longer than 24 hours, and after such detention may be released only upon meeting the conditions of pretrial release set in accordance with G.S. 15A-534. If the defendant is detained for 24 hours, a judicial official must immediately determine the appropriate conditions of pretrial release in accordance with G.S. 15A-534.

(d)   In making his determination whether a defendant detained under this section remains impaired, the judicial official may request that the defendant submit to periodic tests to determine his alcohol concentration. Instruments acceptable for making preliminary breath tests under G.S. 20-16.3 may be used for this purpose as well as instruments for making evidentiary chemical analyses. Unless there is evidence that the defendant is still impaired from a combination of alcohol and some other impairing substance or condition, a judicial official must determine that a defendant with an alcohol concentration less than 0.05 is no longer impaired. The results of any periodic test to determine alcohol concentration may not be introduced in evidence:

(1)   Against the defendant by the State in any criminal, civil, or administrative proceeding arising out of an offense involving impaired driving; or

(2)   For any purpose in any proceeding if the test was not performed by a method approved by the Commission for Public Health under G.S. 20-139.1 and by a person licensed to administer the test by the Department of Health and Human Services.

The fact that a defendant refused to comply with a judicial official's request that he submit to a chemical analysis may not be admitted into evidence in any criminal action, administrative proceeding, or a civil action to review a decision reached by an administrative agency in which the defendant is a party. (1983, c. 435, s. 4; 1997-443, s. 11A.118(a); 2007-182, s. 2.)

§ 15A-534.3. Detention for communicable diseases.

If a judicial official conducting an initial appearance or first appearance hearing finds probable cause that an individual had a nonsexual exposure to the defendant in a manner that poses a significant risk of transmission of the AIDS virus or Hepatitis B by such defendant, the judicial official shall order the defendant to be detained for a reasonable period of time, not to exceed 24 hours, for investigation by public health officials and for testing for AIDS virus infection and Hepatitis B infection if required by public health officials pursuant to G.S. 130A-144 and G.S. 130A-148. (1989, c. 499, s. 1; 2009-501, s. 1.)

§ 15A-534.4. Sex offenses and crimes of violence against child victims: bail and pretrial release.

(a) In all cases in which the defendant is charged with felonious or misdemeanor child abuse, with taking indecent liberties with a minor in violation of G.S. 14-202.1, with rape or any other sex offense in violation of Article 7A, Chapter 14 of the General Statutes, against a minor victim, with incest with a minor in violation of G.S. 14-178, with kidnapping, abduction, or felonious restraint involving a minor victim, with a violation of G.S. 14-320.1, with assault or any other crime of violence against a minor victim, or with communicating a threat against a minor victim, in addition to the provisions of G.S. 15A-534 a judicial official shall impose the following conditions on pretrial release:

(1) That the defendant stay away from the home, temporary residence, school, business, or place of employment of the alleged victim.

(2) That the defendant refrain from communicating or attempting to communicate, directly or indirectly, with the victim, except under circumstances specified in an order entered by a judge with knowledge of the pending charges.

(3) That the defendant refrain from assaulting, beating, intimidating, stalking, threatening, or harming the alleged victim.

The conditions set forth above shall be imposed in addition to any other conditions that the judicial official may impose on pretrial release.

(b) Notwithstanding the provisions of subsection (a) of this section, upon request of the defendant, the judicial official may waive one or more of the conditions required by subdivisions (1) and (2) of subsection (a) of this section if the judicial official makes written findings of fact that it is not in the best interest of the alleged victim that the condition be imposed on the defendant. (1993 (Reg. Sess., 1994), c. 723, s. 5; 2007-172, s. 1.)

§ 15A-534.5. Detention to protect public health.

If a judicial official conducting an initial appearance finds by clear and convincing evidence that a person arrested for violation of an order limiting freedom of movement or access issued pursuant to G.S. 130A-475 or G.S. 130A-145 poses a threat to the health and safety of others, the judicial official shall deny pretrial release and shall order the person to be confined in an area or facility designated by the judicial official. Such pretrial confinement shall terminate when a judicial official determines that the confined person does not pose a threat to the health and safety of others. These determinations shall be made only after the State Health Director or local health director has made recommendations to the court. (2002-179, s. 15.)

§ 15A-534.6. Bail in cases of manufacture of methamphetamine.

In all cases in which the defendant is charged with any violation of G.S. 90-95(b)(1a) or G.S. 90-95(d1)(2)b., in determining bond and other conditions of release, the magistrate, judge, or court shall consider any evidence that the person is in any manner dependent upon methamphetamine or has a pattern of regular illegal use of methamphetamine. A rebuttable presumption that no conditions of release on bond would assure the safety of the community or any person therein shall arise if the State shows by clear and convincing evidence both:

(1) The person was arrested for a violation of G.S. 90-95(b)(1a) or G.S. 90-95(d1)(2)b., relating to the manufacture of methamphetamine or possession of an immediate precursor chemical with knowledge or reasonable cause to know that the chemical will be used to manufacture methamphetamine.

(2) The person is in any manner dependent upon methamphetamine or has a pattern of regular illegal use of methamphetamine, and the violation referred to in subdivision (1) of this section was committed or attempted in order to maintain or facilitate the dependence or pattern of illegal use in any manner. (2005-434, s. 6; 2007-484, s. 4.)

§ 15A-535. Issuance of policies on pretrial release.

(a) Subject to the provisions of this Article, the senior resident superior court judge for each district or set of districts as defined in G.S. 7A-41.1(a) in consultation with the chief district court judge or judges of all the district court districts in which are located any of the counties in the senior resident superior court judge's district or set of districts, must devise and issue recommended policies to be followed within each of those counties in determining whether, and upon what conditions, a defendant may be released before trial and may include in such policies, or issue separately, a requirement that each judicial official who imposes condition (4) or (5) in G.S. 15A-534(a) must record the reasons for doing so in writing.

(b) In any county in which there is a pretrial release program, the senior resident superior court judge may, after consultation with the chief district court judge, order that defendants accepted by such program for supervision shall, with their consent, be released by judicial officials to supervision of such programs, and subject to its rules and regulations, in lieu of releasing the defendants on conditions (1), (2), or (3) of G.S. 15A-534(a). (1973, c. 1286, s. 1; 1975, c. 791, s. 1; 1987, c. 481, s. 2; 1987 (Reg. Sess., 1988), c. 1037, s. 55; 2009-547, s. 5.)

§ 15A-536. Release after conviction in the superior court.

(a) A defendant whose guilt has been established in the superior court and is either awaiting sentence or has filed an appeal from the judgment entered may be ordered released upon conditions in accordance with the provisions of this Article.

(b) If release is ordered, the judge must impose the conditions set out in G.S. 15A-534(a) which will reasonably assure the presence of the defendant when required and provide adequate protection to persons and the community. If no single condition gives the assurance, the judge may impose the condition in G.S. 15A-534(a)(3) in addition to any other condition and may also, or in lieu of the condition in G.S. 15A-534(a)(3), place restrictions on the travel, associations, conduct, or place of abode of the defendant.

(c) In determining what conditions of release to impose, the judge must, on the basis of available information, consider the appropriate factors set out in G.S. 15A-534(c).

(d) A judge authorizing release of a defendant under this section must issue an appropriate order containing a statement of the conditions imposed, if any; inform the defendant in writing of the penalties applicable to violations of the conditions of his release; and advise him that his arrest will be ordered immediately upon any such violation. The order of release must be filed with the clerk and a copy given the defendant.

(e) An order of release may be modified or revoked by any superior court judge who has ordered the release of a defendant under this section or, if that judge is absent from the superior court district or set of districts as defined in G.S. 7A-41.1, by any other superior court judge. If the defendant is placed in custody as the result of a revocation or modification of an order of release, the defendant is entitled to an immediate hearing on whether he is again entitled to release and, if so, upon what conditions.

(f) In imposing conditions of release and in modifying and revoking orders of release under this section, the judge must take into account all evidence available to him which he considers reliable and is not strictly bound by the rules of evidence applicable to criminal trials. (1973, c. 1286, s. 1; 1987 (Reg. Sess., 1988), c. 1037, s. 56.)

§ 15A-537. Persons authorized to effect release.

(a) Following any authorization of release of any person in accordance with the provisions of this Article, any judicial official must effect the release of that person upon satisfying himself that the conditions of release have been met. In the absence of a judicial official, any law-enforcement officer or custodial official having the person in custody must effect the release upon satisfying himself that the conditions of release have been met, but law-enforcement and custodial agencies may administratively direct which officers or officials are authorized to effect release under this section. Satisfying oneself whether conditions of release are met includes determining if sureties are sufficiently solvent to meet the bond obligation, but no judicial official, officer, or custodial official may be held civilly liable for actions taken in good faith under this section.

(b) Upon release of the person in question, the person effecting release must file any bond, deposit, or mortgage and other papers pertaining to the release with the clerk of the court in which release was authorized.

(c) For the limited purposes of this section, any law-enforcement officer or custodial official may administer oaths to sureties and take other actions necessary in carrying out the duties imposed by this section. Any surety bond so taken is to be regarded in every respect as any other bail bond. (1973, c. 1286, s. 1; 1977, c. 711, s. 23.)

§ 15A-538. Modification of order on motion of person detained; substitution of surety.

(a) A person who is detained or objects to the conditions required for his release which were imposed or allowed to stand by order of a district court judge may apply in writing to a superior court judge to modify the order.

(b) The power to modify an order includes the power to substitute sureties upon any bond. Substitution or addition of acceptable sureties may be made at the request of any obligor on a bond or, in the interests of justice, at the request of a prosecutor under the provisions of G.S. 15A-539. (1973, c. 1286, s. 1; 1975, c. 166, s. 27.)

§ 15A-539. Modification upon motion of prosecutor.

(a) A prosecutor may at any time apply to an appropriate district court judge or superior court judge for modification or revocation of an order of release under this Article.

(b) A district or superior court judge may, upon motion of the State or upon the judge's own motion, and for good cause shown, conduct a hearing into the source of money or property to be posted for any defendant who is about to be released on a secured appearance bond. The court may refuse to accept offered money or property as security for the appearance bond that, because of its source, will not reasonably assure the appearance of the person as required. The State shall have the burden of proving, by a preponderance of the evidence, the facts supporting the court's decision to refuse to accept the offered money or property as security for the bond.

(c) Nothing in this section shall affect the legal rights of any surety on a bail bond, bonding company, or a professional bondsman. (1973, c. 1286, s. 1; 1975, c. 166, s. 27; 2005-375, s. 1.)

§ 15A-540. Surrender of a defendant by a surety; setting new conditions of release.

(a) Going Off the Bond Before Breach. - Before there has been a breach of the conditions of a bail bond, the surety may surrender the defendant as provided in G.S. 58-71-20. Upon application by the surety after such surrender, the clerk must exonerate the surety from the bond.

(b) Surrender After Breach of Condition. - After there has been a breach of the conditions of a bail bond, a surety may surrender the defendant as provided in this subsection. A surety may arrest the defendant for the purpose of returning the defendant to the sheriff. After arresting a defendant, the surety may surrender the defendant to the sheriff of the county in which the defendant is bonded to appear or to the sheriff where the defendant was bonded. Alternatively, a surety may surrender a defendant who is already in the custody of any sheriff by appearing in person and informing the sheriff that the surety wishes to surrender the defendant. Before surrendering a defendant to a sheriff, the surety must provide the sheriff with a copy of the bail bond, forfeiture, or release order. Upon surrender of the defendant, the sheriff shall provide a receipt to the surety.

(c) New Conditions of Pretrial Release. - When a defendant is surrendered by a surety under subsection (b) of this section, the sheriff shall without unnecessary delay take the defendant before a judicial official, along with a copy of the undertaking received from the surety and a copy of the receipt provided to the surety. The judicial official shall then determine whether the defendant is again entitled to release and, if so, upon what conditions. (1973, c. 1286, s. 1; 1995, c. 290, s. 2; 2000-133, s. 2; 2001-487, s. 46.5(a); 2013-139, s. 2.)

§ 15A-541. Persons prohibited from becoming surety.

(a) No sheriff, deputy sheriff, other law-enforcement officer, judicial official, attorney, parole officer, probation officer, jailer, assistant jailer, employee of the General Court of Justice, other public employee assigned to duties relating to the administration of criminal justice, or spouse of any such person may in any case become surety on a bail bond for any person other than a member of his immediate family. In addition no person covered by this section may act as agent for any bonding company or professional bondsman. No such person may have an interest, directly or indirectly, in the financial affairs of any firm or corporation whose principal business is acting as bondsman.

(b) A violation of this section is a Class 2 misdemeanor. (1973, c. 1286, s. 1; 1993, c. 539, s. 299; 1994, Ex. Sess., c. 24, s. 14(c).)

§ 15A-542. False qualification by surety.

(a) No person may sign an appearance bond as surety knowing or having reason to know that he does not own sufficient property over and above his exemption allowed by law to enable him to pay the bond should it be ordered forfeited.

(b) A violation of this section is a Class 2 misdemeanor. (1973, c. 1286, s. 1; 1993, c. 539, s. 300; 1994, Ex. Sess., c. 24, s. 14(c).)

§ 15A-543. Penalties for failure to appear.

(a) In addition to forfeiture imposed under Part 2 of this Article, any person released pursuant to this Article who willfully fails to appear before any court or judicial official as required is subject to the criminal penalties set out in this section.

(b)   A violation of this section is a Class I felony if:

(1)   The violator was released in connection with a felony charge against him; or

(2)   The violator was released under the provisions of G.S. 15A-536.

(c)   If, except as provided in subsection (b) above, a violator was released in connection with a misdemeanor charge against him, a violation of this section is a Class 2 misdemeanor. (1973, c. 1286, s. 1; 1983, c. 294, s. 4; 1993, c. 539, s. 301; 1994, Ex. Sess., c. 14, s. 16; c. 24, s. 14(c); 2000-133, s. 3.)

§ 15A-544: Repealed by Session Laws 2000-133, s. 4.

Part 2. Bail Bond Forfeiture.

§ 15A-544.1. Forfeiture jurisdiction.

By executing a bail bond the defendant and each surety submit to the jurisdiction of the court and irrevocably consent to be bound by any notice given in compliance with this Part. The liability of the defendant and each surety may be enforced as provided in this Part, without the necessity of an independent action. (2000-133, s. 6.)

§ 15A-544.2. Identifying information on bond.

(a)   The following information shall be entered on each bail bond executed under Part 1 of this Article:

(1)   The name and mailing address of the defendant.

(2) The name and mailing address of any accommodation bondsman executing the bond as surety.

(3) The name and license number of any professional bondsman executing the bond as surety and the name and license number of the runner executing the bail bond on behalf of the professional bondsman.

(4) The name of any insurance company executing the bond as surety, and the name, license number, and power of appointment number of the bail agent executing the bail bond on behalf of the insurance company.

(b) If a defendant is released upon execution of a bail bond that does not contain all the information required by subsection (a) of this section, the defendant's order of pretrial release may be revoked as provided in G.S. 15A-534(f). (2000-133, s. 6.)

§ 15A-544.3. Entry of forfeiture.

(a) If a defendant who was released under Part 1 of this Article upon execution of a bail bond fails on any occasion to appear before the court as required, the court shall enter a forfeiture for the amount of that bail bond in favor of the State against the defendant and against each surety on the bail bond.

(b) The forfeiture shall contain the following information:

(1) The name and address of record of the defendant.

(2) The file number of each case in which the defendant's appearance is secured by the bail bond.

(3) The amount of the bail bond.

(4) The date on which the bail bond was executed.

(5) The name and address of record of each surety on the bail bond.

(6) The name, address of record, license number, and power of appointment number of any bail agent who executed the bail bond on behalf of an insurance company.

(7) The date on which the forfeiture is entered.

(8) The date on which the forfeiture will become a final judgment under G.S. 15A-544.6 if not set aside before that date.

(9) The following notice: "TO THE DEFENDANT AND EACH SURETY NAMED ABOVE: The defendant named above has failed to appear as required before the court in the case identified above. A forfeiture for the amount of the bail bond shown above was entered in favor of the State against the defendant and each surety named above on the date of forfeiture shown above. This forfeiture will be set aside if, on or before the final judgment date shown above, satisfactory evidence is presented to the court that one of the following events has occurred: (i) the defendant's failure to appear has been stricken by the court in which the defendant was required to appear and any order for arrest that was issued for that failure to appear is recalled, (ii) all charges for which the defendant was bonded to appear have been finally disposed by the court other than by the State's taking a voluntary dismissal with leave, (iii) the defendant has been surrendered by a surety or bail agent to a sheriff of this State as provided by law, (iv) the defendant has been served with an Order for Arrest for the Failure to Appear on the criminal charge in the case in question as evidenced by a copy of an official court record, including an electronic record, (v) the defendant died before or within the period between the forfeiture and the final judgment as demonstrated by the presentation of a death certificate, (vi) the defendant was incarcerated in a unit of the Division of Adult Correction of the Department of Public Safety and is serving a sentence or in a unit of the Federal Bureau of Prisons located within the borders of the State at the time of the failure to appear as evidenced by a copy of an official court record or a copy of a document from the Division of Adult Correction of the Department of Public Safety or Federal Bureau of Prisons, or (vii) the defendant was incarcerated in a local, state, or federal detention center, jail, or prison located anywhere within the borders of the United States at the time of the failure to appear, and the district attorney for the county in which the charges are pending was notified of the defendant's incarceration while the defendant was still incarcerated and the defendant remains incarcerated for a period of 10 days following the district attorney's receipt of notice, as evidenced by a copy of the written notice served on the district attorney via hand delivery or certified mail and written documentation of date upon which the defendant was released from

incarceration, if the defendant was released prior to the time the motion to set aside was filed. The forfeiture will not be set aside for any other reason. If this forfeiture is not set aside on or before the final judgment date shown above, and if no motion to set it aside is pending on that date, the forfeiture will become a final judgment on that date. The final judgment will be enforceable by execution against the defendant and any accommodation bondsman and professional bondsman on the bond. The final judgment will also be reported to the Department of Insurance. Further, no surety will be allowed to execute any bail bond in the above county until the final judgment is satisfied in full." (2000-133, s. 6; 2007-105, s. 2; 2011-145, s. 19.1(h); 2012-83, s. 25.)

§ 15A-544.4. Notice of forfeiture.

(a) The court shall give notice of the entry of forfeiture by mailing a copy of the forfeiture to the defendant and to each surety whose name appears on the bail bond.

(b) The notice shall be sent by first-class mail to the defendant and to each surety named on the bond at the surety's address of record.

(c) If a bail agent on behalf of an insurance company executed the bond, the court shall also provide a copy of the forfeiture to the bail agent, but failure to provide notice to the bail agent shall not affect the validity of any notice given to the insurance company.

(d) Notice given under this section is effective when the notice is mailed.

(e) Notice under this section shall be mailed not later than the 30th day after the date on which the defendant fails to appear as required and a call and fail is ordered. If notice under this section is not given within the prescribed time, the forfeiture shall not become a final judgment and shall not be enforced or reported to the Department of Insurance. (2000-133, s. 6; 2009-550, s. 1.)

§ 15A-544.5. Setting aside forfeiture.

(a) Relief Exclusive. - There shall be no relief from a forfeiture except as provided in this section. The reasons for relief are those specified in subsection

(b) of this section. The procedures for obtaining relief are those specified in subsections (c) and (d) of this section. Subsections (f), (g), and (h) of this section apply regardless of the reason for relief given or the procedure followed.

(b)   Reasons for Set Aside. - Except as provided by subsection (f) of this section, a forfeiture shall be set aside for any one of the following reasons, and none other:

(1)   The defendant's failure to appear has been set aside by the court and any order for arrest issued for that failure to appear has been recalled, as evidenced by a copy of an official court record, including an electronic record.

(2)   All charges for which the defendant was bonded to appear have been finally disposed by the court other than by the State's taking dismissal with leave, as evidenced by a copy of an official court record, including an electronic record.

(3)   The defendant has been surrendered by a surety on the bail bond as provided by G.S. 15A-540, as evidenced by the sheriff's receipt provided for in that section.

(4)   The defendant has been served with an Order for Arrest for the Failure to Appear on the criminal charge in the case in question as evidenced by a copy of an official court record, including an electronic record.

(5)   The defendant died before or within the period between the forfeiture and the final judgment as demonstrated by the presentation of a death certificate.

(6)   The defendant was incarcerated in a unit of the Division of Adult Correction of the Department of Public Safety and is serving a sentence or in a unit of the Federal Bureau of Prisons located within the borders of the State at the time of the failure to appear as evidenced by a copy of an official court record or a copy of a document from the Division of Adult Correction of the Department of Public Safety or Federal Bureau of Prisons, including an electronic record.

(7)   The defendant was incarcerated in a local, state, or federal detention center, jail, or prison located anywhere within the borders of the United States at the time of the failure to appear, and the district attorney for the county in which the charges are pending was notified of the defendant's incarceration while the

defendant was still incarcerated and the defendant remains incarcerated for a period of 10 days following the district attorney's receipt of notice, as evidenced by a copy of the written notice served on the district attorney via hand delivery or certified mail and written documentation of date upon which the defendant was released from incarceration, if the defendant was released prior to the time the motion to set aside was filed.

(c) Procedure When Failure to Appear Is Stricken. - If the court before which a defendant's appearance was secured by a bail bond enters an order striking the defendant's failure to appear and recalling any order for arrest issued for that failure to appear, that court may simultaneously enter an order setting aside any forfeiture of that bail bond. When an order setting aside a forfeiture is entered, the defendant's further appearances shall continue to be secured by that bail bond unless the court orders otherwise.

(d) Motion Procedure. - If a forfeiture is not set aside under subsection (c) of this section, the only procedure for setting it aside is as follows:

(1) At any time before the expiration of 150 days after the date on which notice was given under G.S. 15A-544.4, any of the following parties on a bail bond may make a written motion that the forfeiture be set aside:

a. The defendant.

b. Any surety.

c. A professional bondsman or a runner acting on behalf of a professional bondsman.

d. A bail agent acting on behalf of an insurance company.

The written motion shall state the reason for the motion and attach to the motion the evidence specified in subsection (b) of this section.

(2) The motion shall be filed in the office of the clerk of superior court of the county in which the forfeiture was entered. The moving party shall, under G.S. 1A-1, Rule 5, serve a copy of the motion on the district attorney for that county and on the attorney for the county board of education.

(3) Either the district attorney or the county board of education may object to the motion by filing a written objection in the office of the clerk and serving a copy on the moving party.

(4) If neither the district attorney nor the attorney for the board of education has filed a written objection to the motion by the twentieth day after a copy of the motion is served by the moving party pursuant to Rule 5 of the Rules of Civil Procedure, the clerk shall enter an order setting aside the forfeiture, regardless of the basis for relief asserted in the motion, the evidence attached, or the absence of either.

(5) If either the district attorney or the county board of education files a written objection to the motion, then not more than 30 days after the objection is filed a hearing on the motion and objection shall be held in the county, in the trial division in which the defendant was bonded to appear.

(6) If at the hearing the court allows the motion, the court shall enter an order setting aside the forfeiture.

(7) If at the hearing the court does not enter an order setting aside the forfeiture, the forfeiture shall become a final judgment of forfeiture on the later of:

a. The date of the hearing.

b. The date of final judgment specified in G.S. 15A-544.6.

(8) If at the hearing the court determines that the motion to set aside was not signed or that the documentation required to be attached pursuant to subdivision (1) of this subsection is fraudulent or was not attached to the motion at the time the motion was filed, the court may order monetary sanctions against the surety filing the motion, unless the court also finds that the failure to sign the motion or attach the required documentation was unintentional. A motion for sanctions and notice of the hearing thereof shall be served on the surety not later than 10 days before the time specified for the hearing. If the court concludes that a sanction should be ordered, in addition to ordering the denial of the motion to set aside, sanctions shall be imposed as follows: (i) twenty-five percent (25%) of the bond amount for failure to sign the motion; (ii) fifty percent (50%) of the bond amount for failure to attach the required documentation; and (iii) not less than one hundred percent (100%) of the bond amount for the filing of fraudulent documentation. Sanctions awarded under this subdivision shall be

docketed by the clerk of superior court as a civil judgment as provided in G.S. 1-234. The clerk of superior court shall remit the clear proceeds of the sanction to the county finance officer as provided in G.S. 115C-452. This subdivision shall not limit the criminal prosecution of any individual involved in the creation or filing of any fraudulent documentation.

(e) Only One Motion Per Forfeiture. - No more than one motion to set aside a specific forfeiture may be considered by the court.

(f) Set Aside Prohibited in Certain Circumstances. - No forfeiture of a bond may be set aside for any reason in any case in which the surety or the bail agent had actual notice before executing a bail bond that the defendant had already failed to appear on two or more prior occasions in the case for which the bond was executed. Actual notice as required by this subsection shall only occur if two or more failures to appear are indicated on the defendant's release order by a judicial official. The judicial official shall indicate on the release order when it is the defendant's second or subsequent failure to appear in the case for which the bond was executed.

(g) No Final Judgment After Forfeiture Is Set Aside. - If a forfeiture is set aside under this section, the forfeiture shall not thereafter ever become a final judgment of forfeiture or be enforced or reported to the Department of Insurance.

(h) Appeal. - An order on a motion to set aside a forfeiture is a final order or judgment of the trial court for purposes of appeal. Appeal is the same as provided for appeals in civil actions. When notice of appeal is properly filed, the court may stay the effectiveness of the order on any conditions the court considers appropriate. (2000-133, s. 6; 2007-105, s. 1; 2009-437, ss. 1, 1.1, 2; 2011-145, s. 19.1(h); 2011-377, ss. 6-8; 2011-412, s. 4.2(a)-(c); 2012-83, s. 26; 2013-139, ss. 3, 4.)

§ 15A-544.6. Final judgment of forfeiture.

A forfeiture entered under G.S. 15A-544.3 becomes a final judgment of forfeiture without further action by the court and may be enforced under G.S. 15A-544.7, on the one hundred fiftieth day after notice is given under G.S. 15A-544.4, if:

(1) No order setting aside the forfeiture under G.S. 15A-544.5 is entered on or before that date; and

(2)   No motion to set aside the forfeiture is pending on that date. (2000-133, s. 6.)

§ 15A-544.7. Docketing and enforcement of final judgment of forfeiture.

(a)   Final Judgment Docketed As Civil Judgment. - When a forfeiture has become a final judgment under this Part, the clerk of superior court, under G.S. 1-234, shall docket the judgment as a civil judgment against the defendant and against each surety named in the judgment.

(b)   Judgment Lien. - When a final judgment of forfeiture is docketed, the judgment shall become a lien on the real property of the defendant and of each surety named in the judgment, as provided in G.S. 1-234.

(c)   Execution; Copy to Commissioner of Insurance. - After docketing a final judgment under this section, the clerk shall:

(1)   Issue execution on the judgment against the defendant and against each accommodation bondsman and professional bondsman named in the judgment and shall remit the clear proceeds to the county finance officer as provided in G.S. 115C-452.

(2)   If an insurance company or professional bondsman is named in the judgment, send the Commissioner of Insurance a notice of the judgment, showing the date on which the judgment was docketed.

(d)   Sureties May Not Execute Bonds in County. - After a final judgment is docketed as provided in this section, no surety named in the judgment shall become a surety on any bail bond in the county in which the judgment is docketed until the judgment is satisfied in full. (2000-133, s. 6; 2006-188, s. 2.)

§ 15A-544.8. Relief from final judgment of forfeiture.

(a)   Relief Exclusive. - There is no relief from a final judgment of forfeiture except as provided in this section.

(b) Reasons. - The court may grant the defendant or any surety named in the judgment relief from the judgment, for the following reasons, and none other:

(1) The person seeking relief was not given notice as provided in G.S. 15A-544.4.

(2) Other extraordinary circumstances exist that the court, in its discretion, determines should entitle that person to relief.

(c) Procedure. - The procedure for obtaining relief from a final judgment under this section is as follows:

(1) At any time before the expiration of three years after the date on which a judgment of forfeiture became final, any of the following parties named in the judgment may make a written motion for relief under this section:

a. The defendant.

b. Any surety.

c. A professional bondsman or a runner acting on behalf of a professional bondsman.

d. A bail agent acting on behalf of an insurance company.

The written motion shall state the reasons for the motion and set forth the evidence in support of each reason.

(2) The motion shall be filed in the office of the clerk of superior court of the county in which the final judgment was, entered. The moving party shall, under G.S. 1A-1, Rule 5, serve a copy of the motion on the district attorney for that county and on the attorney for the county board of education.

(3) A hearing on the motion shall be scheduled within a reasonable time in the trial division in which the defendant was bonded to appear.

(4) At the hearing the court may grant the party any relief from the judgment that the court considers appropriate, including the refund of all or a part of any money paid to satisfy the judgment.

(d) Only One Motion. - No more than one motion by any party for relief under this section may be considered by the court.

(e) Finality of Judgment as to Other Parties Not Affected. - The finality of a final judgment of forfeiture shall not be affected, as to any party to the judgment, by the filing of a motion by, or the granting of relief to, any other party.

(f) Appeal. - An order on a motion for relief from a final judgment of forfeiture is a final order or judgment of the trial court for purposes of appeal. Appeal is the same as provided for appeals in civil actions. When notice of appeal is properly filed, the court may stay the effectiveness of the order on any conditions it considers appropriate. (2000-133, s. 6; 2011-377, ss. 9, 10; 2013-139, s. 5.)

§ 15A-545. Reserved for future codification purposes.

Part 3. Other Provisions.

§ 15A-546. Contempt.

Nothing in this Article is intended to interfere with or prevent the exercise by the court of its contempt powers. (1973, c. 1286, s. 1.)

§ 15A-547. Right to habeas corpus.

Nothing in this Article is intended to abridge the right of habeas corpus. (1973, c. 1286, s. 1.)

§ 15A-547.1. Remit bail bond if defendant sentenced to community or intermediate punishment.

If a defendant is convicted and sentenced to community punishment or intermediate punishment and no appeal is pending, then the court shall remit the bail bond to the obligor in accordance with the provisions of this Article and shall not require that the bail bond continue to be posted while the defendant serves his or her sentence. (1995, c. 290, s. 4.)

§§ 15A-547.2 through 15A-547.6. Reserved for future codification purposes.

Article 27.

§§ 15A-548 through 15A-574: Reserved for future codification purposes.

Article 28.

§§ 15A-575 through 15A-600: Reserved for future codification purposes.

SUBCHAPTER VI. PRELIMINARY PROCEEDINGS.

Article 29.

First Appearance Before District Court Judge.

§ 15A-601. First appearance before a district court judge; right in felony and other cases in original jurisdiction of superior court; consolidation of first appearance before magistrate and before district court judge; first appearance before clerk of superior court; use of two-way audio and video transmission.

(a) Any defendant charged in a magistrate's order under G.S. 15A-511 or criminal process under Article 17 of this Chapter, Criminal Process, with a crime in the original jurisdiction of the superior court must be brought before a district court judge in the district court district as defined in G.S. 7A-133 in which the crime is charged to have been committed. This first appearance before a district court judge is not a critical stage of the proceedings against the defendant.

(a1) A first appearance in a noncapital case may be conducted by an audio and video transmission between the judge and the defendant in which the parties can see and hear each other. If the defendant has counsel, the defendant shall be allowed to communicate fully and confidentially with his attorney during the proceeding.

(a2) Prior to the use of audio and video transmission pursuant to subsection (a1) of this section, the procedures and type of equipment for audio and video transmission shall be submitted to the Administrative Office of the Courts by the senior regular resident superior court judge for a judicial district or set of districts and approved by the Administrative Office of the Courts.

(b) When a district court judge conducts an initial appearance as provided in G.S. 15A-511, he may consolidate those proceedings and the proceedings under this Article.

(c) Unless the defendant is released pursuant to Article 26 of this Chapter, Bail, first appearance before a district court judge must be held within 96 hours after the defendant is taken into custody or at the first regular session of the district court in the county, whichever occurs first. If the defendant is not taken into custody, or is released pursuant to Article 26 of this Chapter, Bail, within 96 hours after being taken into custody, first appearance must be held at the next session of district court held in the county. This subsection does not apply to a defendant whose first appearance before a district court judge has been set in a criminal summons pursuant to G.S. 15A-303(d).

(d) Upon motion of the defendant, the first appearance before a district court judge may be continued to a time certain. The defendant may not waive the holding of the first appearance before a district court judge but he need not appear personally if he is represented by counsel at the proceeding.

(e) The clerk of the superior court in the county in which the defendant is taken into custody may conduct a first appearance as provided in this Article if a district court judge is not available in the county within 96 hours after the defendant is taken into custody. The clerk, in conducting a first appearance, shall proceed under this Article as would a district court judge. (1973, c. 1286, s. 1; 1975, 2nd Sess., c. 983, ss. 139, 140; 1979, c. 651; 1987 (Reg. Sess., 1988), c. 1037, s. 58; 1993, c. 30, s. 2.)

§ 15A-602. Warning of right against self-incrimination.

Except when he is accompanied by his counsel, the judge must inform the defendant of his right to remain silent and that anything he says may be used against him. (1973, c. 1286, s. 1.)

§ 15A-603. Assuring defendant's right to counsel.

(a) The judge must determine whether the defendant has retained counsel or, if indigent, has been assigned counsel.

(b) If the defendant is not represented by counsel, the judge must inform the defendant that he has important legal rights which may be waived unless asserted in a timely and proper manner and that counsel may be of assistance to the defendant in advising him and acting in his behalf. The judge must inform the defendant of his right to be represented by counsel and that he will be furnished counsel if he is indigent. The judge shall also advise the defendant that if he is convicted and placed on probation, payment of the expense of counsel assigned to represent him may be made a condition of probation, and that if he is acquitted, he will have no obligation to pay the expense of assigned counsel.

(c) If the defendant asserts that he is indigent and desires counsel, the judge must proceed in accordance with the provisions of Article 36 of Chapter 7A of the General Statutes.

(d) If the defendant is found not to be indigent and indicates that he desires to be represented by counsel, the judge must inform him that he should obtain counsel promptly.

(e) If the defendant desires to waive representation by counsel, the waiver must be in writing in accordance with the provisions of Article 36 of Chapter 7A of the General Statutes except as otherwise provided in this Article. (1973, c. 1286, s. 1; 1981, c. 409, s. 1.)

§ 15A-604. Determination of sufficiency of charge.

(a) The judge must examine each criminal process or magistrate's order and determine whether each charge against the defendant charges a criminal offense within the original jurisdiction of the superior court.

(b) If the judge determines that the process or order fails to charge a criminal offense within the original jurisdiction of the superior court, he must notify the prosecutor and take further appropriate action, including one or more of the following:

(1) Dismiss the charge.

(2) Permit the State to amend the statement of the crime in the process or order.

(3) Continue the proceedings, for not more than 24 hours, to permit the State to initiate new charges.

(4) With the consent of the prosecutor, set the case for trial in the district court if the charge is found to be within the original jurisdiction of the district court. (1973, c. 1286, s. 1; 1975, c. 166, s. 27.)

§ 15A-605. Additional proceedings at first appearance before judge.

The judge must:

(1) Inform the defendant of the charges against him;

(2) Determine that the defendant or his counsel has been furnished a copy of the process or order; and

(3) Determine or review the defendant's eligibility for release under Article 26 of this Chapter, Bail. (1973, c. 1286, s. 1.)

§ 15A-606. Demand or waiver of probable-cause hearing.

(a) The judge must schedule a probable-cause hearing unless the defendant waives in writing his right to such hearing. A defendant represented by counsel, or who desires to be represented by counsel, may not before the date of the scheduled hearing waive his right to a probable-cause hearing without the written consent of the defendant and his counsel.

(b)   Evidence of a demand or waiver of a probable-cause hearing may not be admitted at trial.

(c)   If the defendant waives a probable-cause hearing, the district court judge must bind the defendant over to the superior court for further proceedings in accordance with this Chapter.

(d)   If the defendant does not waive a probable-cause hearing, the district court judge must schedule a hearing not later than 15 working days following the initial appearance before the district court judge; if no session of the district court is scheduled in the county within 15 working days, the hearing must be scheduled for the first day of the next session. The hearing may not be scheduled sooner than five working days following such initial appearance without the consent of the defendant and the prosecutor.

(e)   If an unrepresented defendant is not indigent and has indicated his desire to be represented by counsel, the district court judge must inform him that he has a choice of appearing without counsel at the probable-cause hearing or of securing the attendance of counsel to represent him at the hearing. The judge must further inform him that the judge presiding at the hearing will not continue the hearing because of the absence of counsel except for extraordinary cause.

(f)   Upon a showing of good cause, a scheduled probable-cause hearing may be continued by the district court upon timely motion of the defendant or the State. Except for extraordinary cause, a motion is not timely unless made at least 48 hours prior to the time set for the probable-cause hearing.

(g)   If after the first appearance before a district court judge a defendant with consent of counsel desires to waive his right to a probable-cause hearing, he may do so in writing filed with the court signed by defendant and his counsel. Upon waiver the defendant must be bound over to the superior court. (1973, c. 1286, s. 1; 1975, c. 166, s. 27.)

§§ 15A-607 through 15A-610. Reserved for future codification purposes.

Article 30.

Probable-Cause Hearing.

§ 15A-611. Probable-cause hearing procedure.

(a)   At the probable-cause hearing:

(1)   A prosecutor must represent the State.

(2)   The defendant may be represented by counsel.

(3)   The defendant may testify as a witness in his own behalf and call and examine other witnesses, and produce other evidence in his behalf.

(4)   Each witness must testify under oath or affirmation and is subject to cross-examination.

(b)   The State must by nonhearsay evidence, or by evidence that satisfies an exception to the hearsay rule, show that there is probable cause to believe that the offense charged has been committed and that there is probable cause to believe that the defendant committed it, except:

(1)   A report or copy of a report made by a physicist, chemist, firearms identification expert, fingerprint technician, or an expert or technician in some other scientific, professional, or medical field, concerning the results of an examination, comparison, or test performed by him in connection with the case in issue, when stated by such person in a report made by him, is admissible in evidence.

(2)   If there is no serious contest, reliable hearsay is admissible to prove value, ownership of property, possession of property in another than the defendant, lack of consent of the owner, possessor, or custodian of property to its taking or to the breaking or entering of premises, chain of custody, authenticity of signatures, and the existence and text of a particular ordinance or regulation of a governmental unit or agency.

The district court judge is not required to exclude evidence on the ground that it was acquired by unlawful means.

(c) If a defendant appears at a probable-cause hearing without counsel, the judge must determine whether counsel has been waived. If he determines that counsel has been waived, he may proceed without counsel. If he determines that counsel has not been waived, except in a situation covered by G.S. 15A-606(e) he must take appropriate action to secure the defendant's right to counsel.

(d) A probable-cause hearing may not be held if an information in superior court is filed upon waiver of indictment before the date set for the hearing. (1973, c. 1286, s. 1; 1975, c. 166, s. 27.)

§ 15A-612. Disposition of charge on probable-cause hearing.

(a) At the conclusion of a probable-cause hearing the judge must take one of the following actions:

(1) If he finds that the defendant probably committed the offense charged, or a lesser included offense of such offense within the original jurisdiction of the superior court, he must bind the defendant over to a superior court for further proceedings in accordance with this Chapter. The judge must note his findings in the case records.

(2) If he finds no probable cause as to the offense charged but probable cause with respect to a lesser included offense within the original jurisdiction of the district court, he may set the case for trial in the district court in accordance with the terms of G.S. 15A-613. In the absence of a new pleading, the judge may not set a case for trial in the district court on any offense which is not lesser included.

(3) If he finds no probable cause pursuant to subdivisions (1) or (2) as to any charge, he must dismiss the proceedings in question.

(b) No finding made by a judge under this section precludes the State from instituting a subsequent prosecution for the same offense. (1973, c. 1286, s. 1; 1975, c. 166, s. 14.)

§ 15A-613. Setting offense for trial in district court.

If an offense set for trial in the district court under the terms of G.S. 15A-604(b)(4) or any provision of G.S. 15A-612 is a lesser included offense of the charge before the court on a pleading, the judge may:

(1)   Accept a plea of guilty or no contest, with the consent of the prosecutor; or

(2)   Proceed to try the offense immediately, with the consent of both the defendant and the prosecutor.

Otherwise, the judge must enter an appropriate order for subsequent calendaring of the case for trial in the district court. The trial so ordered may not be earlier than five working days nor later than 15 working days from the date of the order. The judge must note in the case records the new offense with which the defendant is charged, has been tried, or to which he entered a plea of guilty or no contest. (1973, c. 1286, s. 1; 1975, c. 166, s. 27.)

§ 15A-614. Review of eligibility for pretrial release.

Upon binding a defendant in custody over to the superior court for trial or upon entering an order for subsequent calendaring of the case of such a defendant for trial in the district court, the judge must again review the eligibility of the defendant for release under Article 26 of this Chapter, Bail. (1973, c. 1286, s. 1.)

§ 15A-615. Testing of certain persons for sexually transmitted infections.

(a)   After a finding of probable cause pursuant to the provisions of Article 30 of Chapter 15A of the General Statutes or indictment for an offense that involves nonconsensual vaginal, anal, or oral intercourse; an offense that involves vaginal, anal, or oral intercourse with a child 12 years old or less; or an offense under G.S. 14-202.1 that involves vaginal, anal, or oral intercourse with a child less than 16 years old; the victim or the parent, guardian, or guardian ad litem of a minor victim may request that a defendant be tested for the following sexually transmitted infections:

(1)   Chlamydia;

(2) Gonorrhea;

(3) Hepatitis B;

(3a) Herpes;

(4) HIV; and

(5) Syphilis.

In the case of herpes, the defendant, pursuant to the provisions of this section, shall be examined for oral and genital herpetic lesions and, if a suggestive but nondiagnostic lesion is present, a culture for herpes shall be performed.

(b) Upon a request under subsection (a) of this section, the district attorney shall petition the court on behalf of the victim for an order requiring the defendant to be tested. Upon finding that there is probable cause to believe that the alleged sexual contact involved in the offense would pose a significant risk of transmission of a sexually transmitted infection listed in subsection (a) of this section, the court shall order the defendant to submit to testing for these infections. A defendant ordered to be tested under this section shall be tested not later than 48 hours after the date of the court order. A test for HIV ordered pursuant to this section shall use the HIV-RNA Detection Test for determining HIV infection.

(c) If the defendant is in the custody of the Division of Adult Correction of the Department of Public Safety, the defendant shall be tested by the Division of Adult Correction of the Department of Public Safety. If the defendant is not in the custody of the Division of Adult Correction of the Department of Public Safety, the defendant shall be tested by the local health department. The Division of Adult Correction of the Department of Public Safety shall inform the local health director of all test results. The local health director shall ensure that the victim is informed of the results of the tests and counseled appropriately. The agency conducting the tests shall inform the defendant of the results of the tests and ensure that the defendant is counseled appropriately. The results of the tests shall not be admissible as evidence in any criminal proceeding. (1993, c. 489, s. 1; 1994, Ex. Sess., c. 8, s. 1; 2006-226, s. 10; 2006-264, s. 33(a); 2007-403, s. 1; 2011-145, s. 19.1(h).)

§§ 15A-616 through 15A-620. Reserved for future codification purposes.

Article 31.

The Grand Jury and Its Proceedings.

§ 15A-621. "Grand jury" defined.

A grand jury is a body consisting of not less than 12 nor more than 18 persons, impaneled by a superior court and constituting a part of such court. (1973, c. 1286, s. 1.)

§ 15A-622. Formation and organization of grand juries; other preliminary matters.

(a) The mode of selecting grand jurors and of drawing and impaneling grand jurors is governed by this Article and Chapter 9 of the General Statutes, Jurors. Challenges to the panel from which grand jurors were drawn are governed by the procedure in G.S. 15A-1211.

(b) To impanel a new grand jury, the presiding judge must direct that the names of all persons returned as jurors be separately placed in a container. The clerk must draw out the names of 18 persons to serve as grand jurors. Of these 18, the first nine drawn serve until the first session of court at which criminal cases are heard held in the county after the following January 1, and thereafter until their replacements are selected and sworn. The next nine serve until the first session of court at which criminal cases are heard held in the county after the following July 1, and thereafter until their replacements are selected and sworn. If this formula results in any term likely to be shorter than two months or longer than 15 months, the presiding judge impaneling the grand jury may modify the terms. Thereafter, beginning with the first session of superior court at which criminal cases are heard held in the county following January 1 and July 1 of each year, nine new grand jurors must be selected in the manner provided above to replace the jurors whose terms have expired. All new grand jurors so selected serve until the first session of court at which criminal cases are heard held after January 1 or July 1 which most nearly results in a 12-month term, and thereafter until their replacements are selected and sworn. If a vacancy occurs in the membership of the grand jury, the superior court judge next convening the jury or next holding a session of court at which criminal cases are heard in the county may order that a new juror be drawn in the manner provided above to fill the vacancy.

The senior resident superior court judge of the district may impanel a second grand jury in any county of the district to serve concurrently with the first. The second grand jury shall be impaneled as provided in the first paragraph of this subsection. The court shall continue to have two grand juries until the senior resident superior court judge orders the second grand jury to terminate.

In any county the senior resident superior court judge, if he finds that grand jury service is placing a disproportionate burden on grand jurors and their employers, may fix the term of service of a grand juror at six months rather than 12 months. In doing so, he shall prescribe procedures, consistent with this section, for replacement of half of the jurors of the grand jury or grand juries approximately every three months.

(c)   Neither the grand jury panel nor any individual grand juror may be challenged, but a superior court judge may:

(1)   At any time before new grand jurors are sworn, discharge them, or discharge the grand jury, and cause new grand jurors or a new grand jury to be drawn if he finds that jurors have not been selected in accordance with law or that the grand jury is illegally constituted; or

(2)   At any time after a grand juror is drawn, refuse to swear him, or discharge him after he has been sworn, upon a finding that he is disqualified from service, incapable of performing his duties, or guilty of misconduct in the performance of his duties so as to impair the proper functioning of the grand jury.

(d)   The presiding judge may excuse a grand juror from service of the balance of his term, upon his own motion or upon the juror's request for good cause shown. The foreman may excuse individual jurors from attending particular sessions of the grand jury, except that he may not excuse more than two jurors for any one session.

(e)   After the impaneling of a new grand jury, or the impaneling of nine new jurors under the terms of this section, the presiding judge must appoint one of the grand jurors as foreman and may appoint another to act as foreman during any absence or disability of the foreman. Unless removed for cause by a superior court judge, the foreman serves until his successor is appointed and sworn.

(f) The foreman and other new grand jurors must take the oath prescribed in G.S. 11-11. After new grand jurors have been sworn, the presiding judge may give the grand jurors written or oral instructions relating to the performance of their duties. At subsequent sessions of court, the presiding judge is not required to give any additional instructions to the grand jurors.

(g) At any time when a grand jury is in recess, a superior court judge may, upon application of the prosecutor or upon his own motion, order the grand jury reconvened for the purpose of dealing with a matter requiring grand jury action.

(h) A written petition for convening of grand jury under this section may be filed by the district attorney, the district attorney's designated assistant, or a special prosecutor requested pursuant to G.S. 114-11.6, with the approval of a committee of at least three members of the North Carolina Conference of District Attorneys, and with the concurrence of the Attorney General, with the Clerk of the North Carolina Supreme Court. The Chief Justice shall appoint a panel of three judges to determine whether to order the grand jury convened. A grand jury under this section may be convened if the three-judge panel determines that:

(1) The petition alleges the commission of or a conspiracy to commit a violation of G.S. 90-95(h) or G.S. 90-95.1, any part of which violation or conspiracy occurred in the county where the grand jury sits, and that persons named in the petition have knowledge related to the identity of the perpetrators of those crimes but will not divulge that knowledge voluntarily or that such persons request that they be allowed to testify before the grand jury; and

(2) The affidavit sets forth facts that establish probable cause to believe that the crimes specified in the petition have been committed and reasonable grounds to suspect that the persons named in the petition have knowledge related to the identity of the perpetrators of those crimes.

The affidavit shall be based upon personal knowledge or, if the source of the information and basis for the belief are stated, upon information and belief. The panel's order convening the grand jury as an investigative grand jury shall direct the grand jury to investigate the crimes and persons named in the petition, and shall be filed with the Clerk of the North Carolina Supreme Court. A grand jury so convened retains all powers, duties, and responsibilities of a grand jury under this Article. The contents of the petition and the affidavit shall not be disclosed. Upon receiving a petition under this subsection, the Chief Justice shall appoint a panel to determine whether the grand jury should be convened as an investigative grand jury.

A grand jury authorized by this subsection may be convened from an existing grand jury or grand juries authorized by subsection (b) of this section or may be convened as an additional grand jury to an existing grand jury or grand juries. Notwithstanding subsection (b) of this section, grand jurors impaneled pursuant to this subsection shall serve for a period of 12 months, and, if an additional grand jury is convened, 18 persons shall be selected to constitute that grand jury. At any time for cause shown, the presiding superior court judge may excuse a juror temporarily or permanently, and in the latter event the court may impanel another person in place of the juror excused.

(i) An investigative grand jury may be convened pursuant to subsection (h) of this section if the petition alleges the commission of, attempt to commit or solicitation to commit, or a conspiracy to commit a violation of G.S. 14-43.11 (human trafficking), G.S. 14-43.12 (involuntary servitude), or G.S. 14-43.13 (sexual servitude).

(j) Any grand juror who serves the full term of service under subsection (b) or subsection (h) of this section shall not be required to serve again as a grand juror or as a juror for a period of six years. (1779, c. 157, s. 11, P.R.; R.C., c. 31, s. 33; 1879, c. 12; Code, ss. 404, 1742; Rev., ss. 1969, 1971; C.S., ss. 2333, 2336; 1929, c. 228; 1967, c. 218, s. 1; 1973, c. 1286, s. 1; 1975, c. 166, s. 27; 1977, c. 711, s. 24; 1979, c. 177, s. 1; 1981, c. 440, s. 1; 1985 (Reg. Sess., 1986), c. 843, ss. 2, 6; 1987 (Reg. Sess., 1988), c. 1040, ss. 1, 3; 1989 (Reg. Sess., 1990), c. 1039, s. 4; 1991, c. 686, ss. 1, 3; 1995, c. 362, s. 1; 2013-148, s. 3; 2013-368, s. 21.)

Vision Books Order Form

Fax Orders: 1-980-299-5965

Phone Orders: 1-704-898-0770

E-mail Orders: www.visionbooks.org

Mail Orders: Vision Books, LLC
                   P.O. Box 42406
                   Charlotte, NC 28215

Shipp To:
Name_____
Address_____
City_____State_____Zip_____
Phone_____Fax_____
Email_____@_____

Bill To: We can bill a third party on your behalf.
Name_____
Address_____
City_____State_____Zip_____
Phone____(_____)_____Fax_____
Email_____@_____

Pamphlet Number ($15.00 Each)	Qty	Total Cost
_____	_____	_____
_____	_____	_____
_____	_____	_____
_____	_____	_____
_____	_____	_____
_____	_____	_____
_____	_____	_____
Full Volume Set 1-92	92 Pamphlets	1,380.00

Free Shipping Shipping & Handling on Full Volume Orders
Add $1.00 Shipping & Handling per pamphlet $_____

Total Cost $_____

Thank You for Your Support. Management!

DID YOU ENJOY THIS BOOK?

Vision Books, LLC would like to hear from you! If you or someone you know has been falsely imprisoned, we would like to hear your story. If the 'North Carolina Criminal Law and Procedure' has had an effect in your life or if you have suggestions, we would like to hear from you. Send your letters to:

Vision Books, LLC
Attn: Staff Writers
P.O. Box 42406
Charlotte, NC 28215
Email: staff@visionbooks.org

Order Additional Copies:

Fax Orders:	1-980-299-5965
Phone Orders:	1-704-898-0770
E-mail Orders:	www.visionbooks.org
Mail Orders:	Vision Books, LLC P.O. Box 42406 Charlotte, NC 28215

www.ingramcontent.com/pod-product-compliance
Lightning Source LLC
Chambersburg PA
CBHW071407170526
45165CB00001B/200